Praying with Every Heart

Praying with Every Heart

Orienting Our Lives to the Wholeness of the World

Cláudio Carvalhaes

FOREWORD BY
Daisy Machado

AFTERWORD BY
Marc H. Ellis

CASCADE *Books* • Eugene, Oregon

PRAYING WITH EVERY HEART
Orienting Our Lives to the Wholeness of the World

Copyright © 2021 Cláudio Carvalhaes. All rights reserved. Except for brief quotations in critical publications or reviews, no part of this book may be reproduced in any manner without prior written permission from the publisher. Write: Permissions, Wipf and Stock Publishers, 199 W. 8th Ave., Suite 3, Eugene, OR 97401.

Cascade Books
An Imprint of Wipf and Stock Publishers
199 W. 8th Ave., Suite 3
Eugene, OR 97401

www.wipfandstock.com

PAPERBACK ISBN: 978-1-7252-7302-3
HARDCOVER ISBN: 978-1-7252-7300-9
EBOOK ISBN: 978-1-7252-7301-6

Cataloguing-in-Publication data:

Names: Carvalhaes, Cláudio, author. | Machado, Daisy, foreword. | Ellis, Marc H., afterword.

Title: Praying with every heart : orienting our lives to the wholeness of the world / by Cláudio Carvalhaes ; foreword by Daisy Machado ; afterword by Marc H. Ellis.

Description: Eugene, OR : Cascade Books, 2021 | Includes bibliographical references.

Identifiers: ISBN 978-1-7252-7302-3 (paperback) | ISBN 978-1-7252-7300-9 (hardcover) | ISBN 978-1-7252-7301-6 (ebook)

Subjects: LCSH: Prayer—Christianity. | Postcolonial theology. | Liturgics.

Classification: BV210.3 .C36 2021 (print) | BV210.3 .C36 (ebook)

Illustrations copyright © Marc H. Ellis.

Scripture quotations are from New Revised Standard Version Bible, copyright © 1989 National Council of the Churches of Christ in the United States of America. Used by permission. All rights reserved worldwide.

06/14/21

To my mother, Esther Carvalhaes,
who knows prayer more than I ever will,
who has prayed for me my entire life,
and whose life is a beautiful and powerful prayer

Contents

Foreword by Daisy Machado | ix
Acknowledgments | xi
Introduction: Praying with Every Heart | xvii

1. Praying with the World at Heart | 1
2. Praying Truly, with a Lump in the Throat | 21
3. Praying from the Ends of the World | 41
4. How to Pray from the Ends of the World: A Methodology | 67
5. What Is Common about Our Common Worship? A Methodological Critique of White Reasoning in the Process of Renewal of the *Book of Common Worship*, Presbyterian Church (USA) | 75
6. Praying with Black People for Darker Faith | 101
7. Praying with the People of *Axé*: An Interreligious Dialogue | 127
8. Praying with the Earth: A reLent Practice—Praying with a Plant (with Virginia Cover) | 143
9. Praying with Each Other during Infected Holy Week: COVID-19 and the Possibilities of Our Resurrection | 181
10. Praying with the Night | 197
11. Praying with a Lost Heart: A Decolonial Prayer | 213
12. Praying with the End of the World | 233

Conclusion: Orienting Our Hearts to Live Better | 245

Afterword by Marc H. Ellis | 251
Bibliography | 255

Foreword

IT SEEMS ODD TO write this foreword for a book about prayer. Perhaps "odd" is not the right word—maybe "out of step" makes more sense given when this book is being written, a time of pandemic, a time of social unrest, a time when hate and bigotry are being called out in the streets, a time when bigotry and hate are being extolled from a presidential bully pulpit. It would seem to make more sense to write a book that focuses on social action, on civil unrest, on ways to organize and bring marginal people together. It seems that "action" is the more appropriate focus for a time such as this. However, we all well know that after months of social isolation due to the pandemic, many people are also looking inward to find a place of solace, a place of hope, a place of renewal, a place to reimagine a world turned upside down. What better way to find that place than in the age-old practice of prayer?

Prayer has been a reality of all cultures and all religions. It has been practiced in a myriad of ways and for just as many diverse and complex reasons. Prayer has been private and it has been public. Prayer has been a way to protest and it has been a way to unite. Prayer has been about families and prayer has been about nations. Prayer has been one person, face on the ground, and prayer has also been a cathedral full of people lifting their hands in praise. Prayer happens in the simple wooden shack found in any *colonia* along the US/Mexico border and it happens in elaborate and ornate church buildings. Humans have never stopped praying and this book helps us to understand why prayer has remained and still is so very important for us as well. Prayer matters today more than ever and continues to hold a profound meaning that often escapes a simple definition.

Prayer in the twenty-first century continues to be an expression of faith in a Divine being, yet it is also the barely audible cry that escapes us during a long and difficult night. And in the pages of this book in which you, dear reader, will immerse yourself, you will find how and why prayer has also mattered to so many others as well. You will find yourself praying with those whose prayers grace these pages; their words speak to you even if they live a different reality from your own, since we all face loneliness, anger, and illness as well as joy and success, and we all look for hope. The prayers in this book remind us how similar we all are, how much we have in common, how connected we are in our humanity and in our fragility. The prayers in this book, written for and within the context of the twenty-first century, remind us how close the Divine is to us and how much we matter in the grand scheme of things.

Like Cláudio, I too grew up with a mother who was a great believer in prayer. As a teenager I did my best to get home a good forty-five minutes after 3 p.m. when I knew my mom would be praying as she did every day. Yet somehow I always found her in prayer and would reluctantly kneel with her as she prayed over me. I often refused to close my eyes. I know that if I had had a mobile phone I would have been texting a friend about being trapped in my mother's prayer hour. That was a long time ago and yet the memory is vivid as is the fact that in my own life, as I got older, as life became more complicated, as there was a career to build, as there were responsibilities to meet, as personal relationships became complex, as there were victories to celebrate, and achievements earned, I always found myself lifting a prayer. Whether it was a prayer in the wee hours of a lonely dawn or that small whisper of gratitude that escaped my heart after the news that I had been granted tenure, I found that I too turned to prayer in ways I could not have imagined. Prayer had become important for me. Prayer continues to be important for me.

Perhaps you, dear reader, are struggling with the concept of prayer, with how prayer can hold meaning for you, how prayer can fit into your own life. Perhaps you find you have no time for prayer or cannot believe in prayer, but that really does not matter. In this book you will find an entry into new ways of thinking about and reimagining what prayer means or can mean to you, as you witness what prayer has meant to so many others who like you and me struggle with the daily reality of being human in this world of ours. As Mother Teresa reminds us, "God speaks in the silence of the heart. Listening is the beginning of prayer."

—Daisy Machado

High Falls, New York
July 6, 2020

Acknowledgments

Dr. Daisy Machado has written the foreword to the book and I cannot say how immensely grateful I am to her. I vividly remember the first time I heard her speak at Union Theological Seminary when I was a PhD student. Her voice was so potent, so immense, so strong that I knew I was looking up to a giant. Since then, I have never been the same. Dr. Machado is one of the most important presences in my life. She is my master, my elder, and one to whom I listen with devotion. She has made a way out of no way and given all of us Latinxs opportunities to find our own space. Her breadth of knowledge, her wit, passion, and commitment to the poor are immeasurable. Now leading the Hispanic Summer Program,[1] she has reinvented this place of learning where Latinxs and other friends come to learn and be empowered in our journeys. Besides all this, she is a woman of prayer. I am so grateful to you, Dr. Machado.

I want to deeply thank the Jewish liberation theologian Dr. Marc H. Ellis for writing the afterword to this book. Professor Ellis has a history of love for the Palestinians that has cost him a great deal. Yet he has been unmovable in his love for and commitment to them. His prophetic writings have been a light to the world. He has been an endless inspiration to my work and to my life. His latest book, *Finding Our Voice: Embodying the Prophetic and Other Misadventures*,[2] is everywhere present in the background of this book, challenging me in many ways. He has always graciously offered his time to listen to me, to guide me, and to teach me. At the "Chapel of Love" at his beloved Cape Canaveral in Florida, Dr. Ellis has been praying also through daily comments, audios, and breathtaking pictures. Among his many other gifts, Dr. Ellis is a visual artist and some of his paintings are part of this book. What an incredible privilege and honor to have the presence of

---

1. The Hispanic Summer Program, an ecumenical program in theology and religion, trains Latinx church leaders. https://hispanicsummerprogram.org/.

2. Ellis, *Finding Our Voice*.

Dr. Ellis in this book with both his paintings and the afterword. I can't thank you enough, Dr. Ellis.

I am also grateful to Rev. Virginia Cover, the Senior Pastor at Grace Lutheran Church in Camp Hill, Pennsylvania, the pastor of my family. Pastor Cover allowed me to include in this book a wonderful Lenten program she created, and it is now the better part of chapter 8, "Praying With the Earth: A reLent Practice—Praying With a Plant." Thank you for your wonderful work, Pastor Cover.

This book is organized around various modes of language: lectures, church bulletins, texts written straight from the breath of the streets, academic styles. This is how I believe scholarship should be done. During the preparation of this book, I had the luxury of having Jane Redmont as my editor. She is a well-read theologian, a grammarian, a writer herself, and a remarkable editor. She has written an amazing book on prayer.[3] She helped make this manuscript readable. Whatever one cannot understand remains my responsibility. Jane, I am deeply thankful to you!

I am grateful beyond measure to Sudipta Singh and the Council for World Mission, who gave me the gift to pray with people in four different countries, and all of the one hundred people who traveled to these communities to pray with me.

I am grateful to my community at Union Theological Seminary in New York City and all they give to me. I want to deeply thank my Buddhist brother Rev. Kosen Gregory Snyder, my Sensei, whose wisdom and loving kindness are like a daily prayer for me, with me. He gave me the title of the book. My brother and Professor Paul Galbreath is the one who has prayed the longest with me. I am also grateful to Professor Ken Sawyer, who also teaches and prays with the folks at Cook County Jail in Chicago. I was blessed to co-teach a class on prayer with him at McCormick Seminary. So many people to thank who have sustained my life in prayer, in their own ways. Here are just very few of them: Abival Silveira, Adoniran Barbosa, Ailton Krenack, Albert Camus, Archibald Woodruff, Arrelia, Arvo Pärt, B. B. King, Bees, Berenice Rodrigues, Bill Stanley, Birds, Bospo do Rosário, Brad and Jane Wigger, Brook, Caetano Veloso, Carlos Eduardo B. Calvani, Clarice Lispector, Charlie Chaplin, Chico Buarque, Christine J. Foster, Christopher Elwood, Cornel West, Cosme, Delores Williams, Davi Kopenawa, Narges Josephine and Isabelle, Corinthians, Dean Thompson, Donald Mier, Dona Neusa, Dona Maria Pimenta, Dona Leontina, Dona Vasti, Dona Zilda, Éber F. S. Lima, Elizabeth Batina, Eric Clapton, Eloisa Borges Gois, Eny Borges, Esny Cerene Soares, Esther F. S. Carvalhaes, Firmino de Proença, Flowers,

---

3. Redmont, *When in Doubt, Sing*.

Garrincha, Gilberto Gil, Gruimarães Rosa, Grupo O Corpo, Igreja P. I. do Cambuci, Jaci Maraschin, James Cone, Janet Walton, Jane Watt and Chuck, Joãozinho Trinta, John Hoffmeyer, John and Penny Webster, Johnny, José Miguel Wisnik, Ivone Gebara, Katie Mulligan, Karyn L. Wiseman, Kerri Allen, Lauro Ferreira, Legião Urbana, Leonardo Boff, Leonildo Silveira Campos, Leontino Farias dos Santos, Luiz Carlos Garcia, Lula, Mãe Sandra, Mahalia Jackson, Marcos Oliveira, Marcelo Rosa, Melanie Harris, Mercedes Sosa, Miriam Rosa, MST, Nancy Cardoso, Nancy, Lia e Sara, Odair Pedroso Mateus, Oswaldo Montenegro, Padaria Aragão, Paulo, Denise e seus pais, Paulinho, Kátia e a VAE, Plants, Pink Floyd, Profeta Gentileza, Rosevarte de Sousa, Rubem Alves, Santiago Slabodsky, Sara Cazella and the people of Santa Fé, Seu Nelson, Silas Monteiro, Silas A. Pinto, Silvanil Teixeira Ferreira, Storm Swain, Students, Tamanduateí River, the Moon, the Sun, the Rain, the Wind, Tio Francisco e família, Toki, Tom Zé, Trees, U2, Yohana Junker, Zé Lima, my lemon tree, so many stars, and so many others.

I am so grateful to my wonderful in-laws, Rethea and Bruce Deveney, Megan, Adam, Avery, and Marshall. I am grateful every day for Peter Perella, who prays for us without ceasing, and to Tom and Margie Perella and their precious family. My heart goes to my whole family in Brazil who keep me in their prayers every day, especially to my father who lives in me and walks in my feet at every step of my journey. Also the tree Wonder who receives me every time with gladness for a silent prayer, the birds that keep visiting me in my backyard, and my dog Amora, who prays with me every night before we go to bed.

Lastly, I want to thank my family, who have changed my life and to whom I am devoted with all my heart, mind, and soul. My wise wife, Katie, my wonderful daughters, Libby and Cicci, and my amazing son, Ike. They have taught me to pray in ways they will never know. They gave me back to myself and keep telling me about life, about my own ways, what I need to keep changing, and how to love them better. I would not be who I am without each one of them. I pray for them without ceasing.

Chapter 1, "Praying with the World at Heart," is a reprint with changes of Cláudio Carvalhaes, "Praying with the World at Heart" in *Dialog: A Journal of Theology* 52 (2013) 313–20. This essay was also published as a chapter in Cláudio Carvalhaes, *What's Worship Got to Do with It? Interpreting Life Liturgically* (Eugene, OR: Cascade, 2018).

Chapters 3 and 4 are expanded reflections developed out of pages 7–18 in *Liturgies from Below: Praying with People at the Ends of the Earth*, compiled by Cláudio Carvalhaes and published by Abingdon Press (2020). Used by permission.

Chapter 5 is a reprint adapted from "White Reasoning and What Is Common in Our Common Worship?" in *Call to Worship: Liturgy, Music, Preaching, and the Arts* 49 (2017) 19–27.

Chapter 6, "Praying with Black People for Darker Faith," was published in Cláudio Carvalhaes, *What's Worship Got to Do with It? Interpreting Life Liturgically* (Eugene, OR: Cascade, 2018). All rights reserved. Republished by permission of the copyright holder.

Chapter 7, "Praying with the People of *Axé*: An Interreligious Dialogue," was first published in an earlier version as "Praying Each Other's Prayers: An Inter-religious Approach," in *Postcolonial Practice of Ministry*, edited by Kwok Pui-lan and Stephen Burns (Lanham, MD: Lexington, 2016).

Chapter 11, "Praying with a Lost Heart: A Decolonial Prayer," was first published as "A Decolonial Prayer" in *Decolonial Christianities: Latinx and Latin American Perspectives*, edited by Raimundo Barreto and Roberto Sirvent (New York: Palgrave, 2019).

Introduction

Praying With Every Heart

IT WAS MY MOTHER who taught me to pray. For her, one cannot live if not through and by prayer. Dona Esther was born on a farm where her parents worked on a field as *colonos*. A *colono* is someone who works in a "colony," a worker who labors in the fields for somebody else for some form of payment, somebody who tries to establish oneself in a country or a territory that is not one's own. The *colonos*'s situation is like that of the immigrants who work on farms in the United States: meager payment, no rights of any kind, and a very harsh life. In a recent conversation with me, she described her life from her birth to the age of nine. Her mother would wake everybody up at 5:00 a.m., prepare food, and go to the fields with her children: my mother had a little brother and a little sister. She has memories from when she was six years old. When the family got to the coffee plantation in the morning, my grandmother would put my mother, her little brother, and her baby sister under a coffee tree and leave some food and milk for them. My mother would have to take care of the two younger siblings. Sometimes she would have to run and search for her mother in the fields when one of the children would not stop crying.

When she was eight years old, my mother taught her little brother to pick up the leftover coffee beans dropped on the ground by the adults and they filled up a sack with them. With the money from those coffee beans, they were able to buy their first shoes, a little dress for her, and shorts for her brother. But before that, my mother's baby sister got sick one day and the family did not have the money to go to the doctor; the baby died of dysentery and dehydration. Another baby was born soon after, but my grandmother died at the age of twenty-nine, when my mother was nine years old, her brother seven, and her sister two. My grandfather, not knowing what to do and having to support the children, gave them away to families who could raise them. My mother went to school till the second grade. From the ages of nine to seventeen, my mother went from house to house as a maid, baby-sitter, and cleaner. By then living in the city of São Paulo, still working as a maid, she became a member of a local Independent Presbyterian Church and there she met my father. My father, seeing her situation, took her to live with his family. They married when she was twenty. Now, at eighty-nine, she has four children, eleven grandchildren, and seven great-grandchildren.

After my mother talked about her childhood, I asked her, "*Mainha*, how did you survive it all?" She replied: "It was God. Even when I didn't know it was." "But how," I asked, "did you not get bitter going through it all?" She answered: "It was life, how can I complain? It was very hard, very sad, very difficult; we didn't have anything. But it was what we had. I couldn't blame God for my mother's death, and I understood my father: he didn't know what else to do. I always loved my parents." I asked again: "What helped you keep going?" The answer came immediately: "Prayer, my son, prayer sustained my life all the way to this day and will continue to sustain me. Today I live the life of a queen! And I will continue to pray until I go live with the Lord in heaven."

A daughter of parents of various origins, some known and some buried under the forced oblivion of coloniality—Roma, Indigenous, Afro-Brazilians, and Europeans—my mother witnessed poverty and despair vividly. Through it all, she had a heart for the poor that made her radical in her politics. All she wanted was for politicians to help feed the poor because she knew how hard life could be.

I remember how she would not allow me to leave the house in the morning before going to school or to work without first praying with her. If I complained that I was late, her prayer would be longer. I had to pray before my day started. That very practice provided me with a sense of preparedness for whatever the day had in store for me. Her praying with me for the world shaped my heart and my desires. Praying was always to be done with somebody or something in my heart. This made prayer never be a lonely endeavor, even when my mother taught me to go pray in my room. In my room, I used to hold in my hands a globe of the world my father gave me and pray and cry over it, asking God to bless people everywhere.

That is the framework for prayer in which I grew up and within which I am now developing these essays. Praying is always *praying with*: my mother, those who are suffering in hospitals, people on the streets, people in prisons, human and other beings in the whole world. This form and content of prayer gave me a daily exercise in how to orient my heart. They freed me from the strictures of liturgical norms and fixed theological beliefs. "Praying with" has always turned my heart to where the world was hurting and made me focus on the needs of others. To pray was like what I see these days with my puppy Amora, who runs toward anyone who is crying and licks them and offers her presence. Like Amora's reflex, my prayer was also a way of getting closer to someone hurting, licking their wounds, and saying "I am here!" As for the savior complex in my prayers, it diminished with the years. I went from wanting to save the world to being as I am now, a listening presence, praying in deep thanksgiving and weeping together with those for whom I pray.

Prayer has also been a way for me to heal my mother's history and to attend to those like her. It is a way to heal the colonizing and colonized history of my grandparents, who struggled so much to make ends meet and who lost their beloved ones because they did not have money to go to the doctor. Perhaps my life of prayer is my way of offering companionship to those who remain under the coffee trees, not knowing whether their parents will arrive. My prayer was and still is a way of breaking forms of coloniality, the powers that keep the *colonos* under domination and away from any sense of belonging to a territory or country.

I also pray to heal my own anger at growing up poor, at not being able to buy candy or to have the same things as my friends at school. I pray to heal the anger of having to wear used clothes that were not my size, of not being able to buy lunch but to have to bring bread and butter or bread and sugar or, on the best days, bread and egg. I also pray as a form of deep gratitude to my parents because they gave me so much. I pray now with gratitude for my childhood and my secondhand clothes and used shoes, my delicious bread and butter and bread and sugar. I pray for shoe-shining boys who like me could never own the shoes we shined. My heart will always belong to all the shoe-shining kids in the world. They will always belong to me. They are my country and my citizenship. I also pray for a possible future where my children can actually live on the earth. My prayers now are bridges to a future that does not exist but is one that we must create. My daily prayer is the imagination and the desire of another world possible. Prayer is another brick placed toward the building of that bridge. Prayer is a spiritual exercise of the heart that can reshape and heal the past, can orient the heart toward a present of justice and peace, and can move us into a future of real possibilities for life to endure.

João Guimarães Rosa, one of the most important Brazilian writers, a novelist, short story writer, and diplomat, wrote in his novel *Grande Sertão: Veredas* something that I believe could be understood as a prayer:

> Oh, to experience pleasure, to find joy,
>
> We must know everything,
>
> Form our souls in consciousness.[1]

---

1. Guimarães Rosa, *Grande Sertão*, 234.

To pray is to learn how to be happy and have pleasure, but that means shifting from a concept of individual happiness to an understanding of collective joy. For we either move through life together and in solidarity and joy or we die alone in sadness, with individual possessions and a happiness never accomplished.

To pray is to know everything, or rather, always to move toward that place. It is to orient ourselves toward this knowing in ways measured by the heart. It is relearning, reshaping our thoughts, thinking about our actions, acting, checking our thinking, and checking our emotions as we get to know ourselves and the lives of others. We do not live by ourselves; we do not own an identity; we do not work for our own "wholeness." We are more! We are many! We are a compost of soil, water, stars, trees, and air. With the earth, we are a gathering of voices, a plethora of subjectivities, a whole array of emotions, and endless gestures of care and mutuality. To know everything with the heart is to live in deep gratitude and reciprocity to one another, to the earth, to all who have been, who are, and who will be.

Prayer is gaining a consciousness of who we are in solidarity with the world we live in and the earth that hosts us. Thus prayer is fundamentally *more*. Prayer is a way of *giving soul to this consciousness*, that is, of blending consciousness with compassion, action with thinking, emotions with reason, enthusiasm with empathy. To give soul to consciousness is like giving flesh to the bones, to make the consciousness of prayer be not only a reasonable consciousness but also a soulful, playful one. For our prayers encompass soul and body, consciousness and emotions. They teach and train our whole being skillfully to serve, to honor, to laugh, and to prophesy words of life to the world. To give soul to consciousness is to start our knowing with the primal and most fundamental sense that we must not harm: I must not harm others, I must not harm animals, I must not harm plants, I must not harm myself, I must not harm the earth, I must not harm the rivers, I must not harm the forests, I must not harm the fish in the sea. No, I cannot harm. Soul into consciousness.[2]

When we pray something deep must happen in us. We must go to such depth in ourselves that we lose the fear of becoming something else when we are somebody else. The well-being we seek for ourselves is the

---

2. By "consciousness" I mean what has sometimes been translated into English as "conscientization," as used by Fanon as *conscienciser* in *Black Skins, White Masks*; "*conscientização*"—"consciousness-raising" and "critical consciousness"—in Freire's *Pedagogy of the Oppressed*; "archaeology of knowledge" in Foucault's *The Archaeology of Knowledge*; Said's "self-inventory" in *Orientalism*; Kopenawa's dreaming in *The Falling Sky*; and the peasants' imagery and struggles in Cusicanqui's *Sociología De La Imagen* and *Ch'ixinakax utxiwa*.

same well-being as other human beings', whatever race, country, or location they are from. The well-being we seek for ourselves is the well-being of fish, racoons, hummingbirds, cardinals, worms, plants, mountains, rivers, and oceans. In order for that to happen we enter into a form of alterity, of mutual metamorphosis, which some Brazilian scholars call *obliquação*.[3] Prayer is an *obliquação* where we posit ourselves in the place of others. But it is more: it is that moment when I become the other. And still more: it is when I become the other of the other. It is Clarice Lispector, a Brazilian writer whose work influenced the neologism *obliquação*, coined by Alexandre Nodari, who actually writes in this way. While Lispector never used this concept, her work gives fullness to the ways in which this entanglement and perspectivism happen, this form of deep mutual implication occurs. In one of her stories she says: "I had wanted to be the others before I knew who I was. I realized then that I had already been the others and that was easy. My greatest experience would be to be the other of the others: and the other of the others was me."[4]

To pray is to move in this vertigo in which we realize each of us is a multiplicity of others. To pray is to acquire the perspective of others and have that perspective become mine too. To pray is risky because you start supporting and being with what people say is not you. To pray is this *obliquação*, this orientation of our hearts toward elsewhere, a God who lives elsewhere, in the lives of others, and yet to discover that elsewhere also lives within us.

To pray is to pay attention to the world. The world presents itself and I pray and write. I pray by bricolage, as a creative event that needs nothing less than a transformation of the heart into a new mystery. As Lispector says, "Creation is not an understanding, it is a new mystery."[5]

This transformation will teach me to wonder expansively but also to place limits on myself, ways of living and relating that honor and defend the lives of others, be they other humans, animals, plants, water, air, or soil. Each is a mystery in its own multiplicity. That is true *obliquação* in prayer.

As I write, our world is in the grips of the COVID-19 pandemic. Indigenous people, Black and brown people, and all of the poor, whatever their race, are dying in high numbers. The world is burning with cries for racial justice after the death of George Floyd. Social inequality is growing exponentially, and the earth is being ripped apart to the point of exhaustion and is perilously close to permanent unbalance. To pray is to attend to

---

3. Nodari, "'A vida oblíqua': o hetairismo ontológico," 139–54.
4. Lispector, "A Experiência Maior," 23.
5. Lispector, "Brasilia," 961–62.

these events and people. To pray is to hold onto the mountains so they will not fall apart, it is to hold the skies like the Indigenous people in Brazil, so that the earth can continue to exist a little longer. To pray is to be like Sisyphus and push a boulder up the mountain even if it rolls down again. Until the day it does not.

I remember being in Italy in the spring of 2018, visiting the shores of the Mediterranean where the precious little boy Alan Kurdi was found dead after the sinking of a boat of refugees escaping to Europe. His photo, flashed around the world, is engraved in my heart and mind.[6] His body was the presence not only of a Syrian refugee but of the body of our own children. He is a figure of the crisis of refugees and immigrants all over the world. The Afghan-American author Khaled Hosseini wrote the most beautiful book on this experience, *Sea Prayer*, which I read before heading to Italy.[7] When I visited that place I wept uncontrollably. That night, I created a song without words in which I tried to connect my mother's prayer, my prayer as a father, my prayer for all the refugees, and a blessing for the precious Alan Kurdi.[8]

I must confess that this time of ours is turning me more and more toward prayer. I feel as does the Brazilian composer Gilberto Gil, who has said that these devastating times in Brazil, under the leadership of the fascist and rootless president Bolsonaro, inspire him to pray.[9]

I pray to understand the world we live in and to lean closer to those who are suffering. But I only discover what prayer is after I have prayed. Only after. That is why there is a tension always present, combining what I have experienced and what I have become through the lives of others. I pray until I find a way out of no way, until something changes, until something happens and before me are new forms of life, forms of relationships that change and are transformed. To pray is to have our theologies challenged, our cosmologies transformed and expanded.[10]

To pray is to ordain our devotions, to help us know how and what to desire. As a desire, prayer is like a seed that once planted in our hearts, sprouts, and from which a flower blooms vividly. And from that flower, there is fruit, which returns back to the earth to start all over again.

In the times of destruction of everything we know, amid the ruining of the earth and the disappearing of the world, what does prayer have to do

---

6. See Walsh, "Alan Kurdi's Story."
7. Hosseini, *Sea Prayer*.
8. Carvalhaes, "A prayer song for Alan Kurdi."
9. Gil, "Bolsonaro me inspira a oração."
10. Boff, "Post-COVID-19" (I and II).

with it all? How can we pray in ways that can postpone the end of the world? Perhaps this is the main question of this book.

This Book

Prayer is theory and practice together. First-level theology (practice) and second-level theology (theory) together. Prayer is a way of learning to live and to give meaning to life. This book is a kind of theoretical development of my prayer with people who live in the margins, everywhere I have lived. Most fundamentally, this work is deeply shaped by my visits with people from four countries where I traveled during the years 2018 and 2019: the Philippines, South Africa, Jamaica, and Italy.[11] In those places we prayed with people going through hardships and challenges that could not all be thought or spoken. Praying with them was to gain an awareness that we had to stay, linger a little longer with those who were suffering. Being with them reoriented my heart again about how and with whom I should pray.

This book encompasses a large trajectory where each chapter adds an important step to the whole of the journey. While there will be many steps yet to be added to the journey as we go and discover, each chapter adds a fold into the movement of living prayers made of feeling/thinking/doing. Let me note two chapters that come from my book *What's Worship Got to Do with It? Interpreting Life Liturgically* (Cascade, 2018). The first chapter, "Praying With the World at Heart," illuminates the whole journey, establishing the methodology of prayer: we pray with our hearts laid bare in the world, listening to the breathing of the earth and those destitute of any form of dignity. The chapter "Praying with Black People for Darker Faith" comes after chapter 5, "What Is Common about Our Common Worship? A Methodological Critique of White Reasoning in the Process of Renewal of the *Book of Common Worship*." Both chapters together offer a solid case for addressing liturgical racism: the first criticizes a white methodology

---

11. During the years 2018 and 2019, I developed a project with the Council for World Mission (CWM) (https://www.cwmission.org) named "Re-imagining Worship as Acts of Defiance and Alternatives in the Context of Empire," in which a group of us from several countries visited four continents: Asia and the Pacific Islands (Manila, Philippines), Africa (Johannesburg, South Africa), the Americas (Kingston, Jamaica), and Europe (Scicli, Italy). During these four gatherings, scholars, pastors, students, artists, and church members lived with the people in poor communities and afterwards wrote collectively their impressions and experiences of these places in the form of liturgical resources. A book with a collection of these prayers, songs, rituals, rites of healing, eucharistic and baptismal prayers, meditations, and art was published recently: Carvalhaes, *Liturgies from Below*. For more on this project, see chapter 3, "Praying With People at the Ends of the Earth."

in creating liturgical resources, and the second, while bringing an awareness of the history of Black folks, offers white churches a new language for prayer in worship that hopes to challenge the rampant structural racism that lives within the Christian faith.

All this has grown on me and grown in me: the positionality of prayer, its dispositions, commitments, and awareness. To pray is to cast away demons, spirits of death that inhabit people and political, social, and religious structures. Praying is not simple. But I have learned that there is no way to pray if not with a lump in my throat, babbling words, hoping to find ways to name the trauma and the interruptions of life. I have learned that there is no way to pray if I do not carry the whole world in my heart. The only way to pray is to be fully immersed in body, heart, and soul with those I am praying with and for. I have learned that in order to pray one needs to position oneself with those living at the end of the world, where life is taken away, the air to breathe is robbed, and dignity is stolen. I have learned that unless we change the very methodology of forming and performing liturgy and prayers, we will continue to be the cause of oppression and not its solution. I have learned that I need a new vocabulary, a new reasoning, and a conversion in order to move away from structures of power and pray with those who are at the end of the world.[12]

In today's massive pandemic, I have learned once again that unless we pray from the belly of the beast, prayer is nothing more than a set perfunctory gesture. I have learned that unless I pray with those who are not from my faith, I cannot pray my own Christian prayers. I have learned that unless we pray amidst violence, we are not learning how to reorient our hearts. After living with my own changes, I have learned that I have to pray with the night and with that which causes me to fear. And lately, I have gone through a fundamental conversion in my whole way of thinking, feeling, and believing, moving toward the earth. Without the earth I cannot pray, I

---

12. In most of the book, as in the titles of chapters 3 and 4, I speak of the *ends* of the world; elsewhere, as in the title of the final chapter, I speak of the *end* of the world. See that chapter for an explanation of the distinction I draw there. When I use the expression "at the ends of the world" (including in the phrases "people living at the ends of the world" or "people at the ends of the world") in this book, I mean a combination of (1) "the ends of the earth," geographically far away from what we in the "included" consider as far and (2) people who are on the margins in all societies everywhere, those who are most poor and disenfranchised economically, politically, socially, culturally, physically, racially, sexually, ecclesially, and in other ways, who are forgotten and live in places that are abandoned, neglected, torn by violence. When I use "the end [singular] of the world," I add to these two meanings those of (3) in the accepted sense of the time of the end of the world, since for the most excluded people, it has always already been the end of the world; and (4) "at the end of the world" as the ending time of the world which now hangs over us and threatens us due to the human destruction of the earth.

cannot breathe, I cannot survive. Living in this world where violence and death threaten us all, I have learned that we are always on the brink of going mad, of losing our hearts—and of losing heart.

I pray that this book will speak to you in one way or another.

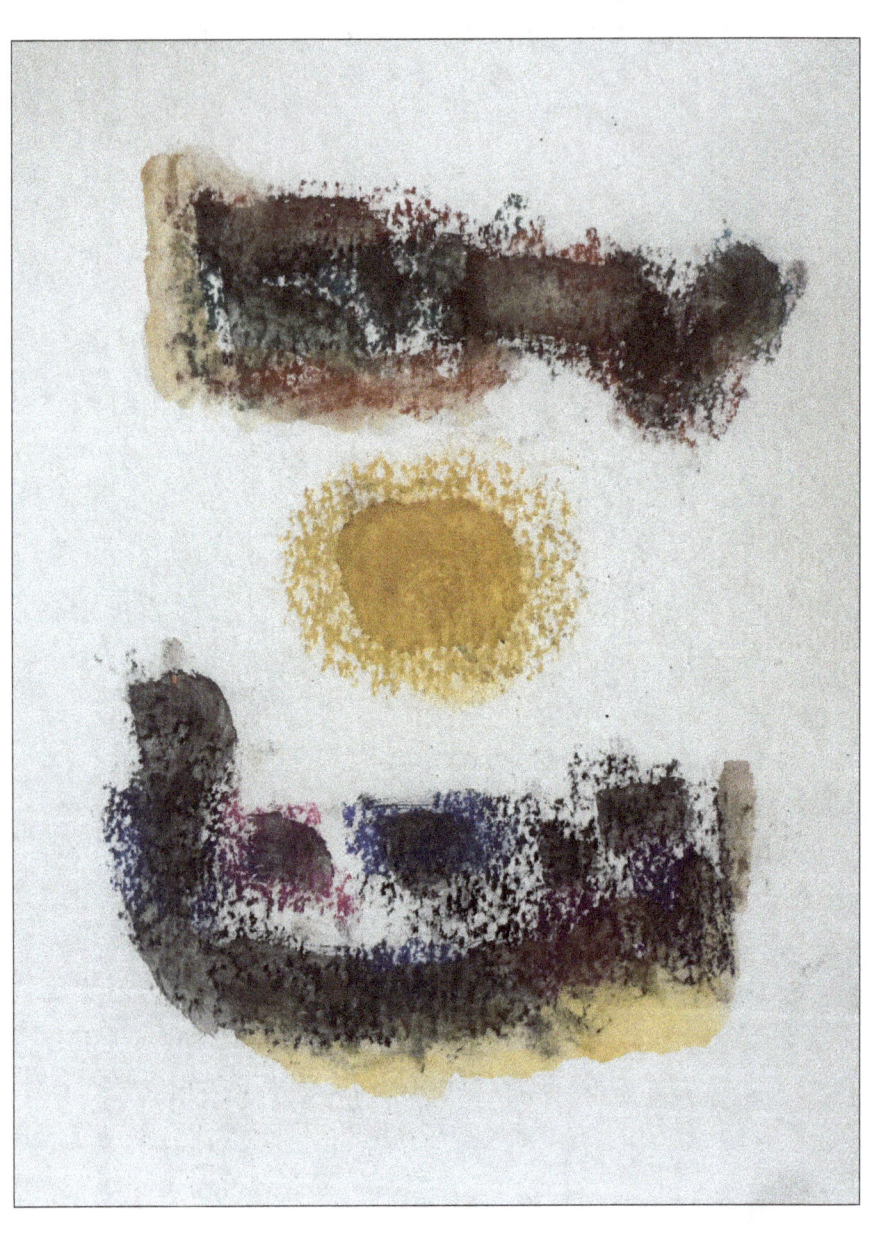

1

Praying with the World at Heart

> Prayer is an invitation to God to intervene in our lives, to let [God's] will prevail in our affairs; it is the opening of a window to [God] in our will, an effort to make [God] the Lord of our soul. We submit our interests to [God's] concern and seek to be allied with what is ultimately right. Our approach to the holy is not an intrusion but an answer.
>
> —Abraham Joshua Heschel[1]

WHERE DO WE START when we pray? Where are the places that we go to pray? What sources do we use to pray? What do we pay attention to when we pray? What theologies, gestures, bodies, communities, commitments inform our prayers? Where does our grammar for prayer come from? To talk about prayers is to talk about that which gives us life. Prayers have the power to create, transform, and hold our worlds together. When I was growing up, my mother would repeat a phrase that I think is from E. M. Bounds, but was used by Billy Graham: "Much prayer, much power. Little prayer, little power. No prayer, no power." My mother has always been a woman of prayer, and if I know the power of prayer today, it is because of her own devotion to prayer. She prayed without ceasing.

My mother would never let me leave the house without a prayer and always reminded me to pray before going to bed. These habits are still within me. Lately, praying has become both easier and more difficult. It has become easier because I do not carry the anxiety I once had to see my prayers answered. I somewhat know, especially when I am not suffering, that God will do whatever God wants to do. On the other hand, it has become increasingly

---

1. Heschel, *I Asked for Wonder*, 28.

more difficult to pray because there are so many disasters piling up in our world today that I do not know what to pray for. Prayer holds together aspects of both agency and powerlessness. In any case, we are called to pray. When I was in my early teenage years, my father gave me a globe with the map of the world. I used to pray holding the globe in my arms, next to my heart. I learned that I always had to pray for the salvation of the world. To this day, I still pray with the world close to my heart. We pray not because God needs our prayers but because the world needs our prayers.

My prayer life has been marked by both the brutality and the gentleness of our daily lives, by the un/bearable, un/framed materiality of our glorious and disastrous reality, by the heaviness and lightness of our bodies, a dizzying search for answers, and awareness of what I should pay attention to when I pray. Below, throughout this chapter, you will see an array of prayer sources. They create, perhaps, an unrecognized theological discourse embedded in a heart filled with vast blessings and emotions and a mind tormented again and again by the disasters of the world and the life of the poor. The events of the world both shrink and expand a faith that longs for a new time and a healed world, where the poor find food and shelter, the economic powers come tumbling down, the afflicted find some solace, and those that are overly comfortable become disturbed by the burning events of our days. I always pray with my community with a broken heart, wrestling with my own faith or lack thereof. While I am still far from "be still my soul . . ." I am learning how to pray. Slowly.

People are in the midst of life and death right now as we read and pray. We have always to pray more. Prayers do have the power to change things! For I believe that "much prayer, much power. Little prayer, little power. No prayer, no power."

Lost Grace

She was at the counter of a drugstore waiting for the medicine. In her arms, her daughter was sleeping. In her hands, a torn paper, the prescription given by a doctor. After a while, the pharmacist came to her and said, "I am sorry, you don't have insurance, we cannot give you the medicine." She did not understand and said, "Medicine for my daughter. Please." The man repeated: "I am sorry, you don't have health insurance; can you pay?" "Yes, yes," she said, and the pharmacist replied: "It is four hundred and fifty dollars." She opened her purse and while holding her exhausted sleeping daughter, she extracted from the purse twelve dollars and thirty-seven cents. While she was putting the money on the counter, with some difficulty, the pharmacist said: "Ma'am,

I am sorry, this medicine is too expensive." She extended her arm, making the sign *"wait"* with her hand while trying to find more money at the bottom of her purse. The pharmacist was embarrassed and the people in line behind the woman were starting to lose their patience. The woman found a couple of nickels and added them to the rest of the money she had placed on the counter. The man said: *"I am sorry, this is not enough."* The woman said, *"Take it, please. Everything,"* she said. *"Medicine, please." "I am sorry"* the pharmacist replied, *"but this is not enough. Please step outside of the line. I need to help the people in line."* The woman said, *"Medicine please, my daughter sick, very sick." "Please step aside,"* said the now impatient pharmacist. The mother did not understand and her exhausted face was filled with fear. *"Please, doctor, please,"* she said. A man in line took the money from the counter and tried to give it to her, but she refused: *"No, please take, medicine for my daughter, very sick, very sick."* The man opened her purse and threw the money inside. *"Please step aside!"* the other customer screamed. The woman stepped aside, saying, *"Please medicine, my daughter very sick. Please."* The pharmacist and the people in the line started to act as if she was not there and kept tending to their business. The woman started to scream, *"Medicine, please!"* while trying to get the money back out of her purse. The pharmacist said, *"Ma'am, if you continue to scream, I will have to call security."* The woman sobbed, *"Sorry, sorry, medicine please, medicine please. My daughter . . . "* While she was crying, she went through the line asking people, *"Money please, my daughter very sick, look,"* showing them the prescription given to her by the doctor.

The people in line started to complain, saying she was bothering everyone, and the pharmacist called security. *"No, please,"* she said, *"medicine only. I go, please medicine my daughter very sick, I go, I go."* Two security guards came, and the woman began wailing so loud that she woke her daughter. Both were crying when the security guards took her, this 5'5" woman with her four-year-old daughter in her arms. As the security guards were taking her out, she cried even louder: *"Señor Jesus, ten piedad, ten piedad! Ten piedad Señor Jesús, mi hija está tan enfermita, por favor les pido que me dé la medicina que mi hija necesita. Por favor, por favor, Jesucristo!"* And she was taken away from the drugstore and placed on the street with the two guards securing the door. She sat on the cold street. She and her daughter were crying, and she was praying, *"Jesucristo, ten piedad."* Jesus Christ, have mercy.

Her prayers were never answered. It appears that God did not have mercy on her. Her daughter went without medicine. Can we say that God had mercy on her? How so? Who was to blame? God? The easy way out is to say that if she were not here illegally, she would not have to go through this. But she was a citizen of this country. We are the arms and legs, hands and eyes, mouths and ears of God's answer. The mother's prayer will never be answered if not through us. Thus, prayer is an exercise in becoming, in our bodies, through our feelings, breathing, and thoughts, always available to the poor. To pray to God is to become that which we pray for. To sing the *Kyrie*—"Have mercy, Lord!"—every week in Christian worship services is to become, by God's grace, God's merciful flesh in the world for the lowly, for those who have no agency, no access, no voice, no place in the world.

To pray thus is an act of love, love for God, love for my brothers and sisters, love for the world. To learn to pray is to learn how to become Christ in the world. To learn how to pray is to walk around in the world with our hearts outside of our bodies, witnessing the least of these being mercilessly crushed. To learn how to pray is to find ways to change things and create conditions of an honored and blessed life for all. Prayer is to make laws that change the mother's situation. Prayer is the opposite of throwing the mother out on the street. It is a whole economic system that demands dignified life for all. And nothing less than that! Politically, socially, culturally, to pray is to become God's love for "the least of these." I will not learn how to pray until I learn how to serve, how to commit to those less favored, how to make sure that the poor are cared for, attended to by the mercy of God in and through us.

Until this woman receives medicine for her daughter, I will never learn how to pray. Every time a prayer like the one this woman uttered is unanswered, a grace is lost. Sadly, we live amidst "lost graces,"[2] possibilities of God's tangible manifestation in our midst, offered to us in order to expand us, to help us become more committed Christians and better humans, but we don't pray, we often miss these opportunities. Lost graces are God's graces offered to us and to which we do not pay attention because we do not pay attention to the poor. We do not have eyes to see, ears to hear, hands to touch, arms to embrace, or boldness to fight for the right causes with the poor.

The Theological Weight of the Circumstances

The Brazilian theologian Ivone Gebara said in a recent article published in Brazil: "In general, theologians reflect very little of the poetic expression of the joys and pain of Christian communities. There is a distance between the work of those who analyze the contents of the religious tradition of our days and those who are responsible for the animation of the community, its feasts and weekly celebrations."[3]

---

2. "Lost grace" is a term used by André Breton in *Mad Love*.
3. Gebara, "Liturgia e Teologia," 60.

Gebara is right. Theologians reflect mostly on the high dogmatics of our theological systems, engage with the philosophical aspects of our beliefs, the historical and linguistic aspects of our creeds, the articles of our books of order, our liturgies and confessions. We do not, however, give much attention to the full exuberance of matters that affect the daily lives of people: the price of the bus or the daily bread, the violence on the streets, the symbols in people's houses, their music, their love life, their joys and dreams. Theologians do not, for the most part, wrestle with people's pains. Whether theologians pray or not, people's daily lives do not often find themselves in our theological books or liturgical books.

Perhaps Gebara says this because her daily life is interrupted by the daily affairs of the people. She cannot seclude herself in a writing retreat. Instead, she always has to stop her writing or research because in the community where she has chosen to live, a couple started a fight, a woman was raped, or children could not get food at school. In her theology, the relationality of people is what helps her understand who God might be and it is in the tapestry of life that God appears and acts in people's lives. Getting deeply involved in the daily life of people, theology must become the breathing of the joys and pains of the people. God has no reason to be/come if not reasoned through the lives of the poor, where God is be/coming all the time. Becoming acquainted with people's daily lives helps us gain a new grammar of faith, and thus a new grammar for our prayers.

Gebara writes, "The world of our circumstances is our life, with its grandeurs and personal and relational miseries. It is from this world that our prayers and our music, even the most sublime ones, are born."[4] The *lex orandi* (law of prayer) is born out of the law of life (*lex vivendi*), the daily life of the poor, as it gives shape to their joys, concerns, and beliefs (*lex credendi*, the law of belief). The task for theologians is to attend to the *lex orandi-vivendi-credendi* of the poor, listening to their prayers and learning with them how to properly pray. It is there, rather than in our liturgical books, that we can find the most powerful and sublime prayers, hymns, and affirmations of faith. There, in the midst of the struggle for justice with the poor, we learn the ethics we need to judge, act, and live. These, Gebara reports, are some of the sayings people say and pray:

> I believe that the world will be better when the smallest one who suffers believes in the small.
>
> You are the God of the poor, a human and small God who sleeps on the streets, God of a torn face.

---

4. Gebara, "Liturgia e Teologia," 59. My translation.

> To receive Communion with this suffering people is to make an alliance with the oppressed people.
>
> All of sudden, our eyes cleared out, cleared out, cleared out! And we discovered that the poor has value, has value, has value!
>
> The people of God marched to the promised land. Moses was walking ahead of them. Today we are Moses when we face the oppressor.
>
> I have so many brothers I can't count, and a beautiful sister whose name is freedom.[5]

These sayings and prayers, like daily actions, feed utopias and transform the world.

Holding the World with Affection

For a Protestant boy like me, it was a surprise to discover a monastery of Protestant nuns in the midst of the mountains in Europe. I always thought that only Roman Catholics had monasteries. And I could never figure out why people would give their lives to be inside of a monastery. Spending a few days with those nuns transformed my vision. In one conversation, I asked them: "Why do you stay here? What is the purpose of your giving your life to live here?" One of the nuns replied, "We are here to pray for the world every day. There are so many people going through pain, turmoil, and suffering, we must tend them, we must care for them, we must stand before God on their behalf. God does not need us to do it, but these people might need us. We hold all of the suffering and the world in our prayers with affection."

Gratitude and Forgiveness

To be grateful in life is a constant challenge. That is why I love to receive communion every week: because it forces me to see the ways that God is blessing my life and I must be thankful no matter what I am going through. At the eucharistic table I must say "God, thank you!" At the table I must learn with the early Christians who organized their prayers around gratitude and forgiveness. At the table I learn with my brothers and sisters that I have been blessed. If I can learn to wrap my days as well as my heart around prayers of gratitude and petitions of mercy, I will gain a kind of wisdom that will help me go through life better. Every day, at least three

---

5. Gebara, "Liturgia e Theologia," 62.

times a day, I must utter a prayer of gratitude and beg for forgiveness. Life is better lived if through *Eucharistia* and *Kyrie*, thanksgiving and mercy. God have mercy, thanks be to God!

Reconstructing Past, Present, and Future

Our prayers have the power to recreate the past, reshape the present, and invent a future where the Reign of God can happen. Time and time again, we must create prayers that take the conditions of the world, inform us of the tragedies of the world, and offer a new way of being, acting, hoping, learning, and believing. Pedro Casaldáliga, a prophetic bishop in Brazil, wrote a mass to celebrate the past-present-future of the *Quilombolas*, heirs of African slaves in Brazil. In this prayer, past, present, and future are remembered, renamed, reframed, and reorganized. The mass begins with the following prayer:[6]

> We are coming from the bottom of the earth,
> coming from the womb of night,
> made into meat at the butcher,
> we have come to remember.
>
> We are coming from the death of the seas,
> coming from the dark and muddy basements,
> heirs of the *banzo*[7] we are,
> we have come to cry.
>
> We are coming from the black rosaries,
> coming from our *terreiros*,[8]
> from the cursed saints we are,
> we have come to pray.
>
> We are coming from the shop floor,
> coming from sounds and shapes,
> of art denied we are,
> we have come to create.

---

6. Casaldáliga and Tierra, "Missa dos Quilombos." My translation.

7. *Banzo* is the feeling of something lost, left behind, a longing for something one had once but does not have anymore. The Africans, when brought to the American continent, used to mention this feeling of *banzo* about their homeland, people, things, life.

8. *Terreiros* are houses of worship in Brazil for Afro-Brazilian religious services.

We are coming from the depths of fear,
coming from the deaf currents
a long lament we are,
we have come to praise.

A de Ó (Recited)

From the Exile of life,
the mines at night,
the meat sold,
the Law of the Scourge,
the *banzo* of the seas ...
to the new *albores*![9]
we go to Palmares[10]
with all the drums!

We are coming from the rich stoves,
coming from the poor brothels,
of sold meat we are,
we have come to love.

We are coming from the old slave quarters,
Coming to the new slums,
of the margins of the world we are,
we have come to dance.

We are coming from the trains of the suburbs,
coming in crazy pendants,
with life between the teeth we arrive,
we have come to sing.

---

9. *Albores* here can mean "new mornings."

10. Palmares was a large, well-known free community in the state of Alagoas, Brazil, made up of Africans turned into slaves who rebelled against slavery and of other societal outcasts; it existed from 1605 until it was suppressed in 1694. A famous leader of Palmares was Zumbi, who was born there in 1655. When he was a child he was captured by Portuguese colonial forces. He was taught Portuguese and Latin. At the age of fifteen Zumbi rebelled, escaped, and returned to Palmares, where he became a leader of that *mocambo*.

We are coming from the big stadiums,
coming from samba schools,
dancing the samba of rebellion we come,
we have come to sway.

We are coming from the womb of Minas
coming from the sad *mocambos*,[11]
of silent cries silent we are,
We have come to charge.

We are coming from the cross of the power mills,
We are bleeding the cross of Baptism,
tagged by iron we were,
We have come to scream.

We are coming from the top of the hills,
coming from the lower parts of the law,
from the unnamed graves we arrived
We have come to cry out loud.

We are coming from the ground of the *Quilombos*,[12]
coming from the sound of drums,
the new Palmares we are,
We have come to fight.

These prayers, said in unison, shape not only people of African descent in Brazil but also fall upon the whole society of Brazil as a form of history from below, a way of telling white folks what coloniality did to the precious Black people of Brazil. The whole prayer is structured around "We have come from" and "we have come to," showing not only the diverse origins of the people who are praying but also the places they are going now, opening up spaces of creation and life in the present. Naming who they are, they embrace their past of utter pain and struggle and prepare the way for a future of struggle empowered by their ancestors, organized by their songs, energized by their gifts, strength, wisdom, and all of the movements of their souls and bodies. Such a prayer has the power to scare away the white patriarchalism

---

11. *Mocambos* were villages like Palmares, formed by Africans who freed themselves from slavery.

12. *Quilombos* are like *mocambos*.

and racism still in place in Brazilian society and to create a new world of justice and hope, one that is already happening under the feet of those who are praying. Stepping onto this new holy ground, their and our holy ground, all of us in Brazil are impacted by its power, the power of this holy ground and holy people. By praying the Quilombos' prayers with them, I learn to honor them. I dance with them. I sing with them as I become one of them, loving them deeply and fighting now the same fight of justice and hope. That is why we must pray each other's prayers!

Psalms

My mother taught me the best way to contextualize the use of the Psalms for our days. Here is a story that my fifty-six-year-old brother Joe told me about Psalm 121.

For almost four years Joe could not find a job and his situation was getting worse and worse. He lost a very good job he had, then he lost his car, and he was several months late on his house payments. His wife got sick, his daughter had to stop going to school, and in spite of it all he went to the streets of São Paulo every day looking for any job he could find. His shoes had holes in them. One day, he went to my mother's house for lunch. There is a long corridor from the gate at the street to the door of her house. He rang the bell and entered. As he walked towards our mother, his head was down, his body tired. Our mother went to meet him and as soon as she saw him walking down the corridor she called, "Son, look up! Look up right now! I ain't gonna let you look down this way!" He was absolutely exhausted, his soul and body beaten up, lonely, with no strength or hope to continue anymore. Our mother approached Joe, held his head up with her small but strong hands and said: "Look up, son! For your help will come from the Lord . . ." He started to cry and could barely stay standing. My eighty-year-old mother had to hold his body and crying with him she said, "Look up and say with me: 'I lift up my eyes to the hills—from where will my help come? My help comes from the Lord, who made heaven and earth.'" Joe could not say a word, but my mother said: "I am going to continue to say it until you say it with me: come on . . . I lift up my eyes to the hills . . . Say it . . . 'I lift up my eyes to the hills—from where will my help come?' With me now: 'My help comes from the Lord, who made heaven and earth.'" In the midst of tears of exhaustion, with his head still held up by my mother's hands, Joe started to whisper some words with the salty taste of his tears: "I lift up my eyes . . . I lift up my eyes to the hills . . . I lift up my eyes to the hills . . . " "Continue with me now, son: 'My help comes from the Lord, who made heaven and earth.'" And she continued the psalm for him. She knew it by heart: "He will not let your foot be moved; he who keeps you will not slumber. He who keeps Israel will neither slumber nor sleep. The Lord is your keeper; the Lord is your shade at your right hand. The sun shall not strike you by day, nor the moon by night. The Lord will keep you from all evil; he will keep your life. The Lord will keep your going out and your coming in from this time on and for evermore." They ended up saying the whole psalm on their knees. "Look up!"

With the help of Psalm 121, my mother was able to give my brother perspective, new hopes, and empowerment. By re-positioning my brother's body, she helped him reposition his soul and his mind towards God. With his head up, he could see God's vastness beyond his immediate surroundings and was reminded of God's grace. He was able to add another possibility for his life, to let something new grow inside of him that did not exist before and bring a part of him back to life that was already killed by the adversities of life. Within a year of that day, his life changed. Today my brother has already retired. He and his family are doing well. Psalm 121, proclaimed by his almost illiterate mother, saved his life.

Praying with Brothers and Sisters of Other Traditions

If my references and prayer life were confined to the Christian tradition, my life would be narrow and my God incredibly small. While we have a wealth of prayers from many Christian churches throughout history, I believe we can gain more of life and of God if we learn to pray the prayers of sisters and brothers of other traditions. My work and my hope are that, increasingly, we will be able to pray each other's prayers and sing each other's songs, blessing ourselves with each other's blessings.

So I learned to pray in silence with a Buddhist cylindrical prayer wheel from Tibet. A spindle made of metal, the prayer wheel has a piece of paper inside with a *mantra*, a sacred phrase to be repeated by the one who prays. The way to pray is to spin the wheel. As we spin the wheel, it serves as a series of spoken prayers and spreads the prayers around the world. It is indeed a beautiful silent way of praying! The Brazilian theologian Leonardo Boff once said, "I prefer the silence of Buddha to the endless babbling of the theologians."[13]

I am challenged to learn to pray with Mahatma Gandhi, who said: "Prayer is not asking. It is a longing of the soul. It is daily admission of one's weakness. It is better in prayer to have a heart without words than words

---

13. Boff, "Prefiro o silêncio de Buda." My translation.

without a heart." The admission of my weakness can be compared with the *Kyrie* in the Christian tradition. Gandhi reminds us that what is at stake in prayer is what our heart carries, not exactly what we say.

With Rumi, the thirteenth-century Persian poet, jurist, theologian, and Sufi mystic, I utter the words, "I am like a bird from another continent, sitting in this aviary. The day is coming when I will fly off, but who is it now in my ear who hears my voice? Who says words with my mouth?"[14] As a colonized foreigner, I never know whose voices I am speaking, who is whispering in my ear, and who is speaking the words in my mouth. Rumi helps me to pray and find a better way back to the multitude that I am.

With Lalla Ded, a fourteenth-century mystic of the Kashmiri Shaivite sect, I learn to deal with my own darkness.

> I didn't believe in it for a moment
>
> But I gulped down the wine of my own voice.
>
> And then I wrestled with the darkness inside me,
>
> Knocked it down, clawed at it, ripped it to shreds.[15]

Our prayer life must learn to pray in another language, another religious tradition, another culture, and another heart, many other hearts. Endlessly. Until we finally learn how to pray.

Praying without Ceasing

> My body is suffering
>
> It is my great torpor
>
> I am languishing
>
> I give you a thousand thanks, my Lord
>
> My bones are shaken up
>
> My shadow becomes invisible
>
> My soul is confused
>
> Pierce me, my Lord
>
> My God
>
> Open to me the gates
>
> Of eternal servitude

14. Rumi, "Who Says Words with My Mouth?," 2.
15. Děd, *I, Lalla*, introduction.

Throw me your cholera (anger)[16]

In the Temple of Zion.[17]

A friend has problems with drug addiction. He stole almost everything that had value from his parents' house in order to buy drugs. He is still wandering around the streets of Fortaleza, Brazil, but his parents do not even know if he is still alive. Another friend used to read the obituary section of the newspaper every morning to see if his son was still alive. Yet another friend had to visit her son in jail because addiction caused him to steal and be incarcerated. The proliferation of drugs throughout the world is consuming innumerable lives. The war against drug cartels initiated by the Clinton administration was a failure and it continues to have no results, even with the millions of dollars spent. The drug cartels rule over many places around the globe. Los Angeles is filled with drugs. Hong Kong lives under their rule. The streets of São Paulo are now filled with people dependent on crack. They live in a region nicknamed "Crackolandia," in eternal servitude, living the *cholera*, the anger of life. The local state and other social and religious organizations are hopeless in their efforts to help them. The descent into drugs is a descent into hell and there are very few that make it back. How do we pray for and with them? How does our prayer create new ways to fight, to struggle, to find new life possibilities? How can we walk and pray with people in the grips of drug addiction?

It is not only drugs. More and more our societies are inhabited by people with some kind of disorder. We live in brutal times, where the pressure for distinction and high expectations for success are combined with high anxieties and no space for failure or opportunity for gentleness. People living with addictions, disorders, and disabilities of many kinds face cruel hardships in life. People with mental illness are completely forgotten.[18] And then there are those who receive the news of terminal illness. Death opens its jaws while people are still living. Insults and violence, atrocities, death and lack of control, anger, life at the edge of the abyss. So many people go without help and so many people who want to help do not know what to do. Moreover, social threats in society run the risk of contributing to social collapse on a daily basis. People are trafficked and enslaved, children turn into soldiers, women are battered at every corner of the earth, and the news of disasters is relentless.

---

16. In Portuguese, the word for anger and the word for cholera are the same.
17. Buarque and Lobo, "Salmo." My translation.
18. Flatow, "DOJ Finds Unconstitutional Solitary Confinement."

My mother is now eighty-nine years old and she still visits my cousin in a mental institution every week. She also goes every week to a nursing home to pray for the elderly and visits hospital rooms, offering a prayer for the sick. In times of pain, prayer is fundamental. When we are in pain, creed does not really matter. What matters is the help, consolation, and hope for healing that can come from any corner of the world, under any name, through any medium. Pain is an equalizer of religions and healing options. Whoever is in pain knows no boundaries in their search for healing. The presence of God through family, friends, and loved ones is an answer to a prayer people do not even know how to pray. God's answer to our prayers comes in unexpected ways. In our social life, economy, and culture, immediate relief of pain is always demanded, and it is hard to wait on God. So we must be countercultural and pray and say like the psalmist, "Stay with God! Take heart. Don't quit. I'll say it again: Stay with God" (Ps 27:14 MSG).

In the company of the psalmists, we will continue to wait and pray for each other until God's healing fills the earth. Until then, we will embrace each other and all who are waiting for God, and pray for them ceaselessly.

I share with you three more prayers we can pray daily without ceasing, with or without faith, for us, for our family and friends, and for the world:

> God, grant me the serenity to accept the things I cannot change,
>
> Courage to change the things I can,
>
> And wisdom to know the difference.[19]

> All shall be well, and all shall be well, and all manner of thing shall be well.[20]

> Stay with us, because it is almost evening and the day is now nearly over.[21]

"A Future Not Our Own": Prayers, Seeds, and Tears

> It helps, now and then, to step back and take a long view.
>
> The Kingdom is not only beyond our efforts,
>
> it is even beyond our vision.

---

19. The Serenity Prayer, frequently prayed in Alcoholics Anonymous, other twelve-step groups, and other settings. Originally a longer prayer by theologian Reinhold Niebuhr. See Sifton, *Serenity Prayer*.

20. Julian of Norwich, *Revelations*.

21. Luke 24:29 (NRSV).

We accomplish in our lifetime only a tiny fraction
of the magnificent enterprise that is God's work.

Nothing we do is complete,
which is a way of saying that the Kingdom always lies beyond us.

No statement says all that could be said.
No prayer fully expresses our faith.
No confession brings perfection.
No pastoral visit brings wholeness.
No program accomplishes the Church's mission.
No set of goals and objectives includes everything.

This is what we are about.
We plant the seeds that one day will grow.
We water seeds already planted,
knowing that they hold future promises.
We lay foundations that will need further development.
We provide yeast that produces effects far beyond our capabilities.

We cannot do everything,
and there is a sense of liberation in realizing that.
This enables us to do something,
and to do it very well.

It may be incomplete, but it is a beginning, a step along the way,
an opportunity for the Lord's grace to enter and do the rest.

We may never see the end results,
but that is the difference between the master builder and the worker.
We are workers, not master builders.
ministers, not messiahs.
We are prophets of a future that is not our own.[22]

---

22. On many internet sites, this prayer is attributed to Archbishop Óscar Romero of El Salvador, but it seems to have been composed by Bishop Ken Untener of Saginaw, Michigan, drafted for a homily given by Cardinal John Dearden of Detroit in November 1979 for a celebration of departed priests. As a reflection on the anniversary of the martyrdom of Bishop Romero, Bishop Untener included it in a passage titled "The Mystery of the Romero Prayer."

Ours is the task of *ora et labora*,[23] praying and working for this world and a world not our own. When we pray and work, we re-signify life, work, and a world to come. A work of hope. Quoting Nietzsche, Brazilian theologian and educator Rubem Alves reminds us that trees grow slowly. He wants to plant trees, even knowing that he will never eat of their fruits. Alves's happiness is in knowing that he is providing for a future, where these trees will offer shade and fruits for future generations.[24]

As Christians and human beings made in the image of God, we are responsible for and with this world and all its people. Ours is the work of spreading seeds of peace, health, healing and love, seeds watered by the very tears of our eyes. Praying with tears and seeds in our hands, this is our *ora et labora*, our prayer and our work. However, this is not enough. To the *orare et laborare* we must add *et saltare*, which is the Latin word for "to dance." Unless we learn to dance we will not be able to pray and work. By dancing, we learn to live the fullness of life, for there is no life or religion without dancing. We would do well to heed some other words of Nietzsche, "I should only believe in a God that would know how to dance."[25] To pray, work, and dance! And back again. To pray, work, and dance with our knees, our hands, and our hips as well. Tears added to the sweat of our bodies. Thus, prayers in the flesh as much as in our hearts and souls. Fully committed to God, to the well-being of our sisters and brothers, especially the poor, fully committed to the world and to the joy of life.

Decolonial Wound

Praying with the world at heart is like carrying a decolonial wound.[26] For we know the histories of stealing, death, pillaging, erasure of people and the earth. But as Mercedes Sosa sings:

> *Tantas veces me mataron*
>
> *Tantas veces me morí*
>
> *Sin embargo estoy aquí resucitando*
>
> *Gracias doy a la desgracia y a la mano con puñal*

---

23. Ora et Labora, "Pray and Work," is the motto of the Benedictine monastic order.
24. Alves, "Sobre Política e Jardinagem," 26–30. My translation.
25. Nietzsche, *Thus Spake Zarathustra*, 24.
26. The words "decolonial" and "decoloniality" will appear throughout this book. I understand much of my work as decolonial. Two of the principal decolonial thinkers write: "Decoloniality becomes a process of recognizing the colonial wounds that are historically true and still open in the everyday experience of most people on the planet." Mignolo and Vazquez, "Decolonial AestheSis."

> *Porque me mató tan mal*
> *Y seguí cantando*

> So many times they killed me
> So many times I died
> However, I am here resurrecting
> I give thanks to the misfortune
> and the hand with a dagger
> Because it didn't actually kill me.

We carry the wound of many deaths within us. This resurrecting in the midst of death is a way of living and a way of prayer. And a prayer that entails both death and celebration and gratitude. Our sisters' and brothers' prayers never disconnect suffering from celebration, life from death. Did somebody say death? We pray. Did somebody say life? We pray. Did somebody say life and death? We are grateful! We pray in the midst of words, but we also pray in silence when not to say anything is the only way to respond. Prayer with and against lack! Love against death! Re-existence against violence! Yes, we are praying! Prayer as a balm in Gilead, to heal the historical wound of colonialism, of oppression, the wound of horrors and disasters, the undeniable wound of death. Prayer in hopelessness, in powerlessness, hope in celebration. Howling, wailing . . . Nobody knows the troubles we've seen! Longing for a day of peace that I never knew, longing for what I never had, longing for a world now impossible but on its way. Stretched to my core, I pray! For my prayers are seeds! Seeds that will produce trees whose fruit my grandchildren will be able to eat. So I pray! For them to survive! For the trees to grow. Perhaps, one day, the colonial wound will disappear.

The Lord's Prayer, Revisited by Rubem Alves

In hope of this healing, I offer a version of the Lord's Prayer written by the Brazilian theologian, educator, and poet Rubem Alves. Shall we pray?

> Father, mother, with meek eyes
> I know that you are, invisibly, in all things
> May your name be sweet to me,
> The joy of my world.
> Bring me good things that delight you:
> Gardens
> Fountains

> Children
> Bread and wine
> Tender gestures
> Unarmed hands
> Bodies embracing
> I know that you desire to give me my deepest desire
> The desire that I have long forgotten
> But you never forget.
> Make manifest your desire, so that I can laugh.
> May your desire be made manifest in our world
> In the same way it pulsates within you.
> Grant us contentment in the joys of today
> Bread, water, sleep . . .
> That we may be free of anxiety.
> That our eyes would be as humble with others as your eyes
> are with us, for if we are ferocious,
> we will not be able to welcome your kindness.
> Help us to not be deceived by evil desires, and free us from that which burdens our eyes with death. Amen.[27]

May God teach us how to pray with the world at heart.

---

27. Alves, *Perguntaram-me Se Eu Acredito Em Deus*.

2

Praying Truly, with a Lump in the Throat

If you are a theologian, you will pray truly.
And if you pray truly, you are a theologian.

—Evagrios the Solitary[1]

Introduction: Praying With

I HAVE PRAYED SINCE I was in my mother's womb. All I do in life is pray. To pray is to keep myself alive, to breathe life into the world. To pray is to discover worlds that I have not known, heard, or experienced yet. I never pray alone. On the contrary, the event of prayer is always an event of *with-ness*, a way to be with somebody, fully, intensely, listening, silencing, speaking, breathing together. I pray with God, with somebody else. To pray with somebody is to be told of a God unknown. Being with somebody is to have God birthed into my life, again and again. And to the God I receive, every time I praise, I honor, I am grateful. I am deeply transformed, changed, moved from my own places of comfort and security. To pray with somebody is to have my horizons shifted, broken, undone, reinvented. That is why praying is such a troubling act: because we act and are acted upon, word and performance giving shape to my soul, marking my body, disturbing my mind, moving my emotions, challenging my allegiances, changing my faith, reinventing my life.

I pray for those alive, but I never forget those who died. I always pray with them. I cannot stop praying for those who have left us. For instance, I pray every day for Oscar Alberto Martínez Ramírez and his almost two-year-old daughter, Valeria.[2] They drowned trying to cross the Rio Grande from Mexico to United States. I cannot stop praying with them. I weep their

---

1. Evagrios, *On Prayer*, no. 61.
2. Kaufman, "Story Behind Horrific Photo of Man and Toddler Drowning."

death every day. I pray with the refugees and their disgraced lives. I pray with immigrants on the move. I pray with people who have become homeless. I pray with children who do not have anyone who loves them and those living under violence. I pray with people with mental illness, I pray with people at the margins, I pray with all those who can't make it.

I also pray with nature. I pray with trees being murdered, the ocean life being destroyed, the birds being decimated, the bees being killed by pesticides, with the earth being poisoned by chemicals, the mountains being extracted, the rocks and minerals becoming things. They are myself, living beings just as I am a living being.

When I pray with all of them, I am working on my memory, on forms of belonging, on my commitments with God, trying to figure out who I am and how I must live. When I pray I learn to desire what matters, what can keep us all alive, what should be searched, stopped, rebuilt, paused . . . what needs life breathed into many forms of living.

When I pray I am using the Christian understanding of "religion," which comes from the Latin verb *religare*, meaning to reconnect, to place together again. So when I pray I am reconnecting with God, with myself, with others, with the earth, and I am placed back together with those who are at the end of our forms of life, the ones we are taught and ordered to discard and forget.

When I pray I try to unlearn most of what was taught: I try to get out of my Western forms of rationality, my exclusive monotheism, the double bind of God caught in "transcendent vs. immanent" frames, my superior forms of feeling human, my desire for things I don't need, my belief that I am enough with myself, my unconscious forms of progress and development.

When I pray I make vows, commitments that will orient my life. To these vows I bow down in faithfulness and steadiness.

When I pray I am emotional, I am deeply moved within me, I am thrown into a place I can't control, I can't fathom, I can't imagine. When I pray I wonder. I have learned that praying is to be in awe, to be taken by wonder. I am always in the company of stars, fungi, air, universes, mountains, little creatures. When I pray I silence. I listen deeply. I drop any grasping and am thrown into a field of impermanence. When I pray, my whole body prays with me. My body rests in its breathing, lightens up into unknown forms of life, rays of color and states of mind that make all of my senses alive. When I pray I feel the currents of rivers underneath moving within the earth with a gush of might that I can only honor.

I also pray with my soul, asking my fears to be taken away. Oh my soul, why are you so restless within me? Every time I dialogue with my soul, I have to be prepared to listen back. I pray for evil to be won over, for my uncontrollable desires be controlled, for loneliness not to scare me too much. I pray for all the evil within me to be taken away, to be transformed into blessings. I pray for constant healing, for gratitude never to leave my heart. I pray for the grudges to go away, for forgiveness to wash me fully, for speed not to consume my days. I pray that my atrocities, my monstrosity, my envy, my jealousy, my anger, my frustrations, my desire of death be turned into a field of good energies.

Then I am thrown back into the *with-ness* of life, being together, entangled, and responsible for every single thread of life that makes me who I am, always becoming in this endless life with no death. Universes without end. When I pray I am often lost, figuring out somebody else as a way to come back to myself. But then, I hear my children's voice and I am back somewhere deep within me. I hear the birds and I am reconnected. I hear and see the dancing moves of the trees, the presence and the absence of animals and people who are here and gone, and I am awakened.

People ask me if I believe in prayer. I say first that prayer doesn't make any sense. What can prayer do? Why do we think we have extra powers to change anything? How arrogant we are to even ask anything of God, of life. Having been in violent, death-driven places, I cannot say prayer can do something. Prayer does not protect anyone, does not bring food to anyone's table, it does not provide a doctor for those dying. In fact, prayer does not do a thing. So I do not believe in prayer. I can't! But then, I must continue my answer by saying that I absolutely believe in prayer. How can I not believe in prayer?

As I mentioned in the introduction, my mother taught me to pray and I never leave the house without praying. To leave the house without a prayer is like leaving the house naked, unprotected, unhinged. Prayers can do wonders, make miracles, transform people. Prayers are castles of protection for the weak, a king's bed for the weary, bread for the hungry, a hug for the lonely, a gentle smile to the fearful. Prayers are a breath of life into the world that can shift the flow of movements and webs of connectivity. Prayers heal, cast away the demons, and bring life that was never there. Have you been to a church where people need God? I mean truly need God for survival? If you know such a church, you know that prayers enact miracles! How arrogant can I be not to believe in prayer? How can I think that my rationality is my only measure of life and my compass of life? How dare I not pray every day and for everything? Oh yes, I so believe in prayer. Absolutely! I would joyfully pray with those who, like the poet Paul Valéry, say, "What should we be without the help of that which does not exist? Very little."[3]

---

3. Valéry, *Outlook for Intelligence*, 42.

The Interior/Exterior Life of the One Who Prays: When We Truly Pray

The Jewish liberation theologian Marc Ellis writes about the prophet and the prophetic. In a poetic book called *Finding Our Voice: Embodying the Prophetic and Other Misadventures*, Ellis wrestles with the voice of the prophet and the prophetic. He writes, "When we speak for others, we speak for ourselves. Our voice is entangled. Even the primal prophetic is negotiated. Our voice is not only for others or ourselves. Our voice is an intermediary, a way of bridging the gap between I and the world."[4]

When we pray, we speak for others, we claim their rights, we describe their situations, we demand justice, we utter a scream with the hopes that it will get somewhere where things can be changed. But when we weep for those suffering, we are also crying for ourselves, claiming our own lives. Our voice is always blurred since there is no separation between others and ourselves. We are a "we" intrinsically connected, entangled. When we pray we are responsible not only for the prayers we utter but also for those for whom and with whom we pray. Because at the end of the day, we are always praying *with* somebody. Ellis writes that "our voice is not only for others or ourselves. Our voice is an intermediary, a way of bridging the gap between 'I' and the world,"[5] and I would add between us and each other, between "we" humans and animals and the earth. That means that we must be careful with the ways we pray for and with, and careful about the bridges we build. Bridges must always have a double movement, coming and going, crossing and staying.

As Christians, we must pay attention to the ways we pray and how our prayer can be a way to confirm our own sense of selves in the lives of others. For example, how much is our prayer a construct of our desires, a play of mirrors, a way of turning others into ourselves, with the same abilities we have, the same forms of thinking, believing, and living we are used to? Prayer can be very dangerous, for it carries a mighty seed of coloniality, of control, of measurement—especially where Christianity is a part of power dominance. Because through prayer, we can be more an apparatus of governments than agents of a kin-dom[6] of life-giving, prophetic voice and confrontation. From where do we pray when we pray to God? With whom do we pray and where are we praying with them?

---

4. Ellis, *Finding Our Voice*, 28.

5. Ellis, *Finding Our Voice*, 28.

6. The use of *kin-dom* has been popularized by Mujerista theologian Ada Maria Isasi-Diaz. See Isasi-Díaz, *Mujerista Theology*.

When Christians universalize our object of love, our sense of justice, our ways of living, we are praying mostly for ourselves and our own religion. We are mostly bringing peace to our hearts and civic confirmation of our patriotic life. When our prayers confirm the exclusive ways of our religious tribes, the racial structures of our thinking and feeling, the normativity of gender and sexual rules, we are praying only with ourselves. In this self-centered prayer, naming somebody else is just a disguise to keep us within the bounds of our own beliefs without being transformed. For instance, when prayers are more concerned with the protection of countries and with the keeping of state borders, we have lost the powerful ways prayer can undo not only individuals but also nations.

To pray is to be fundamentally transformed. When we pray, truly pray, we are thrown outside of ourselves and into the lives of others. When we truly pray, house doors are unlocked and opened for immigrants, and we break down refugee camps and welcome immigrants and refugees into our rural and urban communities. When we truly pray, our racism is challenged, and we start to see everything differently. To pray truly is to understand with Frantz Fanon that "the black soul is a construction by white folk,"[7] and we start to see history as a pile of white events that have always taught us to be racists, fearing minorities and their unknown forms of freedom and ways of living. When we pray, truly pray, our religious, civic, sexual, secular, and sacred patterns are undone. Constitutions are rewritten. Borders are broken down. Violence within the Christian religion is denounced. Patriarchalism and the power of men go tumbling down, bigotry and intolerance are not accepted, white supremacy is erased. When we pray truly, we do not accept that any religious leader becomes rich. No one who gets rich with religion is accepted in this communal gathering of praying people. We all must have the same. When we truly pray, we pray against capitalism, as capitalism is the work of the devil, creating inequalities and distorted historical views of Jesus, who never owned anything. We learn with Mary's true prayer:

> God has brought down the powerful from their thrones,
>> and lifted up the lowly;
>
> God has filled the hungry with good things,
>> and sent the rich away empty. (Luke 1:46–55 NRSV)

As we fight to change the world, when we pray, truly pray, we are the ones transformed by the ones we are praying for and with. In that way, to pray is to be prophetic. As Ellis writes:

---

7. Fanon, *Black Skin, White Masks*, 145.

> The prophetic is about Thou and I, separated and intertwined. The political and economic systems of every time and place have to be scrutinized. Judgment is essential. The political and economic systems of society are called to task precisely when they crush the weak. In the Bible, the widow, the orphan, the poor and the stranger are victims of unjust systems. Their very being, their Thou, is under assault by a system that remakes persons into objects, it. To justify such an unjust system, God is objectified as well. People as objects. God as object.[8]

The I and Thou is also a way to understand the individual and the social systems, the political and the personal, the natural and the cultural, prayer and belief. All integrated, all part of each other, shaping, moving, and making us who we are.

Another way that we need to think/feel when we truly pray is the way we relate with nature. Meadows are not distant places. The earth is not a background to our living. Animals are not things and they are not less than humans. Trees and plants are living beings who deserve the same respect that we give to people. Fungi and coral reefs are fundamental to our living. When we truly pray, we see the web of life, where nature and the cosmos are deeply connected, not the bottom of a pyramid of values or a resource to be exploited for profit and money. If we pray truly, we do no harm to the earth and all its precious living beings. That also means that if we pray truly, we learn to pray with the Indigenous people. We stand near them, with them, for their survival and fullness of life.

Eliane Brum is a Brazilian journalist living with the Indigenous people in Brazil, a prophet in the ways Ellis understands the word. When she describes her work, she describes herself. When she talks about her craft we can perceive how we can see each other as praying people, praying and working, *ora et labora*, in the world. Brum writes, "Being the journalist I am, means putting on the skin of the Other. And the Other's skin is language, the first world we each inhabit."[9] There is something to the fact that when Native people who have other languages now fight for their lives, but in the language of the colonizer, they turn the language of the colonizer into a "language of insurrection." Brum's language is her body and to speak the language of insurrection means she needs to inhabit a body of insurrection as well, trying to connect the world of those disgraced by the system and those graced by the iniquities of colonized political and economic frameworks. In order to do that, she lives with the people she

---

8. Ellis, *Finding Our Voice*, 28.
9. Brum, *Collector of Leftover Souls*, 3.

is writing about for a while in order to understand their language, their views, and their ways of thinking and feeling. She describes her work in almost the same ways Ellis describes the prophetic:

> I make my body a bridge between such diverse Brazils. . . . Resisting the domestication of our eyes by reaching for the singularity of each person's life is what allowed me to stitch each small report together. . . . Reality is an intricate fabric, sewn not only from words but also from textures, smells, colors, gestures. Marks. From voids, excesses, nuances, and silences. Ruins. . . . A news story also demands an initial radical movement: crossing the wide street of yourself. This is perhaps the most profound and also the hardest act. It demands that you uninhabit yourself to inhabit the Other, the world that is the Other. We become capable of accomplishing this only by listening with all of our senses, the kind of listening that palpates what is said as much as what goes unsaid, what sounds and resounds as much as what is silent.[10]

Again, how can our prayers become a bridge? How can our prayers go from speaking to becoming a deep listening event? How can we truly listen to people we are praying with? However, unless the praying person is doing exactly that, one is not truly praying. For to pray is to listen viscerally, to the point of uninhabiting ourselves from what we believe so we can try to hear as fully as possible the one we are praying with. How can we truly pray by inhabiting ourselves knowing that to uninhabit ourselves is impossible? Nonetheless, we try! We try to listen attentively, so deeply that the other starts to matter more than my own life, as if my life depended on the one I am listening to. Our lives being deeply tied to the ones we are praying for and mostly with is to pray truly. For my prayer is what can give life to me and the other, working prayer, *ora et labora*. If, for Brum, "writing is a physical, carnal act,"[11] to pray is also an act of incarnation. To pray is not only to put my mouth where my gestures are but to put our bodies where we pray. To go be with those we are praying. Otherwise we cannot truly pray. Unless we are with those we are praying with, we do not fully pray. Brum lived for three months with a woman who was dying. She truly prayed with her. To stay with someone who is sick, to be with those who are homeless, to be with those who are at the borders, this is a true prayer. When we breathe the same air as those who are suffering, we realize that our prayers must demand much more than words in our hearts. Prayers demand a kind of work that

---

10. Brum, *Collector of Leftover Souls*, 5, 6.
11. Brum, *Collector of Leftover Souls*, 9.

breaks with systems, that disrupts and troubles ways of living and being. But this is so hard. When is it that we pray? Truly?

The Desert: Solitude

We must understand the call to uninhabit ourselves with care: the processes of colonization often strip away the very core of one's beliefs, the relation between one's cosmologies and the ways of living with the earth. In order for one to uninhabit oneself, one must be aware of at least two things: one must know one's own inner worlds and the sources, materials, forces, and combustions by which one is formed, and one must be able to engage in a power analysis of one's privilege, positionality, desires, and goals. In other words, one must look inward and outward at the same time.

The look inward is only possible if one can carry together both a sense of solitude and a sense of connection. In some forms of Christian spirituality, we see an emphasis on individual, detached forms of life that tend to isolate one person with God without much connectivity with a larger world. That means I must pray for what I want, for what I need, without the demand of desiring the same for my neighbor. But Christian spirituality is not a race where the one who prays more will get more. We don't pray to get something. We don't pray to own anything. We pray to become somebody else. We pray to affirm ourselves in collective ways. My identity, fully learned within myself, gives space to a larger sense of humanity. This larger sense of humanity can only be constituted by ways of an exterior presence, an outside gaze, toward somebody who is not the repetition of my own self. However, when one is placed in a situation of social isolation, in a situation of not having anything, then to pray for food, health, and home makes total sense. This is when the Christian religion should come to organize these needs in a collective sense. The life-giving prayers then are prayers for the needs of all, for everyone to have what they really need.

When we think of a collective sense of Christian prayer or of the Christian faith, we think about the well-being of the other. Where can we find this form of prayer? When the resources of the community are shared and given to the members? When the church pays people's health insurance, or house payments, or credit card bills, or college tuition? Josh Robinson, a pastor and friend of mine, sent me a picture of an offering envelope saying, "Pastor, I took $20. I will bring it back in a week." We are not aware of people's needs and we do not want to know anything about them. Members of our middle-class churches can only continue to be accepted as members of their churches if they continue to pay their mortgage. If they don't and they become homeless, what church will support these families? When I was pastor of a tiny, poor church in the outskirts of São Paulo, Brazil, we were trying to raise money to buy a piece of land and build our own building to serve the community. But people's needs were much more pressing than any building. After an enormous effort on the part of the congregation to raise three hundred dollars for our building, the roof of one of our members' house fell in, and all the money had to go to fix his home. When the church is a true community, prayer takes on another meaning. African American churches in this country often have a strong program to give youth awards and support their entrance into college. Some churches pay bills of members in financial difficulties. Some churches provide food or medicine for the families around the community

We tend to separate the inside and the outside of ourselves; when we pray, the inward and the outward move together. This division comes from our divided notion of the sacred or God. What is inside might not be outside, but it is the confluence of these realms that makes who we are. Marc Ellis writes of how we must pay attention to our interiority as well as our exteriority, as a single movement, to discover our own voices:

> Solitude and solidarity define our lives. Art and poetry come from this tension. Our words about God come from there. As poetic hope. Not less. Not more.
>
> God-talk as poetic hope. The prophetic as embodied poetic hope. On the edge of despair. Attempting to pry open the possibility of meaning in our lives and world . . .
>
> The prophet embodies the—possibility—of God. Much more than prayer. Is the prophet embodied prayer?
>
> On the threshold of meaning. In history. Of God. Like love and beauty, always *en route*. Starting over each day . . .
>
> When the prophet hears "liturgy," he thinks "death." The incense is too much at religion's High Noon altar. As if any God worth her salt wouldn't think the same. Imagine God desiring worship in an unredeemed world. Scandal!
>
> The prophet's liturgy is vigilance. The prophet constantly fights the demons of despair. The prophet's field of battle is the world and the no-hope hope that envelops him.[12]

Prayer is also a part of the prophetic performance, dealing consistently with this binomial structure: solitude and solidarity. Finding oneself and God in this relation. Solitude is the awareness of oneself and the ability to stand with oneself fully, all connected. Solidarity is the awareness of one's

---

12. Ellis, *Finding Our Voice*, 15, 16, 22, 27.

surroundings and the world at large, with the ability to keep vigil with those who have their lives in danger. Solitude and solidarity can both bring despair and peace. The ability to find peace within oneself makes the one who prays able to go through despair. The grounding that only solitude brings to oneself is the deep relation with the earth. Grounding is becoming one with the earth. That sense makes us be at home in the world. The awareness of pain around the world brings compassion that makes us move towards those who are suffering. Grounding and compassion are the two feelings/ thoughts that help us move through life. Spiritual practices that help us find grounding and compassion are technologies of the self that make us live full circle within ourselves and the world.

But we do not learn that just by thinking or praying. We need spiritual ritual practices that help us orient our desires, our bodies, and our minds. We have learned to run, to move, to conquer, to own, to fill our lives with actions and accomplishments, creation, and progress. We need spiritual practices to unlearn this way of living and learn other ways. No wonder Jesus went to the desert frequently. It is a place that brings a sense of isolation, either real or imagined, where one is confronted by a sense of wilderness, both outside and inside, that brings challenges and wonders. In the desert one learns to live with oneself, to slough off or work off one's worries, fears, and anxieties. For Jesus, the wilderness was a place to feel, to listen, to be. "Rooted in re-tellings of the exodus traditions, the desert or wilderness was a spatial metaphor for a period of self-reckoning or transition, of deep psyche confrontation that had to do with exile and diasporic uncertainty," says biblical scholar Maia Kotrosits.[13]

The retelling of stories, the wonderings, the learning about oneself in a place filled with various other forms of life brings a certain clearing, perhaps openings that make us see ourselves in ways that break prejudices, hatred, anger, internalized oppression, and the desire to conquer, to own, to acquire. The desert is alive, the desert carries a call, it brings us to different parts of our interior lives. "The road of cleansing goes through that desert. It shall be named the way of holiness," said the ancient desert elders, invoking the prophet Isaiah.[14] Holiness is to find the oneness in ourselves, to understand ourselves as connected with every little creature, with rocks, plants, trees, stars, animals, and people. It is a process of folding and unfolding. The fullness of the desert unfolds into complete emptiness. This emptiness scares

13. This was given to me in a conversation with the wonderful scholar Maia Kotrosits, Assistant Professor of Religion at Denison University and author of *Rethinking Early Christian Identity: Affect, Violence, and Belonging* (2015) and *The Lives of Objects: Material Culture, Experience, and the Real in the History of Early Christianity* (2020).

14. Chryssavgis, *In the Heart of the Desert*, loc. 97, Kindle.

us. We live lives filled with so many things to sustain us that we forget that we already have what we need to survive. The desert also leads us to discern the causes of our suffering, our desires or cravings, the ways we have been formed, and our historical traumas. The desert can be a place where we have no other place to go but inward. Terrifyingly so. The desert gives us the company of our loneliness. To pray alone is to take oneself into a place of solitude in order to learn how to be in solidarity with someone else. This tradition of monastic life and doing laundry is also present in Christian and Buddhist monasteries where prayers, meditations, tending the earth, cooking, or doing the laundry must be done as a prayer, truly, mindfully.

Solidarity: Living with the Absurdities of Our Time

The look inward strengthens us to look outwards, in solidarity with others. At the same time, the more we are in solidarity with others, the more we need solitude. From the fall of 2018 to the spring of 2019 I traveled to four continents. I saw much pain, death, disaster, ruin, and destruction. I heard the noise of the absurdity of life in many ways in distinct sounds. I was reminded of the Latin meaning of the word absurd. *Ab-surdus* is a sound so loud that it makes one deaf. Having grown up in Brazil, a country of daily absurdities, immense inequalities, white supremacy, racism, and destruction, I have that noise within me.

Having witnessed as a pastor the *ab-surdus* among undocumented people in United States, and then, on that multi-continental journey, the signs of climate change, the brutal violence of nation-states, the utter poverty of so many, the many forms of suffering of the people of the Philippines, South Africa, Jamaica, and refugees from Syria, Africa and other countries around the Mediterranean Sea, I felt my heart fall to the ground. And yet, standing with people who participated in this global project of prayer, I felt a deep sense of solidarity run through my body. Seeing people's forms of resilience and creativity, their refusal and denial, their challenges and resurrections, made me think and feel that life is always bigger than we can even imagine.

In all of that I had a sense of solidarity paired with the absurdity of it all. A sense of togetherness that saved me from falling into the abyss of despair. After witnessing several accounts of evil, violence, and death, I cannot tell these stories without the strength of life, the resilience of people and the ways life bursts out everywhere. What I felt every time I traveled was a mix of feelings enmeshed in the tasks of preparing and doing the event, being with people, listening to many stories, writing prayers, and feeling that indeed, something can be done through prayer. And yet I have a clear sense that the prayers cannot capture the intensity of situations. My solidarity is always bursting into shouts of glory and on the verge of drowning in a river of tears, asking for God's mercy.

The interior and the exterior of ourselves, never fully divided is how we inhabit the world. To uninhabit parts of ourselves is to inhabit other forms of being within and without. During these travels I realized how unbalanced I was and how much I did not pay attention to my interior life. I was so anxious with everything I had to prepare and the things I was seeing that I became overwhelmed. Before I went to the Philippines, I knew that people who work against injustice there could be arrested by the police. When we got there, the national council of churches told us that we could be arrested by the police and gave us instructions of how to proceed. That was beyond my limits. I was so anxious that I developed tinnitus, an intermittent sound in my ears. *Absurdus*! I got desperate and had to ground myself in God, engaging in prayer, meditation, and therapy. I needed to have strong bonds of connection, voices that kept holding me saying, "come back, don't go there." Voices from loved ones became repeated signposts that helped turn me around and turn to the better places within me. I learned to be peaceful at the threshold of the abyss. The earth called me back, as did the birds, my family, those whom I love. They were there: deep solidarity bringing me to a solitude where I needed to hear myself, and myself in relation to others. Then, rooted and grounded, I was ready to be in solidarity with others.

Only when I am connected, organized around solitude and solidarity can I pray truly, a prayer of revolution, a prayer that changes me and others, and the world around me. Rabbi Abraham Joshua Heschel describes the revolution that prayer brings:

> Prayer is meaningless unless it is subversive, unless it seeks to overthrow and to ruin the pyramids of callousness, hatred, opportunism, falsehoods. The liturgical movement must become a revolutionary movement, seeking to overthrow the forces that continue to destroy the promise, the hope, the vision.[15]

A revolutionary prayer can infuse with passion the liturgical life of a community and create movements of transformation; it can help us denounce violence and inner and outer destruction and enable us to announce a life without poverty. A revolutionary prayer makes us aware of the ones with whom we are in solidarity so that we can count ourselves among those who are fighting for life, especially for those who do not count amidst those

---

15. Heschel, "On Prayer," 262.

who are included. Our work is to be with and pray with those beyond the commons, what is understood as "the public." In *The Undercommons: Fugitive Planning & Black Study*, Stefano Harney and Fred Moten make us see that the conditions of oppression and death and disaster of our world are not only bad for the poor, or the Africans, or the immigrants or the refugees. This situation we are living in is death for all of us. The difference is that it kills the refugees faster than the citizens of the world. The "undercommons" are those who are under the line of full citizenship, of full humanity. We can add refugees to the list of people mentioned here:

> If you want to know what the undercommons wants, what black people, Indigenous peoples, queers and poor people want, what we (the "we" who cohabit in the space of the undercommons) want, it is this—we cannot be satisfied with the recognition and acknowledgement generated by the very system that denies a) that anything was ever broken and b) that we deserved to be the broken part; so we refuse to ask for recognition and instead we want to take apart, dismantle, tear down the structure that, right now, limits our ability to find each other, to see beyond it and to access the places that we know lie outside its walls. We cannot say what new structures will replace the ones we live with yet, because once we have torn shit down, we will inevitably see more and see differently and feel a new sense of wanting and being and becoming. What we want after "the break" will be different from what we think we want before the break and both are necessarily different from the desire that issues from being in the break.[16]

To uninhabit ourselves is to inhabit ourselves with those living in the undercommons, to have them live inside us as ourselves, as the other of our own selves. Together, our prayer is the continued destruction of systems that keep people under the power of official and unofficial necropolitics; by necropolitics I mean a politics that gives life for those who belong to the system and organizes a political structure of death and dying for those who are the excess to the system, the undercommons. Any prayer that prays for any government and its necropolitics is not a true prayer, and it is against the gospel, serving only those who keep the system. Woe to them! Prayers of understanding, niceness, and conformity are only prayers that serve to protect those in the commons. This is prayer turned in on itself.[17] To pray, truly, is to "turn

---

16. Harney and Moten, *The Undercommons*, loc. 21, Kindle.
17. See Jenson, *The Gravity of Sin*.

shit down," as Harney and Moten write, to break and to stay in the break—in solidarity with those in the living undercommons.

We live in the midst of nation-states creating ruins everywhere. Nationalisms, patriarchalisms, white supremacy, neoliberalism, and extractivisms[18] are expanding colonized powers. Destructions, killings, lack of health, dignified ways of living, the earth burning. Everything is eroding. The Brazilian singer Gilberto Gil, now almost eighty years old, was persecuted during military coups in Brazil in the 1960s. He was put in jail, exiled, and suffered a great deal at the hands of the military. Eventually Gil went back to Brazil and continued his career. Now that Brazil has a president who supports torture and the killing of minorities, he says this about this president, "Bolsonaro, inspire me to pray." The prayer Gil is mentioning is the integration of the interior and the exterior life of someone who knows that to survive evil, one must pray, truly, paying attention to that which grounds us so we can continue in solidarity with those in the undercommons. Solidarity, via solitude.

Praying with a Lump in the Throat: Sacramental Prayers

I remember a scene in Ai Weiwei's documentary *Human Flow*.[19] Ai was interviewing a survivor of the war in Syria. They were in an abandoned place where there were open holes in the ground where people were buried. An older man, walking between those holes, took identity cards from his pocket, identified several members of his family, and said, "Look, here is my wife, my daughter, my cousin, my sister, my son, they are all buried here. They are all gone. What do I do now?" And he started crying as if it were the only thing in the world left to do. After that testimony, I prayed with a lump in my throat.

I keep thinking about the Palestinians and the Dalits. Their lives and conditions exhibit the most horrendous forms of violence, brutality, defacement, social decomposition, abandonment, open chambers of fire, slow death, utter ethno-caste destruction. They are people who go through rituals of humiliation and destitution. Every time I remember them, I pray with a lump in my throat.

---

18. "*Extractivismo*, as extractive capitalism is known in the Américas, indicates an economic system that engages in thefts, borrowings, and forced removals, violently reorganizing social life as well as the land by thieving resources from Indigenous and Afro-descendent territories." Gómez-Barris, *Extractive Zone*, loc. 189, Kindle.

19. Ai, *Human Flow*.

Reading Nancy Pineda-Madrid's *Suffering and Salvation in Ciudad Juarez*, I could not help praying with a lump in my throat:

> Far more often than not the pain of others, particularly that brought on by institutionalized power, remains sequestered from public view. We find numerous ways to keep the social suffering of our time at bay, distant. It slips in and out of our awareness with the passing stories we read in our daily newspapers. Undoubtedly we realize that recognizing social suffering will be personally costly. It is far easier to view the pain of others as a misfortunate occurrence, the poor luck of the draw, rather than as a product brought about by unjust systems and structures.[20]

The brutal deaths of hundreds of girls and women in Ciudad Juarez described by Pineda-Madrid are, like Elaine Brum's journalism, a bridge made with her body, a deep listening that sheds light on people in the shadows. Tragedy gains a shape with Pineda-Madrid's writing. She offers us a gift to be in solidarity with those who suffer and die. And I pray. Truly. With a lump in my throat.

I remember the first time I saw the art of Doris Salcedo, a Colombian visual artist and sculptor, and immediately felt a lump in my throat. There was something there that was way too recognizable, too vivid, too real, and yet unable to be fully grasped, understandable, given to the fullness of any form of rationality. Before Salcedo's art, we must respond with all of our senses, since it is our body that can identify the full force of the transgression and the loss that are portrayed. There is something to the devastation, desolation and mourning of extreme forms of violence that we can only recognize in our bodies, perhaps with a feeling of a lump in the throat.

Salcedo's art is a mirror of our guts after they have been shuffled and turned over by the filthy hand of violence, convulsing our inner organs and shutting down the light that shines on us. Salcedo's work represents the telling of the stories of people who were lost, who were abandoned, who faced disasters, with violence breaking into their lives and leaving them drifting, their selves shattered to different pieces and places, with traumatic memories, their beings filled with pain and mourning. Salcedo's work is a work of listening, containing years of research and interviews with suffering people. Her work does not restore what is lost or destroyed, but it helps us mourn, and the work of mourning is fundamental. It makes us engage our wounds and the violence lodged in our bodies. Salcedo helps us create a sense of solidarity with those who have been there, for they are us. We could have been they.

20. Pineda-Madrid, *Suffering and Salvation*, 59.

Doris Salcedo's work is much like a Christian sacrament, in the sense of Augustine's definition of a sacrament as "the outward sign of an inner grace." Sacraments show externally what happens inside of us. Salcedo's work does that too.

The sacraments are also the presence of an absence. Without the absence of God, we would not need to have a sacrament. We celebrate the mourning of a God who also died mercilessly and brutally. The humiliation, the defacement, and the destitution of Jesus's mind, body, and soul were too vivid, beyond horror, like the works Doris Salcedo shows us. God's presence in Jesus was taken away from the world. Jesus massacred, killed, to the point of making social memory only the pain, the thorns, the cry, and the shame of Jesus's naked body—just like so many people in our world today. The cross and the lynching tree.[21] That is why the death of Jesus is so close to the violence lived by so many in our world. The cruelty around the world, the deaths perpetrated by the state are what we live today too. That is why for marginal communities the lives of the martyrs are so important.

Third, Salcedo's works of art and the Christian sacraments work within the framework of *memory, grief, and agency*. For Salcedo, the memories of lost ones are fundamental to the re-compositions of social and individual memories. Grief is a work that must be done collectively and individually. Agency is in the making and in the participation in the work of art.

For the Christian sacraments, the grief of the tragic death of Jesus is a weekly or daily act to remind us of the ones who continue to be defaced and humiliated in our world daily. The subversive memory of Jesus is the reinstating of new possibilities, of what the past and present can still do, the actualization and the experience of a living God who is absent but also fully present! The work of remembering and the work of grief enable us to restitute ourselves to a point of self-restoration perhaps when we feel that we can respond and move forward. It is the absurdity of the resurrection that makes us think that life after a horrendous death is possible.

Fourth, both the sacraments and Salcedo's work make visible what is invisible and give us new ways of living. Salcedo's work gives a name to our loss, helping us see our inner and outer lives under states of oppression and unspeakable violence. In this way, her art helps us orient our interior life within a social life marked by horrors and fears. By making loss and responses visible, her work of art calls back to life what was thrown into abjection and forgetfulness, helping us to identify and remember the shame and the unnamable tragedies people go through. Between the horror and the wonders of her art, she tells us what is *still there*, in our social-spiritual

---

21. Cone, *Cross and Lynching Tree*.

life and histories; she helps us find some form of strength by going deep into it and helping us find our way around it all. It is a both/and event: Salcedo's art helps us not to hold back what is fundamental to what happened to us, what made us who we have become, but also, to move on with it with some sort of healing.

Holy Week teaches us that we need to learn to linger in loss and death for a while. Jesus's companions could do nothing from Friday until Sunday. They did not have the assurance that we have today. Death was a full death, and nothing could change it. Until it was changed! Holy Week and Salcedo's work help us learn that sometimes we have to linger in difficult places.

Salcedo's work *1,550 Chairs Stacked Between Two City Buildings*[22] in Istanbul and her 280 chairs placed at the Palace of Justice in Bogotá[23] remind us of the absence of the bodies that were taken away. Chairs are sacramental reminders of someone's absence. The arrangement of candles in Bolívar Square in Bogotá[24] to remind us of the civil war victims is an invitational piece of art where viewers become participants, adding candles to the installation. Witnessing and participating in her work, people come together and see that we all inhabit a humanity that is frail and susceptible to disasters and tragedy. About her art work *A Flor de Piel*,[25] where she compressed rose petals together to show a woman tortured and killed. Salcedo says: "I look for the most fragile thing and there is nothing more fragile than a body in pain." That saying reminded me of James Cone's saying that theology starts where it hurts. How can we, artists and theologians and liturgists, help our communities to do the work of memory, grief, and agency? How can we pray truly, with a lump in our throat?

Ñe'é

Eliane Brum tells us of the word Ñe'é in the language of the Guarani-Kaiowá, an Indigenous people who have been murdered since colonization and yet resist. She says, "Ñe'é means word and soul, it is word-soul."[26] The word Ñe'é encapsulates in many ways the meanings of her work. She writes with the soul and her words are not only words but her soul itself. We can learn from her about the meaning of prayer as well. She says that, as a reporter,

22. Netke, "1550 Chairs Stacked Between Buildings."

23. *Noviembre 6 y 7* (2002). See the website of the Museum of Contemporary Art, Chicago: https://www3.mcachicago.org/2015/salcedo/works/noviembre_6_y_7/.

24. Voon, "Doris Salcedo Fills a Public Square in Bogotá."

25. Thompson, "A Flor de Piel."

26. Brum, *Brasil*, loc. 1927, Kindle.

> Inhabiting bodies, converting this experience into words, is something visceral, definitive of what I am. All of how I view the world is mediated by an incommensurable love for the infinite absurdity of reality . . . Ñe`é. It is a word and soul at the same time. It is in this other language, neither mine nor yours, that I find something that defines my search. In the vortex of the between worlds, I want to be a word that acts.[27]

Yes, prayer lives in between worlds, the worlds that I inhabit with my soul, the worlds with which I am fully, words and soul, in solidarity with people and the worlds that also make who I am, and the worlds to which I belong. Prayer is the soul uttering a word, a word that acts and composes our soul and our living. When I pray truly, I am blessed by words that expand my soul and my soul breathes into words that help me act. Words that mediate an incommensurable love for the infinite absurdity of reality.

If I am to pray truly, I must pray with somebody else, take into consideration all these words, with all their souls, and the lumps in my throat, so that I can make words into life, words into soul, soul into words. Ñe`é.

---

27. Brum, *Brasil*, loc. 16, Kindle.

3

Praying from the Ends of the World[1]

Faced with pain that rips apart, we cry out in one voice,
> **intercede with us,**
> **O solidarity Lord.**

Faced with death that wounds
and marks with pain,
> **give us the strength of an embrace**
> **and the peace that your love gives us.**

Faced with injustice that kills
and cries out for conversion,
> **move us to transform the world**
> **and let all death become a song.**

In the face of desolation and crying,
faced with impotence and frustration,
> **come to our side,**
> **sustain us with your life, Lord.**

You are the God of the poor, the One who sows hope,
> **you are the God of solidarity,**
> **the One who gives love.**

---

1. This chapter is based on portions of Carvalhaes, *Liturgies from Below*, published by Abingdon Press (2020).

You are God with us, the Eternal, the Great I am:
> God of the embrace, God of song, God who caresses,
> God who strengthens, God who surrenders, God of action.

O Lord of Solidarity: Your kingdom come to the mourner,
lean your ear to the cry,
> your sons and daughters are coming
> to show your great love.[2]

From Places of Violence: The Dissonance between Belief/Prayer and Action

IN A TOWNSHIP IN Johannesburg, a group of people from several African countries and I were walking around to learn about the situation of the people there. We came to a church where people were worshiping. The gate had a lock and we could not enter. We said, "We are Christians from various places, can we go inside?" "No," came the response, "no stranger can come in." A conversation ensued during which the members of that little church said, "This is a very dangerous neighborhood, so we come here to church to feel safe. But it is also very dangerous to be here in the church because people come and steal from us." In the same place, there were feelings of freedom and a state of being locked in and fearful. There people prayed.

At a gathering of women in the Philippines, the women were crying. They had lost their sons to the war on drugs President Duterte declared. None of the seven women knew why their children had been killed; most of them had been killed "by mistake." We held a worship service and as they told the stories of their dis-grace, we could hear their wailing. They could barely talk. We were there to pray.

In Jamaica, behind a mountain of garbage, one of the dumpster places of the city, lives a group of people abandoned and forgotten by everyone. They are remnants of a community into which the police came, raped the women, threw children out of a third-floor window of a building, and killed all of the men. How could we pray?

Breonna Taylor, George Floyd, and Ahmaud Arbery in the US, and João Pedro Matos Pinto in Brazil, are Black people killed by the police. The world is burning. A colonial disaster of global proportions has taken over the whole planet. Violence and death are alive, vivid, palpable, and visible

---

2. The prayers in this chapter are part of the book *Liturgies from Below* (see n. 1 above), and many of the prayers from the project are available at the website of the Re-Imagining Worship Project; see http://reimaginingworship.com.

in proportions much greater than we can count in words. Psalm 139 can be said in this new way for our days:

> Where do I go to escape the presence of violence?
> If I go to Manila, violence mounts everywhere,
>   killing Indigenous people.
> If I go to Johannesburg, violence engulfs
>   the spirit of the South Africans in the townships.
> If I go to Minneapolis, Louisville, or Rio de Janeiro,
> blood on the streets
>   overwhelms over our eyes.
> If I go to Jamaica, the violence of discarded people
>   is beyond our reach.
> If I go to Europe, the violence of turning away refugees
>   exposes their sheer desperation.

How can we pray in those places? How can we pray in situations where it seems there is nothing to be said and yet everything to be processed, learned, and explained? To go where violence abounds is to ask the question "Should there be a God?" To pray in those places is to face the absurdity of life and also discover the resilience that only those living in these situations can muster. To go there is to discover ourselves being reviled and killed. How can we let our own people be treated this way? How can we do this to ourselves? Why do we keep destroying people and the earth mercilessly without care of any kind? How should we even pray? And if we pray, to whom do we pray when we pray to God?

How can we reconcile our beliefs with the life of the world? Marc Ellis has said that "systematic theology is a reduction of cognitive dissonance." We try to turn down the volume of absurdity and dissonance, but can we even do that? Systematic theology committed to knowledge without bodies, blood, or (lack of) breath cannot do much to reduce the cognitive dissonance. Can the written prayers of the church even respond to the pain of the world? In one of my classrooms, a well-known visiting lecturer said to our students, "Recite the prayers of the prayer books for twenty years, and only after that can you write your own prayer." While this is a way to uphold the tradition of the church and a proper understanding of proper prayer, I wonder if the prayers in our prayer books can still hold the pain of the people and the flooding of violence everywhere.

We are all feeling, in one way or another, that we are moving toward an impending collective death. The vast majority of people around the earth are poor. Social and economic inequality is growing. Oxfam reports that "the world's 2,153 billionaires have more wealth than the 4.6 billion people who make up 60 percent of the planet's population."[3] We live in an alarming Earth catastrophe that does not always make headlines; some call our era the *anthropocene* (the era when the human being—in Greek, *anthropos*—determines and dominates what happens on the planet) but also *capitalocene, plantationocene,* or *chthulucene*.[4] Humans, who have placed ourselves above any other form of life, are extracting more from the earth than its limits permit, and the earth is losing its balance. Global warming, the melting of polar ice caps, uneven seasons, droughts, overpopulation, forest devastations, the warming of the oceans, the extinction of many species are everywhere. Geopolitical configurations are marked by an expanding movement of migrants and refugees due to climate change and civil wars. Democracies are collapsing, nation-states are dissolving into dictatorships, public spaces are contested or shrinking, and fear is the political emotion of our time. Many forms of destruction and violence are becoming normalized, and the consequences of an unrestrained neoliberal economy are thrusting us toward a place of no return.

In these calamitous times, what prayers are we called to pray? The condition of our world begs for prayers and forms of prayer different from the ones we have prayed thus far. As we witness the pain of the poor, the collapsing of the world we know, the natural disasters around the globe, there seems to be no prayer that can respond to it all. Where should our prayers come from? What prayer may Christians offer to God and the world?

If we are to pray today from real historical and social locations, from places of deep pain, and from places that are almost entirely foreign to us, we Christians must learn a new grammar for our faith. We must learn new prayers and new ways to pray.[5] We will have to look at tradition differently and use our current prayer books with fresh eyes. Our prayer will have to delve into other prayers, the ones made in the midst of disasters, to engage with

---

3. Oxfam, "World's Billionaires Have More Wealth."

4. Haraway, "Making Kin."

5. Paul Holmer, in *The Grammar of Faith*, writes that prayer consists of structural languages that shape people's ways of being. The grammar of faith, for him, is marked by language *of* faith and not language *about* faith. Theology is done by the one praying and is not a comment or reflection on proper theology done elsewhere. Theology is a personal event. "Theology," he writes, "must always move toward a present-tense first person mood" (*Grammar of Faith*, 24). With Holmer, I believe that every individual prays from their people's lived experiences. Prayers are the ritual and contents of theology. In other words, theology happens in the moment when one is praying, with one's personal and collective presence, with the conditions, situations, and limitations of one's life. When we pray in places of hurt and violence, our theologies pulse with sweat and blood, and a new grammar of faith ensues. See Holmer, *Grammar of Faith*.

the earth more fully, in order to respond to the excruciating poverty and the demise of our planet. We also need to be more open to other religions in order to become a different kind of church. I wonder if the grammar of the prayers we currently have and use is enough to sustain us, or the world.

If God's voice in the world can be expressed in our prayer, we are called to be radically converted in our ways of praying. We are called to go deeper within ourselves, to relate more deeply with nature, and to be radically converted toward forms of action that heal, recuperate, reconfigure, restore, and restitute our communities, the earth, and our social and natural systems. May it be anathema, we pray—any form of government that sustains war, that oppresses people, animal, mountains, oceans, and the whole earth! Instead of placing us apart from the world, prayer can reconcile us back into a deep sense of communities. And blessed be those who understand that we live *en conjunto*, together, all with the same rights and responsibilities.

Only a prayer that has its ear attached to the earth and hears the cries of the oppressed, a prayer that has its eyes upon those who suffer, and hands stretched in solidarity, can help us pray better and help us realize our distance from God and a world in flaming pain. If prayer is about loving God, then prayer is also about building a house for the abandoned, becoming a wall of protection for the vulnerable, and giving our life away for those who are on the brink of disappearance. When we lose our entitlements, our class protections, our fear of others, and realize our deep connection with the poor, the stars, the animals, and the whole earth, prayer becomes breathing God's breath in the world.[6] Prayers are a continuation of Jesus's life, and thus prayer must express a radical commitment with the poor. The building of a common happiness and place of safety for those vulnerable is an absolute imperative in our world today.

Many Christians have created a faith that avoids the poor. Some of our denominations have become gated communities protecting a privileged class. However, in different parts of the world, there is a Christian renewal thriving amidst the poor, at the bottom of economic systems, on the fringes of Empire. This neo-Pentecostal Christian renewal is taking place through worship, ritual, and prayer. It is exploding everywhere,[7] offering a new grammar of faith that gives strength, mission, and purpose to those abandoned by the state and exposed to social threats, chaos, and loss. These churches are embracing the poor, speaking from places where abandoned people live, and from there a new grammar of faith has been developed, often giving people tools to survive in the midst of violence, social and

---

6. See chapter 1, "Praying With the World at Heart."
7. Sung, *Desire, Market, Religion*; and "Pentecostals: Christianity Reborn."

personal trauma, illness, anxiety and depression, deep economic hardship, and close acquaintance with death. In the midst of these conditions, people worship to ask God for protection, to ask for healing, and to imagine promises of a better financial life and happiness. Their churches offer something real, local, named, visceral, that resonates within these realities, most of which we, in our context, cannot imagine how to engage.

Many of us would surely criticize this form of Christianity and say that it is not good theology, not the best way to help people worship God, not the appropriate way to help people find their sense of self-worth. Meanwhile, on this side of the world, the First-World-traditional-bourgeois-white-middle-class theologies that sustain many of our dying churches serve to appease social upheaval and maintain a psychologically neutralizing boundary, a rationalization for self-protection in faith, and an impediment to getting closer to those who are racialized and those living in the lower classes under the sign of poverty and violence. While many of the neo-Pentecostal churches exploit people, they also offer sanctuary and hope to those who are impoverished and suffering miserably by creating new songs and prayers—new ways to pray, sing, and listen to the word of God. Theirs is a grammar of faith whose prayers find fertile ground in the hearts of those who are unwanted around the world, but wanted by God.

Praying with the Wretched of the Earth: Learning a New Grammar of Faith

Blessed and supported by the Council for World Mission,[8] a group of some one hundred people from various Christians traditions, theologies and types of churches, of different races, ethnicities, sexualities, and walks of life in fifty or so countries, gathered together during 2018 and 2019 in four different countries on four continents. The group of participants in the project (named "Re-Imagining Worship as Acts of Defiance and Alternatives in the Context of Empire") was made up of pastors, theologians, students, artists, and activists. Our purpose was to learn how to pray with local communities and to create liturgical resources for Christian communities around the world. This project was rooted in God's demand for us to live a life of compassion, listening to those who are suffering and learning how to pray with them. We hoped that together, in the desire of God and the strength of our faith, we would respond to the challenges of

---

8. The Council for World Mission is a worldwide partnership of Christian churches, many of them with roots in Reformed tradition, focused on global resource-sharing for local mission. https://www.cwmission.org.

our world today. We reached and stretched toward an alternative to both the traditional prayer books of Christian liturgies and neo-Pentecostal cultic prayers. Always, the main question for us, as for me in these pages, was "How are we to pray with the unwanted of the world? How can our prayers not only address the disasters of the world but also offer, in God's love, hope and actions of transformation?"

During the four gatherings, we lived and engaged with people who are poor and disenfranchised and wrote prayers and stories of people who live the Christian faith in abandoned places. The encounters were short but intense. Eventually we produced a rich and varied collection of liturgical resources—prayers, songs, rites of healing, baptismal and eucharistic prayers, meditations, and art—from varied communities contending with violence, migrants and refugees, drugs, land grabbing, war on the poor, attacks on women, militarization, and climate change. But first, we listened. And we prayed.

After living with communities of people on four continents, we realized that we had actually been *learning how to pray*. When we prayed, we were not only praying with those affected by violence and poverty, we were also praying for ourselves. By praying with those living in inhumane conditions, we were challenged to change. Wrestling with many contradictions, with heavy and full hearts, bringing together our own struggles and the ones from the communities we visited, we created prayers for our own churches, not for the poor, with the hopes that we might learn how to pray for ourselves and move into deep change, for the sake of the most poor. In a circular movement, we were also, through our own prayers, praying with those at the ends of the world.

Our project brought together a mix of voices, those of the travelers—the visitors—who participated in this project and those of the people who accepted and welcomed us to be with them for a while. We continued to wrestle with the tension between witness and solidarity on the one hand and "poverty tourism" on the other. In our prayers, we came to profess and confess both. Our work was only a gesture toward a necessarily longer and deeper stay with those who suffer at the ends of the world, until we are finally in and of the same place, together. From the ends of the world, we came out praying, singing, creating art, crying out loud for the mercy and power of God. The experiences reflected in the resources we created aim to give churches and Christians a new methodology and a new vocabulary to pray, so that we might reorient ourselves in the world. Figuratively and concretely, we became part of a wave of liturgies coming from the bottom up.

Manila, Philippines

In Manila we experienced what the world will become in the future. After many years of colonialism, the Philippines is fertile ground for fascism. The country is controlled by a few rich people, and neoliberalism is the preferred weapon of the state. A fascist government led by Rodrigo Duterte is in place, using martial law and extrajudicial killings as necropolitics, expelling Indigenous people from their lands and selling the country's natural resources to agribusiness. The government is in the hands of China's economy and US militarization and does not know how to address poverty. The fifteen richest Filipinos have fifty-seven billion dollars—more money than the remaining 79.6 million people together. Hundreds of thousands of jobs have been lost in the agricultural sector due to the spread of agribusiness. There are no workers' rights, and most jobs offer low wages.

On this leg of the journey, a diverse religious group of two dozen people from more than fifteen Asian countries gathered to begin this work. At first none of us had any idea of what would happen or what kind of result we would have. We trusted each other and stayed together from beginning to end. We laughed and cried and shared life together. This bonding provided a model for the gatherings to come on other continents.

In Manila, we visited four communities: 1) Indigenous peoples' communities in the Province of Rizal, victims of militarization, forced evacuations, demolitions, and extrajudicial killings. They are continuously harassed by land grabbers, mining companies, and the government military forces. 2) Workers' organizations in the province of Bulacan and Southern Tagalog areas. The workers are victims of unfair labor practices, and two workers' organizations located in different communities are currently on hunger strikes. 3) Urban poor communities, victims of demolition because of development aggressions. 4) Peasant communities in the Batangas and Kalinga Areas, victims of land conversions, militarization, demolitions, and extrajudicial killings.

On the first day, after engaging in a powerful worship service and being welcomed by our hosts, we heard a presentation about the socioeconomic and political situation of the Philippines and an introduction to the communities we would be visiting. After this, a member of the National Council of Churches of the Philippines spoke to us about safety. We were advised to be alert about how we talked, both with people with whom we gathered intentionally and with people we met on the street, and not to use social media. We were also told that if the police were to put us in jail, a group of lawyers would try to help, but that even with its planning and anticipating, the Council of Churches was not able to promise that nothing bad would happen to us.

When we returned each night from our visits to poor communities, we were emotionally exhausted. We had seen so much pain and death that we were deeply disturbed. We met mothers who had lost their sons to police brutality and to the war on drugs and mothers who wailed in pain during our worship services. We wept with Indigenous children whose schools have been bombed by the government and paramilitary movements because they were considered havens for revolutionaries. We cried with workers who earned so little that they did not have enough money to take back home and thus needed to sleep on the streets.

It was after these visits and during the two subsequent days of writing liturgical resources that we finally felt life coming back to us. Writing prayers was a life-giving time when we found ways to address people's pains and to connect God to real-life situations and to liturgy. It was during this process of writing that we found the life of our faith and the faith of our life.

As part of the project, we were tasked to write prayers to engage our own rage and anger. One of the prayers written by a group of participants was filled with curse words. In any other place or time, this prayer would have been considered blasphemous and outrageous, but within this group, as theologically diverse as we were, there was a deeper understanding at stake. These prayers were about the life of the disenfranchised under the brutality of the Empire. They were about the pain of our brothers and sisters in such a way that cursing was a "theological" way of expressing that for which we had no words. We all prayed those words together.

In the midst of all this, a source of immense joy was learning from local Christians in all the communities we visited. The church is well and alive in the Philippines!

Johannesburg, South Africa

In Johannesburg, we experienced the remarkable development of South Africa in the midst of its still deeply entangled history of racism and colonialism. The brutal history of apartheid has racist historical consequences that continue to plague the country. The South African theologian Vuyani S. Vellem expresses it as follows: "Racism in our times is thus an ethos, an imperial spirit, innate to the socio-political, ecclesial organization and institutions of management and learning in our society."[9] Trapped in these "fraudulent, race-blind, normative invisibility and elusiveness of race, doubt," the presence of racism has the power to "castrate the goals and agency of black

---

9. Vellem, "Cracking the Skull of Racism," 23.

Africans against this problem."[10] Still sunk in a deep wound opened by white settlers, South Africa is still wrestling to find ways out of this complex situation. Here we questioned whether and how we could help when the situation was so difficult and seemed to require years of knowledge. In spite of these challenges, we tried to learn both from our insurmountable limitations and our struggle to write something about experiences and events that seemed indescribable. Holding on to these dilemmas, we gathered, thirty African scholars and I, not only to talk about South Africa but to make a composition of African spaces and situations and to pray from that web of issues, histories, pain, violence, and struggles.

We visited four communities: 1) Marikana, where there is exploitation of workers that closely resembles slavery, as capitalist corporations profit at the expense of human dignity by taking away the community's resources. 2) Soweto, a township of the City of Johannesburg Metropolitan Municipality in Gauteng, South Africa, bordering the city's mining belt in the South. Its name is an English syllabic abbreviation for South Western Townships (So-We-To). Formerly a separate municipality, it is now incorporated into the city of Johannesburg. Soweto has become synonymous with the South African struggle, as we think of protest and the 1976 Soweto uprising. Soweto is also the home of many liberationist leaders. In Soweto, Moroka has become Johannesburg's worst slum area, where residents have erected their shanties on plots measuring six by six meters with only communal bucket-system toilets and very few running water taps. 3) Alexandra, another township in the Gauteng province of South Africa, commonly known as "Gomorrah" among local residents. It is one of the poorest urban areas in the country and at one point made the news during xenophobic attacks by residents on foreigners living in their midst. 4) CBD, another community in Soweto, where we were able to experience the life of economic and political refugees. Johannesburg gave us the opportunity to interact with the brutal effects of wars, economic looting, and political instability. It also helped us to engage the realities of displaced communities that are mostly undocumented local residents and refugees.

Being in these townships as foreigners was a source of anxiety and fear for us. The shacks where people live, their difficult living conditions, and the violence within the villages showed us how Empire destroys entire communities by moving, shifting, and dumping people into places that they do not know and where they have to fight for their lives by being set against each other.

---

10. Vellem, "Cracking the Skull of Racism," 24.

As our group came back from our visits to the communities, the conversations about liturgy became very difficult. We discussed the notion of praying for "those who are lost," since this form of prayer implies that "we" are not lost and have accomplished something that places us above "them." Questioning the very task of liturgy and its workings was paramount to this process. This group left nothing unchallenged or uncriticized, and in so doing, showed an extraordinary commitment to name uncomfortable feelings and to wrestle with thorny situations.

Kingston, Jamaica

The third leg of this global project took place in Kingston, Jamaica. In keeping with the model of the workshops held in Manila and Johannesburg, this workshop had a variety of participants from American countries, an ecumenical group of scholars, pastors, students, and church leaders who came with the desire to create something new in the realm of liturgy. We examined evidence and causes of such realities as violence, urban displacement, land grabbing, neoliberal policies, corruption, climate change, poverty, hunger, and violence. We divided into four smaller groups for our visits to local communities.

We visited Tivoli Gardens, where seventy-three people were shot in a massacre by the state in 2010. Local residents claim that the government figure of seventy-three dead was low and that at least one hundred and possibly two hundred people were killed. With our leader and guide, social activist Lloyd D'Aguilar, we heard the searing testimonies of people who survived the shootings and visited neighborhoods abandoned by the government with no concern, care, or help. Our group also experienced the ways in which religion can transform the lives of the people. It was powerful to walk the street markets of Kingston and hear people speak of Mr. D'Aguilar as "our good Samaritan."

We also visited August Town, Trench Town (the home of Bob Marley), and displaced street workers in both of those districts. All these communities struggle with poverty and neglect. Our people walked on the streets and in marketplaces with pastors and local leaders and listened to their stories and to those of community residents. We also heard the heart-wrenching testimonies of workers who were going to be displaced from the market where they had lived for the last fifty-five years because the place was sold to the owner of a nearby shopping mall. We were able to have a worship service organized by Jamaica Theological Seminary with the vendors about to be evicted.

We spent time, too, at the Bobo Shanti Rastafari community in Bull Bay, a thriving community of Rastafarians in the woods. Members of our group were able to participate in worship services and to learn about the community's life and beliefs and its proposal for a new society. Finally, our visits took us to two rural communities in Low River and Manchester. These small rural farming communities received our group with joy and taught our people how to care for the earth as they do. We also heard about their struggles to survive against extractivism and big corporations.

After our visits, participants spent two intense days of writing resources. Their experiences with poverty provoked differing reactions; some participants experienced more difficulties than others in fully giving themselves to the poor. Thus, we were reminded that our presence in Jamaica and in our group was not to defend a personal position nor to share a paper or intellectualize the situation, but to be a witness to the people, to become a sounding board for their cries, and to learn how to pray with the poor, as church. The mix of participants—local participants and people from South, Central, and North America—helped us to understand the plight of the Jamaican people, and it shaped our efforts to create a new grammar for the Christian faith through prayers, songs, and liturgies of liberation. In Jamaica, we were able to engage with the local situation more fully with regard to the content of our faith and through our liturgical resources. Bob Marley's "Redemption Song" echoed throughout the days.

Every gathering on each of the continents produced something new in the context of unique challenges. At this particular gathering in Jamaica, we experienced liturgy unfolding into many new possibilities. Liturgy has the power to offer inner and outer transformation, and doing liturgy together was a way of connecting with people, our own selves, and our faith in a new way. At the same time, this liturgical work was also a way of seeing our immeasurable distance from those who are suffering, our inability to say things properly, our powerlessness before such suffering, and the insufficiency of trying to do what we were hoping to do.

Scicli, Italy

The fourth and last meeting of this global project took place in Scicli, Italy. This small town in southern Sicily on the shores of the Mediterranean Sea receives and welcomes refugees and immigrants from the African continent, Syria, Iraq, and other parts of the world. We were hosted by the Mediterranean Hope Refugee and Migrant Programme, a migration project recently conceived by the Federation of Protestant Churches in Italy in association with other Protestant churches in Europe. Federation members helped us to understand the situation of migrants and refugees and we heard testimonies from people who had dealt with violence across the globe. This gave us a window into a reality we do not pay much attention to and helped us to gain a new language for our prayers. All the participants in our ecumenical group were troubled by the ways in which European countries mistreat migrants and carried in their hearts a desire to create something new to respond to these situations in ways that help to shape our Christian spirituality and mission. We intended for our worship services to reflect the voices of the poorest people in Europe by offering solidarity, resistance, and defiance to the forces of death of Empire in this particular context.

The first day of our visit, we gathered to learn about the overarching effect of European laws on immigration and the powerful resistance work of the Christian churches in Scicli. We learned from Ciccio Sciotto, a pastor of the Italian Waldensian church, about the ways in which the European continent is closing borders. We were also offered theological perspectives to better understand migration. Pastor Sciotto spoke of migration starting when Adam and Eve were expelled from the garden of Eden and then explained human movements as part of the world's history. He described how Italians were shipped to other countries and how Italy exported violent groups such as the Italian mafia. The problem, he said, is not migration but how we talk about it, condemning migrants and refugees without addressing the sources and reasons for the intense movements of people on our planet and in our regions. We then heard stories from refugees and immigrants about their difficulties, including that of two young boys who came in small boats from Libya to Italy and struggled to survive near-death experiences several times during their journeys. We shared a meal with refugees at Mediterranean Hope; this became, for us, the event that most closely mirrored what the realm of God can be. We were all deeply moved by it.

One of our unforgettable moments was having dinner with refugees from many countries at the Casa delle Culture, a sanctuary receiving people in conditions of particular fragility and vulnerability from around the world.[11] We were able to break bread together and gesture kindness to each other. Since we could not speak each other's languages, we smiled and served each other in the best way we could. We heard some of the guests' stories and at the end, we played and laughed out loud with all of these precious children.

---

11. Casa delle Culture is part of the Mediterranean Hope Refugee and Migrant Program of the Federation of Evangelical Churches in Italy (FCEI). See https://www.mediterraneanhope.com/casa-delle-culture-scicli.

As we had in Manila, Johannesburg, and Kingston, after our two days of visits we engaged in two days of writing liturgical resources. It was difficult to figure out how to pray with those affected by policies of death and destruction. We wept and prayed together using theater, art, singing, and writing in collective ways. The result was beautiful, powerful, and challenging.

A new movement is required for this time: not to abandon the prayers of the church, but also to pray new prayers in new ways—for others and ourselves, in a constant movement of God's grace into an expansive mindfulness, transformation, and recreation of ourselves and the world. This will mean learning how to pray differently, to be faithful to Jesus in these devastating times by praying with and for the unwanted—those who are the "undercommons,"[12] including not only humans, but also the whole earth and other animals, because their conditions of living are also the conditions of existence for all of us.

Our prayers must help us navigate new changes and challenges. Through our collective prayers, with those we are called to listen to, serve, and fight for, God calls us to live our faith in much deeper ways, understand the world we are living in broader ways, and make a radical commitment with the poor in the name of God. Praying with one another teaches us that we are never done. Through prayers, we can imagine a radical moral imagination of new worlds! By the grace of God, we can birth these new worlds through *ora et labora*—our prayers and our work in solidarity.

> *A lost voice. Squatting in my little street corner this very dark night. It is cold and the darkness is scary. Who can hold me—the hand of God. Is there a God out there? God if you are there—if you can hear me—hold me through the night. I really want to sleep but my belly is rumbling. Please don't let them find me here, stop them from taking and hurting me. God—if you are there—hear my voice!*

Prayers and Empire

The extensive context of the four-continent project was and is (the) Empire: institutions, networks, individuals, mindsets that control power, money and authority embedded in nation-states, tradition, rationalities, reasoning, science, references, epistemologies and knowledge production, illustrations, academic work, dualities, fake news, values, policy, patriotism, social construction, culture, history, forms of identity, race, gender, patriarchy, heterosexuality, wars,

---

12. Harney and Moten, *The Undercommons*, locs. 26–30, Kindle.

forms of religion, religious care, prayers, songs, worship. We call ourselves out as we name this. We are all entangled in Empire and longing to know what we can do to find awareness, conscientization, and contribute to fracturing the porous walls of dominance and injustice.

The variety of knowledges in these prayers complicates any easy targeting of colonizer from the North and colonized from the South. Our group of about one hundred people show how colonized and colonizer are not only in external, fixed locations but inside of us all. Modernity has won the world and made it impossible to live without the present work of colonization and coloniality. Our hearts have become racist, imperialist, and colonizers just as much as we are colonized. A closer look at these prayers reveals a vast array of power dynamics with voices filled with colonized and decolonized struggles. This aspect of the group, coupled with the fact that we were not only praying with the poor but sometimes thought that we were praying on behalf of the poor, makes it impossible to idealize these prayers as a completely decolonized project. No! This is not a full decolonized project but a decolonial work in progress. It is a work made of expectations and guilt, embarrassment and attempts, limitations and desires, awkwardness and confusion, frustration, and joys. Even the use of colonial metaphors expressed by us who are colonized evidences the insidious nature of oppression: the language available to us for liberation in many cases is itself colonized. Nonetheless, this project also showed how people are trying to figure out the coloniality of our times and to respond to these forces of Empire in many ways. We start here praying with all the complexities, hopes, absurdities, im/possibilities, and beliefs that a new world structure is possible.

We who participated in the project have various forms of entanglement with Empire, but with the prayers that emerged from it, we seek to change how we think about ourselves and the world. We imagine that we can be transformed and offer resistance as we do the work of decolonization. As Frantz Fanon wrote, "The oppressed will always believe the worst about themselves.... Imperialism leaves behind germs of rot which we must clinically detect and remove from our land but from our minds as well."[13] Prayers must help us to transform our thinking, feeling, and ways of living. To pray with the wretched of the earth is to work on the cognitive dissonance between the Christian faith and its practices, the Christian Empire and the Christianity that works as resistance to the same Empire.

How does placing colonized people at the center of Christian prayers affect the praying of Christian colonizers? Considering the complexity of the colonized and the colonizer in this work is paramount. All of the people

---

13. Fanon, *The Wretched of the Earth*.

participating in this work had large or small ties to this complex relationship. Races and ethnicities mixed, sexualities and genders blurred, high and low classes combined, theologies and liturgical practices were placed in dispute and tension.

The power of prayer offers resistance to the Empire: to orient our hearts, embolden our souls, strengthen our spirits. No Empire can resist the work of the Spirit who keeps things alive, shows us ways out of no ways, breaks down barriers and walls, and makes us sing a song of victory and freedom at last!

Lex Orandi, Credendi, Vivendi, **and** *Natura*

How do we connect our faith, the *polis* and the *oikos* (community and economy) of God? We have received from the tradition of the church the expansive notion of the *leges* (plural of *lex*, law in Latin) of the church: *lex orandi, lex credendi,* and *lex agendi* or *lex vivendi*.

How does the *law of prayer* challenge Empire?

How does the *law of our beliefs* defy the self-enclosed sense of self that is not correlated to the earth and its suffering?

How does the *law of vivendi*, the way of life, our ethical mode, based on a just way of living, help transform the logic and practice of our prayer-beliefs within a sordid economic system?

Often the relationship of the *leges* happens within a theological inner circle that protects the boundaries of faith by analyzing liturgy with liturgy. In spite of all of the dialogue liturgy has with other areas of knowledge, the praying and believing of liturgy seem to be encircled within a tradition that looks mostly inward upon itself. We juxtapose liturgical things with liturgical things: gathering with word, water bath with eucharist, word with sending, and so on.[14] We need to expand these notions of the *leges* and put prayer at greater risk through a perhaps frightening series of "external" juxtapositions: placing prayer alongside wars, praise alongside all forms of violence, confession alongside poverty and patriarchy, word alongside ecological destruction, sending forth alongside refugees and migrants. This is what I am proposing: the relation of the internal *leges* with the "outside" of the church's worship, including nature, and all the world that is not human.

If we think about these juxtapositions, we can easily realize how much the church has kept its worship sacred by avoiding "worldly" issues. The naming of these issues is tangential and irrelevant to sacred ritual. The

---

14. On liturgical juxtaposition, see the work of Lathrop in *Holy Things*; *Holy People*; and *Holy Ground*.

multi-continental project—and my proposal in these pages—connects the inside of the church with the outside by organizing our center not from tradition, but from the voices of the poor, from the places of pain and violence. It is women losing their children to state violence that makes us define our prayer. It is the extreme poverty of people without humane living conditions that shapes our faith. It is refugees drifting in the midst of the sea without help who define our worship. It is global warming and drought that make us confess and ask for God's mercy. It is violence against women that makes us pray prayers of anger. It is the utterly desperate condition of a vast majority of people that is the *lex* of our prayer, faith, and life.

There is a need for another *lex*, a liturgical law for our time. This law has been more recognized in the past than in our modern-day traditions. It is the *lex natura*, the law of nature. Given the climate disaster that is coming to us all with all its effects and already taking place all over the globe, *lex natura* becomes a pre-condition to the laws of prayer, belief, and way of life for our common survival. *Lex Natura* must be our guiding principle in praying by providing an orientating ground from which we can learn how to pray, to believe, and to act. Thus, to pray becomes an orientation toward Gaia, the earth, in this time of Anthropocene. *Lex Natura* helps us to pay attention to the cries of the earth, the burning of God's *oikos*, the desolation of peoples' lands across the globe, and the extinction of many species. We are called to *ora et labora* with the earth and with those who live everywhere on the earth.[15]

Praying Locally: Challenging Christianity's Universal Dominion

The goal of our group of liturgists was to learn and work from the self-determination of people, their resources of daily life, their art, dreams and struggles, their vulnerabilities and forms of resistance, paradoxical structures, and idiosyncratic languages. By attending to these forms of life, our prayers mark the historical, patriarchal, political, economic, sexual, cultural, and class loci of enunciation of our utterances in order to show the dynamics of power at stake in each place. These locations, sites of enunciation of the poor, became fundamental to our understanding of the Christian faith, theologies, liturgies, reading of the Bible, sacraments, and prayers.

This work/ing of prayers from the ground shifts and creates both a new vocabulary and new forms of prayers for the Christian faith by "simply" *praying with* the poor. These prayers do not seek to change the poor, but

15. See Carvalhaes, "*Lex Naturae.*"

fundamentally ourselves, the ones praying to God. When we pray with other people, our field of recognition shifts and changes. Being with people who are not within the horizon of our ways of knowing and living places us in a new territory where we must reframe, transform, and restore our own ways of knowing, of making sense of the world and of ourselves, since we are now "affected" by the presence of somebody else, with whom we are now praying. To come to the knowledge of somebody else's praying, believing, and living, I must change my own ways of praying, believing, and living.[16]

Prayer that shows the dis-ease within the Empire in Christian liturgical resources disrupts assumed liturgical ways of thinking, believing, and being that shape people that are marked by an expansive whitening/witnessing of European liturgical local histories made universal. Instead of prayers demanding to be prayed, prayers come from a belief in the sovereignty of local people praying to God and each other their own struggles with their own voices and full bodies. These prayers beg us to darken our liturgical resources.[17]

To pray with is to bear witness, to walk together, to be a companion, from the Latin *com-pane*, "with bread," sustaining, filling the path with enthusiasm, with God, offering a shield. To pray is to take sides with the ones with whom we are bearing witness, protecting, giving ourselves, transforming our sense of self, changing our consciousness, telling the story from the perspective of the ones with whom we are praying.

One of the challenges of this process of praying with the wretched of the earth is to figure out our own condition, our own complicity with power, our distance from those suffering, the relation between "our" inclusion and "their" exclusion. This methodology sheds a light into our common history and we are challenged to read it differently, asking who owns what and how, who has been a part of this "common" history, who has been erased, to whom do we pay attention and honor, to whom do we not, and in all of it, why?

When we pray from the underside of Empire, the entire dynamics of prayer, its content, forms, mechanics, social places, tonalities of voices, breathing intervals, body strength, heart condition, and rationality change, since everything starts elsewhere, namely, where it hurts. There, from these places of pain, our voices quiver, we are always at the edge of our strength, we can't speak, we mostly scream when we can. I remember that when I was growing up in Brazil, my voice always quivered.

16. When we read prayers of people far from us, we are always challenged. For those here in the US, especially white people, see Du Bois, *Prayers for Dark People*; Mbiti, *Prayers of African Religion*; and Tutu, *African Prayer Book*.

17. See chapter 6, "Praying with Black People for Darker Faith."

When Christianity is on the side of Empire, it controls the sources of domination, and as such it prescribes the proper prayers, while not allowing prayers in forms of rupture, dissonance, screams, curses, woes, "disrespect," demands, breaks, and radical transformations. Instead, it keeps our emotions under a certain understanding of humanity, mostly defined by forms of doctrinal control, allowing people to pray in some ways, and at the same time denying prayers as social reaction against oppression and consequent radical social responses.

Amidst theological quibbles and fables and edited histories chosen by official liturgical theologies, liturgical resources have been composed to actually prevent such radical prayers from ever touching the horrors done by humankind—especially when such horrors go beyond the suffering of white middle- and upper-class folks. Liturgical history is often the repetition and confirmation of official history through dogmas and documents, confined to very well-crafted liturgical texts, restricted to the inner conflicts of doctrinal interpretation, recollecting doctrines and forms of belief that only serve to confirm the official history, which is always a "universal" history of Christianity created by local peoples living in Europe, wholly accepted and necessarily regurgitated everywhere else. Our common ground is not somebody else's history but the common struggle of those from below.

If we are to pray with the Jesus who was killed by the violent state of his time, we must create liturgical resources in the shadows of colonization, modernity, and slavery. Only by reading the history of liturgy with those who are damned, whom Frantz Fanon called the wretched of the earth, can we start to be faithful to Jesus. Thus, the only way to pray a Christian prayer today is to pray with those who are exploited, crushed, killed, and oppressed, on the sides of our societies; to pray against liturgical thinking that is still wrapped up in white supremacy, colonial capitalist power, and the slavery mentality of those who have invaded and plundered lands everywhere, destroyed local people's history, and massacred their offspring. And are still doing it.

Thus, to *pray with* the poor is to take a step beyond our comfort zone moving to a different location to begin our theological thinking. To be on the ground with those suffering without any security of their own is to gain awareness of our own groundlessness, of our distance from those with whom Jesus lived and taught us to pray. Praying with the poor shifts the center of prayer. Oaths are shifted, commitments are challenged, emotions are evoked and expanded, beliefs are questioned, compassion is issued, and theological positions are placed at stake.

A New Grammar of Faith

Prayer is the grammar of faith, and doctrine is the grammar of colonization—at least for the most part. The history of Christian prayer, associated with powers of destruction, has created a grammar of faith that has been also a form of wounding. The colonizers made us repeat their words, words that made sense only to them. Words that could translate only their own stories, their own pain and forms of living. Surely, they reasoned, the prayers of the church can be said by people anywhere and that can be the healing of entire communities.

We need a new grammar of faith, a grammar that is born from the streets, from the abandoned corners of the earth, from the wisdom of the people buried under the powers of dominance, exploitation, and extermination. We need a new grammar of faith that can help us sense the dissonance between the promise of the presence of God and the dissonance of the felt absence of God in the miserable situations of so many.

In each place we went, we witnessed pain and hurt. We experienced the cognitive dissonance between the language of our faith and the conditions of violence present in each location. Thus, these workshops were about the possibility for all of us to be transformed by the Holy Spirit as we were present to a certain incarnation of Jesus, one whom we, as a church, mostly avoid. This event was a life-changing experience, a denunciation of our detached liturgical resources, and a call into a life of deeper connections and fullness sparked by prayers resounding with the pain and joy of the unwanted.

We witnessed how Empire can make us feel terribly frail, and at the same time we experienced how prayers permit us to discover a God who is much more vivid than our imagination. We discovered how prayer is a way to find ourselves in the midst of others, a way to breathe in the wonder of God and to create conditions of resistance. Prayer helps us to "organize" forms of consciousness that give us a sense of agency grounded in the power and love of God. Although it may seem that prayers are almost nothing with which to fight Empire, they can crack its walls with their sound and persistence. As we read in Ezekiel 22:30, we must "stand in the breach" between the Empire and the unwanted, the powerful and the least of these, the center and the periphery, listening to the local stories of the margins, learning their wisdom and knowledge, providing spaces for sustenance and expansion. Prayer carries an immense possibility of breaking the structures of evil and violence, within and outside.

In one way or another, praying in situations of suffering changed us. Most of the workshop participants' testimonies pointed to that transformation.

Many of them never thought that the church could be so important and could mean so much to so many people. At the same time, it is impossible to capture the experiences of the people who participated. Through this project, many of us experienced how it is possible for Christians to be challenged, to decolonize ourselves and reclaim patterns of words and actions in liturgies that can open fissures within the walls of Empire. We realized that by creating liturgies from the places where vulnerable people live, we ourselves gain a more radical voice, one closer to where Jesus lived.

Christians must build expansive practices of compassion and solidarity with those who are deemed to die. We must realize our deep connections with all from the lower classes, all the poor, of any religion or color, and expand this solidarity with animals, rivers, ocean, birds, and the whole earth. Prayer reminds us that through God, we understand that to become human is far more than the indoctrination of any human dominion. Instead, we learn that we are always collective, in our communities and with other species and the earth. Through our prayers and liturgies, God transforms the world through us. Only through that confluence of mutualities and belonging does our prayer become God's breath in the world. In that way, prayer becomes a continuation of Jesus's prophetic life, expressing a radical commitment with the poor. A new grammar of faith.

What is the grammar of our prayers when we write them with an empty stomach, a bleeding wound, a terminal illness, without any provision of health care or medical intervention? What is the grammar of our prayers when there is no redemption anywhere? When our prayers and liturgies are disconnected from the forces of death, we cannot reach the forces of life. When we pray under the power of Empire without vividly naming the powers of death, we are offering a soft support to the powers of destruction and domination. Soft, but support: enabling conditions for the hard power of destruction to continue.

When we pray our liturgies within situations of terror, we need a grammar that names and responds to that situation, a grammar of awareness, of rebuke, of resistance, of transformation, of life pulsing in the midst of death. We do not have such a liturgical grammar for our prayers and for that we need to engage our worship to God and our worship services from a different perspective, not that of the rich or the comfortable, but of the poor and those being attacked mercilessly. The Hagars and the cast-out concubines of our time also need prayers, anamnesis, and liturgical care. We need liturgies that can rage against all forms of destruction and prophesy against local injustices by helping to dismantle violent forms of power that kills: patriarchy, racism, sexism, economic injustice, and Earth extractivism.

In sum, how can we create a grammar of faith that pauses and reckons deeply with violence, and at the same time, carries the urgency of those who are about to die?

Christian women and feminist scholars have developed an entirely new way of doing liturgy. Some of the liturgies respond to violence against women based on their own experiences with evil structures. Others speak from and to other concrete situations and life transitions.[18] These practitioners and scholars "do liturgy" not for the sake of some male liturgical traditions, but for the sake of the healing and well-being of women. In the same way, Pentecostal churches are responding in prayer to the disasters of our world. Other Christian communities have developed the work of liturgy from the context of local experiences of suffering, vulnerability, and strength that can offer resistance to the political-economic forces of Empire.[19]

When Christians are not seen as a danger to any of the powers that be, the church has lost its core meaning and purpose, and prayers and liturgies are only a perfunctory act of self-conservation. "Prayer is meaningless," wrote Rabbi Abraham Joshua Heschel, "unless it is subversive, unless it seeks to overthrow and to ruin the pyramids of callousness, hatred, opportunism, and falsehoods."[20]

Prayer as a Circular Movement

Prayer does something. It is a potent ritual action. Prayer effects a deep circular movement within us, moving between our inside and outside without separation. When we pray to God, our prayer first changes us and then, while the movements of our hearts go toward God, our prayer has ripple effects into the world, affecting the course of our individual and communal life. Prayer effects changes in our personal and political thinking, feeling, actions, and ways of being. In the United States, when there are disasters or mass gun shootings that kill many people, including children, or even now in the midst of COVID-19, politicians typically say they are sending "thoughts and prayers" to the victims. But most of the time,

---

18. The sources are vast and diverse, including Walton, *Feminist Liturgy*; Procter-Smith and Walton, *Women at Worship*; Procter-Smith, *Praying with Our Eyes Open*; Procter-Smith, "Liturgical Responses to Sexual and Domestic Violence"; and Berger, *Women's Ways of Worship*.

19. Among other works, see Stewart, *A Watered Garden*; Galbreath, *Leading into the World*; Lathrop, *Holy Ground*; Copeland, "Eucharist and Some Black Bodies"; West, "Liturgy: Church Worship and White Superiority"; Haldeman, *Toward Liturgies that Reconcile*; Johnson, *Divine Communion*; and Junker, *Prophetic Liturgy*.

20. Heschel, "On Prayer," 263.

this is empty rhetoric, since nothing else happens, nothing really changes. The public quickly learns from the rote repetition of this expression that prayers do not really matter.

In these cases, however, we can see an obvious circularity: prayers and thoughts not accompanied by sociopolitical and economic actions and changes are not really genuine prayers. When we think of our prayers, we have to remember Jesus saying, "You will know them by their fruits" (Matt 7:16 NRSV). When we pray, the fruits of gratitude, solidarity, justice, and compassion are seeds that, once planted in us, make the soil of our hearts and communities rich and grow into new gardens of collective harvest and bounty. When we pray together no one should go hungry or go abandoned. When we pray, genuinely, for families who have lost their children to gun violence, to jail, or to poverty, a whole network of life and solidarity must come to fruition and be turned into laws against guns, against social disparity, against systems of death and exclusion. If prayer has a live and full circularity within one's body and spirit, the whole community will breathe this prayer and be connected in love and true solidarity. Prayer can be the starting point for change.

Praying is about bringing people into re-existence. We are called to pray into re-existence those hidden and forgotten in the shadow of oblivion, into abject and obscure places where life is considered a thing to be disposed of. To pray people into re-existence is to bring them closer to our hearts and our neighborhoods, rewriting laws and offering a new way of organizing and living our social life. For those abandoned at the ends of the world, we pray God to bring them into full existence against the necropolitics of Empire that only tortures and exterminates the poor. We are called to pray like the women in the movie *Pray the Devil Back to Hell*, who, amidst civil war, prayed the devil away from their lives by facing warlords so that children could get out of the hands of armies and return to a peaceful life.[21]

Our times demand courage. We must do more than hope. Waiting is often a form of apathy or complacency. As the Spirituals says, "We are the ones we've been waiting for."[22] God is calling us all to offer solidarity, and the way to do it is by giving our hearts to it. As we get closer to those who are suffering in our communities, we may feel lost and unsure what to do. We may experience a mixture of gratitude, exhaustion, longing, impotence, pain, discomfort, excitement, and confusion. At the same time, we may learn as we go that prayer has the power to keep us going! Our hearts may

---

21. Reticker, *Pray the Devil Back to Hell*.
22. Sweet Honey in the Rock, "We Are the Ones." See https://www.youtube.com/watch?v=UHsJHZpOJCc.

be open to courage in ways that we will only know as we pray, work, sit, meditate, listen, and act.

There are actions done with people around the world that can help spark our imagination. For instance, we can take a line of actions from Babasaheb Ambedkar, who wrote the Constitution of India, a social reformer and liberationist. Fighting with and for his own people, the Dalits, he proposed: *educate, agitate, and organize*. From Catholic Social Teaching, a methodology to change social reality using this pedagogical pattern: *see, judge, and act*. From the large social movement around the world called the Landless Movement, a pattern of actions with the most impoverished people: *occupy, resist, produce*.

Korean-American theologian Anne Joh bluntly says of solidarity:

> You don't just pull solidarity out of your ass. Solidarity/solidarities is an act now or for hopeful futures. It's un/learning ways of cultivating relations with others, it's learning to hear, embrace, to speak and to even fight differently. Solidarity is a labor of love, repentance and choosing to risk oneself in being with another whose life and living, whose histories and politics may not even resonate or be in direct opposition from what may be familiar to oneself. Solidarity is being with another in acts of dissensus that most likely will be the target of systemic and social wrath. Stand up. Speak/shout up, act up![23]

Whatever path we take, praying with those who are at the ends of the world will be hard. It takes an immense amount of courage and a conversion of the heart. As Professor Mayra Picos Lee reminded me during our journey, when I was feeling lost and frail,

> Courage comes from the Latin *cor*, which means heart. Courage means "with heart," or to pour one's heart into action. As such, your courage reflects your heart's strength, which needs those moments of confusion and chaos to pump harder and to become stronger. This is the gift of growing one's heart in adversity, the story your project tells in so many ways from so many places and through so many people, including you!

Dear readers, take heart, and draw closer to those who are suffering—with full ears, compassion, courage, solidarity and hearts open to be completely transformed.

---

23. Wonhee Anne Joh, Facebook post, July 19, 2019, 8:50 a.m. Joh is the author of *Heart of the Cross* and editor of other works, such as Kim and Joh, *Feminist Praxis against U.S. Militarism*.

4

How to Pray from the Ends of the World

A Methodology

THE METHODOLOGY OF THIS work is associated with the methods of liberation theologies. It starts in communities that are hurting. It lingers with people hurt by economic oppression. It expands, complicates, and enriches its vision through an intersectional reading of reality, through social and economic lenses but also through the lenses of gender, class, race, culture, psychology, and ecology. It relies on Indigenous and local knowledges and resources that help us see what is at stake in our communities, the questions of life and death around us, and how to respond with Christian resources.

Christianity is not a religion of individuals disconnected from the world seeking for some individual success or living for themselves alone. Rather, it is a faith that throws us into the world. The very core of being a Christian is to be thrown into the world to live Jesus's life amidst those who are hurting. The work of the Holy Spirit in the Christian faith is to connect individuals with communities. To be a Christian is to be in community! A community only exists because of the individual and the individual can live and thrive only through being continuously challenged by the community. This reality can be summarized in the African word *Ubuntu*. Retired archbishop of Cape Town, South Africa, and Nobel Peace Prize winner Desmond Tutu defines *Ubuntu* in these words:

> Ubuntu is very difficult to render into a Western language. It speaks of the very essence of being human. When we want to give high praise to someone we say, "Yu, u nobuntu"; "Hey, so-and-so has ubuntu." Then you are generous, you are hospitable, you are friendly and caring and compassionate. You share what you have. It is to say, "My humanity is caught up, is inextricably bound up, in yours." We belong in a bundle of life. We say, "A person is a person through other persons." It is not, "I think therefore I am." It says rather: "I am human because I belong. I

participate, I share." A person with ubuntu is open and available to others, affirming of others, does not feel threatened that others are able and good, for he or she has a proper self-assurance that comes from knowing that he or she belongs in a greater whole and is diminished when others are humiliated or diminished, when others are tortured or oppressed, or treated as if they were less than who they are.[1]

This! This is what the church must be. *Ubuntu*! The church as a communal gathering with all its challenges and demands, inspired by the Holy Spirit, empowered to be an agent of transformation in the world, honoring each person, promoting justice, protecting life for all. Collectively, we as Christians push forward into the liberation of all communities.

One of the ways we do this is by thinking together, what Paulo Freire called conscientization, which counters social numbness, a sense of being in the world by oneself, with "a critical form of thinking about the world."[2] This form of critical thinking also includes faith. The gospel of Jesus Christ is always a counternarrative. It is a counter-emotional life; it is a counter-way of living, counter to a world living in self-destruction. The gospel of Jesus leads us to struggle against injustice as we seek for collective peace. A true Christian faith reflects critically on the world we live in and questions why some people are pushed away from basic resources of life. This critical faith begs for a theological work that must be done with and among the poor. This means we need to be sent by the Spirit to where people are hurting the most, which is where God chooses to live. In theological language, we talk about God's "preferential option" for the poor. This preferential option does not deny love to anyone. It does not choose some over others in terms of ontological value or even religious affiliation: all are truly loved by God and deserve God's encompassing love. What the expression "preferential option for the poor"[3] signals is that God is always at work on behalf of those who are suffering at the hands of oppressors. It is something like this: if a forest is on fire and another three forests are not, we will bring water to and care for the forest that is burning. In the same way this is true for our ecological world, this is also true for those who suffer because they have been unjustly kept away or taken away from basic resources that can help them live better.

---

1. Tutu, *No Future without Forgiveness*, loc. 31, Kindle.
2. Freire, *Pedagogy of the Oppressed*, 95.
3. This term "preferential option for the poor" is a hallmark of liberation theology in Latin America and part of the theological, political, ecclesial, sexual, and ethical thinking and practices within communities throughout the continent.

Thus, Christian churches should make a move toward the forests on fire, which are the places of poverty near their communities, in order to sit and listen, to stop and learn about those who are hurting. Perhaps those who are hurting are the unhoused people around the block, or immigrants waiting for day labor at a street corner, farm workers picking tomatoes in nearby fields, families in the city or neighborhood surviving on meager resources, single mothers struggling to educate their children while working in two or three jobs, or children and youth who don't have support for education, refugees invisible to society, a polluted river, a community exploited by agribusiness, workers with very low salaries and poor working conditions, people in prison.... I am not suggesting that each congregation build bridges with all of these. Pick one. Begin anywhere. But begin. Create a network. Move out toward a suffering group in your community.

Those churches to whom reaching beyond their comfort zone or their own population is new can create partnerships with churches that are already in those places and learn how to pray together. Since prayer and work go together (*ora et labora*), we have to learn how to pray and how to live from those prayers. For these initial steps in partnerships with churches that serve poor and disenfranchised people, we have to learn to approach each other with care, caution, imagination, compassion, and kindness. We need to learn as much as we can about people who live near our communities, listening to them and inviting them to be with us—as well as going to be with them where they are. We must do what Judith Butler calls us to do, to *think in alliance*: "For me," she says, "the task is not to find a single or synthetic framework, but to find a way of thinking in alliance."[4] In the words of Brazilian Indigenous leader Raoni Metuktire, "We can't accept any use of violence anymore... the success of our generation is to obtain success in cooperation."[5]

To this *thinking in alliance* and cooperation, I want to add *praying in alliance* or *in cooperation*. This thinking-praying-cooperating in alliance includes cooperation between Christians and Christians of other denominations, Christians and people of other religions, Christians and atheists. Since we are moved by the Holy Spirit toward others, what we hope to do is not to find liberation just for our community but liberation for everyone and every community. Thinking and praying in alliance also means to pray with animals and mountains, rivers, flowers, seeds, fields, animals, soil, and wind. We are all intertwined in life, made of stardust, part of a cosmic

---

4. Butler, "Thinking in Alliance."

5. Raoni Metuktire, "Instituto Raoni," Facebook video, August 31, 2019, https://www.facebook.com/watch/?v=521680488602310.

movement, within this same earth. As Martin Luther King Jr. said in his "Letter from Birmingham Jail," "We are caught in an inescapable network of mutuality, tied in a single garment of destiny. Whatever affects one directly affects all indirectly."[6] We are all part of a whole, but this whole includes vast and deep differences: praying with others entails both learning to be part of a whole and acknowledging our deepest differences.

As we move forward to think and pray together, we start with praxis: by practicing our prayers together. We start praying with what we have within these encounters and that connectivity will transform, correct, and expand our prayers. Our prayers are praxis, our first theology, and then we do the second level of theology as we write it, after our praxis. In other words, we reflect our faith on the ground, by praying with people who are different from ourselves, and then we do a second reflection, which is to come back to worship with our congregations to pray the prayers we learn from living with the larger community. For as long as it is necessary.

Below is a suggestion of steps for you to engage your community. You can adjust them to your local congregation and context.

1) Teach your church how to pray with the poor. Use liberation theology's resources that can help you learn about God's preferential option for the poor. Engage your community to go out and do mission by praying with people—for instance, one of the groups I mentioned above in my examples. This work does not prioritize giving money to other organizations; it is not meant to create an environment for the people with whom you are building bridges to come to church, but to have people from your congregation move outside of the church building and into the places where people who are suffering live—and, among other things, to pray with them there.

2) Examine your community, starting with your neighborhood, and then your town or city, to see where people are hurting economically. From this economic perspective, you will see why few people have so much and so many have so little. Connect with groups working with poor communities like the Poor People's Campaign[7] to help you have a deeper systemic view of problems around you. From the ways we establish the law of our living together, the *eco-nomos*, we witness many forms of violence and hurt that are present and that you will need to become aware of and try to attend to.

3) Choose one community or group of people with whom you want to connect. Make contact, listen to them, see what their needs are and ask if you can be a part of their lives. Only say that if you mean it—if you are open to your own transformation.

---

6. King, "Letter from Birmingham Jail," loc. 219, Apple Books.
7. See https://www.poorpeoplescampaign.org/.

4) *Before you go*, learn why this community or group is there. If it is people who are homeless, learn the history of public policies in your city or state that have contributed to this situation. Is it lack of medical assistance? Possibilities of jobs? Education opportunities? What is their agency? Their forms of survival? Check if there are other organizations working with these people already and add your presence. Evaluate strategies of action: interview people, live with people, learn what they eat, what they celebrate, what their challenges are. A pastor friend told me about a church that wanted to bring in people who were homeless to attend church regularly. When coffee hour came, the guests ate all of the donuts. The church members were outraged by their lack of manners. This is evidence that our good intentions toward others are never enough. We ourselves must change.

5) Find strategies for communities to get to know each other. Listening deeply is paramount.

6) Every time you meet with those "outside the gate," go back to your church and, with the people in your congregation who were part of your initial outreach, start to pray, naming the real, concrete situations of that community. May your prayer be an opportunity for conversion and transformation. Continue to pray and meet with the community you visited. Invite them in and create opportunities for other forms of community experiences such as shared meals and gatherings to get to know each other's needs.

7) Find ways to create prayers that become common for both groups, prayers that can inhabit the worship space but that can go beyond the sanctuary. See how prayers can change the ways the church creates the budget. How can this new community with which you are building a relationship be central to the ways the church worships and lives in the world? What needs to be changed? Uses of space? Mission provision? Offerings? What are the priorities of your church now? How can you make sure that each person who is homeless can have a house in which to live?

8) Then, continue to create prayers with your church and the people you are engaging with, adding the prayers of this experience with the prayers of your own church or denomination. Anyone can say their prayers. What prayers can be prayed? With whom? What does your prayer say about your God? What do your prayers say about what or who your God is?

Martin Luther King Jr. wrote in his "Letter from Birmingham Jail,"

> I have traveled the length and breadth of Alabama, Mississippi, and all the other southern states. On sweltering summer days and crisp autumn mornings I have looked at [the South's] beautiful churches with their lofty spires pointing heavenward. I have beheld the impressive outlines of her massive religious

education buildings. Over and over I have found myself asking: "What kind of people worship here? Who is their God?"[8]

As we move into these practical ways of praying and engaging with other communities, with whatever strategies we find necessary for each community, we must answer this question: *Who is our God?*

---

8. King, "Letter from Birmingham City Jail," 299.

5

What Is Common about Our Common Worship?

A Methodological Critique of White Reasoning in the Process of Renewal of the *Book of Common Worship,* Presbyterian Church (USA)[1]

Before the Introduction

THE STRUCTURE OF THIS essay is somewhat strange. It hopes to show the reasoning that often undergirds and orders the ways of thinking and ordering liturgy and worship in Christian churches. Books of common worship are markers of this form of liturgical reasoning, often an unmarked white form of reasoning. But what is this white liturgical reasoning? That is what I try to show here. In order to do that, I will start showing the process of renewal of the *Book of Common Worship* of the Presbyterian Church (USA), the denomination of which I am a member and in which I am an ordained minister.[2] I was invited to be a part of this process. As I describe the movement of renewal of this prayer book, I show some of its very problematic core issues, which is what constitutes white liturgical reasoning. Once I get to that point, I make a detour to show how a white reasoning was historically created and how it functions. Once this detour is made, I go back to the renewal process of the book of common prayer and wrestle with the very notion of the "common" in this book. As I finish it, working with an expanded sense of *leitourgia*/liturgy, I end with an example of how to think about the season of Pentecost not from a white universal liturgical reasoning but from a historical situation. The death of George Floyd defines the season and where we

---

1. An earlier, shorter version of this essay was first published as Carvalhaes, "White Reasoning and What Is Common."
2. As much as it might not look like it, this work is a work of love.

should align ourselves as Christians. It all might feel cumbersome, but I hope that, at the end of this long essay, it will make sense.

Introduction

This essay began as a contribution to the process of renewal of the *Book of Common Worship* of the Presbyterian Church (USA).[3] I had hoped that this reflection could help us in the Presbyterian Church to pay attention to the ways in which our liturgical methodology was marked not only by a distinctive theology but also by certain class, race, gender, and sexual commitments. I did not intend to be adversarial to my sisters and brothers or to dismiss the beautiful work that was already in process. Instead, I hoped to bring a vision from the underground, to surface a perspective from the fringes of our society and church that could expand the racial colors of our common faith, bringing light from the Black, brown, yellow, and red people of our society, from those who are undocumented, from sexually excluded people and disabled people, in order to expand the possibilities of our worship services.

This work was just a small movement in the now vast and growing field of worship and diversity. I attempted to investigate, rather briefly, how the mindset of what I call white reasoning has placed minorities into the fringes of the *leitourgia*, liturgy, the "work of the people." We, the racially, sexually, and otherwise minoritized and minority people and communities are at the receiving end of this liturgical enterprise, turned into peripheral categories by "universal" white reasoning. We are expected to receive the wisdom of our white brothers and sisters, ritualizing our loves and faith according to the grounds of wisdom and tradition handed to us. One form of knowledge, universalized, has served to deter other forms of knowledge in the name of "tradition."

My point was not, and is not, to dismiss the wisdom collected in the prayer book, since the gathering of wisdom necessarily needs people of all races, gender, and sexual orientations. The problem was the very absence of other people and other forms of thinking that would constitute a more complex notion of the common, at least to the point of not working with an unmarked and given sense of "common." Thus, my hope was *to expand the notion of what was "common"*: to open spaces for other wisdoms, practices, and thinking from people historically colonized and designated improper, whose liturgical practices and thinking are often considered "low liturgy," "popular," "contextual," or even "cultural" liturgies, as if the so-called

---

3. Presbyterian Church (USA), *Book of Common Worship* (2018).

universal liturgy were not also based on a particular cultural and contextual understanding of the body, of life, of race, sex, class, and worship itself.

Throughout this essay, I attempt to evoke and encourage different or expanded ways of thinking, acting, gesturing, performing—indeed, different ways of living. I write with a performative mind. My main wrestling ground is an all-encompassing white reasoning that purports to be neutral, universal, and pure but instead is fundamentally patriarchal, heterosexual, colonizing, and grounded in exclusion.

Leitourgia: Revising the Methodology of the *Book of Common Worship*[4]

What is our understanding of the word *leitourgia* as we undertake the process of BCW revision, or for that matter, any prayer book revision in a mainline Protestant denomination, beyond the PC(USA)? When I ask this question I am inquiring not only into the meaning of the Greek word, but also into the theological sense of the assembly it brings with it, the understanding of "the people" we have in mind when we undertake our worship book revision.

In other words, I am asking, "What is the role of the assembly, of the people, in this project? Who and where are the people we are working with as we revise and renew the *Book of Common Worship*?" These fundamental questions need to be addressed prior to the decisions about what prayers and practices we will choose and give to the people—the assembly—to shape their worship life. The meaning of *leitourgia* as "the work of the people" with which we are working (either implicitly or explicitly) will define both what "work" and "people" "mean when we engage in this process of renewal. With that, we may ask some obvious questions: What is actually the work of the people? Can the people, not (only) the ordained people, create liturgy? Who can create access to the holy things and decide who have access to them? What can people do in worship? To what fundamental "holy things"[5] should we ascribe and according to whom? What rubrics should be assigned? What are the holy

---

4. In September 2015, a group of mostly white people, mostly men, leaders and liturgy experts in the PC(USA) and liturgical experts from other denominations, gathered at McCormick Theological Seminary in Chicago to continue the process of the renewal of the *Book of Common Worship*. This was not a decision-making group but a consultant gathering asking a variety of people to offer their wisdom to the people of the church who were leading the renewal. I had hoped to speak this at the meeting, but time constraints did not allow me to do so. I continue to believe that if we fail to attend to this concern, we will have failed our call and our people.

5. See Lathrop, *Holy Things*.

things—symbols, ritual sequences, forms of prayer—we are going to offer to our people? What proper action or behavior will we allow in our worship spaces? What sources are we using and authorizing? And before all this, what kind of liturgical theological choices are we making?

All of these questions bear witness to the notion of "common." Who is the *common* in this book of prayer or whose *common-ality* are we talking about? I am not concerned in this discussion with the number of prayers of confession, the litanies we create, the clarity of the movements, whether eucharistic prayers are to be short or long, whether the presider should raise their hands when leading, how many feet away from the table they should stand, or how we condense, combine, and/or collapse services. I know this will be there.

What is at stake for me is the common or the measurement by which we decide what being human is all about. What form of humanity is contemplated here under the generalized sense of common? What forms of thinking, of relations, of human experiences, of knowledges, practices, and wisdom are we talking about when we talk about a "common" book of prayer?

"Common prayer" often means a form of experiences and way of living that shapes the beliefs, hopes, and troubles of one group that prays and worships together. Books of common worship are a historical report of one group of people at the expense of others. If not, why do we not have prayers and songs and litanies and confessions that are fully antiracist and deeply committed to the eradication of the systemic racism that kills and imprisons Black people? Why do we not have relentless woes and curses against white supremacy at each liturgy? Why do we sustain a bland universal form of worship that does not name the violence against LGBTQI people at every corner of our common history? Why do we never talk about colonization and the ongoing genocide of Indigenous people and the endless de-sacralization of their sacred lands? Caught in the dualism of the transcendence/immanence of God, these books are always above the earth, never praying with the earth but holding up a sovereignty that rules over the earth and over other animals or forms of life.

In that way, books of common prayer are religious documents of white supremacy and white civilization, soft colonial support for politics of exclusion, white jurisprudence, and control of land and riches, a hidden manifesto on class struggles, and a clear orientation of the heart, the mind, and the body towards particular forms of social, political, economic, and religious control and dominance. It is hard not to add the books of common worship to the other civilizational documents mentioned by Walter

Benjamin: "There is no document of civilization which is not at the same time a document of barbarism."[6]

The content and forms of our prayers have to do with power dynamics and how this form of power is dispersed within our forms of relationship to oneself and self with others. We must ask what understanding of self is proposed in our prayer, and self in relation to what? Also, how is the earth part of this common sense of life? Over against what strictures (strict structures) will we work in order to make sense of our sense of God in the common life of the people? The *Book of Common Worship* will surely enhance and close off spaces for liturgical possibilities, imagination, and context, giving a full sense of humanity and what is common. Moreover, we must say that in comparison to the 1993 *Book of Common Worship*, we can name several changes, namely, material in three languages, more emphasis on freedom (in both the rubricized prayers and the insistence in commentary sections that liturgy is contextual), and new sections on both the care of creation and justice and reconciliation. In this way, the Presbyterian *BCW* is already much more open to creativity and is more contextual and more expansive than other denominational books of common worship.

My work is to try to figure out what kind of reasoning is underneath this process, the reasoning that will make us describe what it is to be human, humus, Earth, relationships, God, and each other. Thus, our work is not to keep asking how many prayers we need to add to the book but rather, to ask a more difficult question that comes before and that has to do with the *methodology* of our book of common worship, its theological commitments, the people we are serving, the worlds of injustice we are dismantling and the worlds we are creating, all marked at the beginning and at the end of this project, sometimes clearly noted, sometimes hidden in a given, expected sense of *leitourgia*.

One of the main issues for me has to do with the place in which we are to start as well as our relationships and the forms of power dynamics that exist among us. These issues define our class belongings, our access to material and other goods, our relation to race, social access, and power. Since we hope to locate ourselves in the best sources of our tradition, often our liturgies get swallowed into a clear un/conscious purpose to reflect unspoken locations, as if the liturgy and its starting location float somewhere universally in order to keep local people and its class commitments protected. Who are we "representing"? Who are we working with and for? To what purpose? We just assume that we are doing the work of God for "all" and that is enough. This reflects a strong sense of acquired power through tradition.

---

6. Benjamin, "On the Concept of History," VII.

A pastor friend of mine is trying to bring poor youth into the churches she is working with, but time and again these young people have nothing to do with our liturgies or our ways of being in the world. Are they the very reason for our desires to create the forms of our worship? Are we working for those who lack institutional power to find their own way within our society? Must they conform to the institution and the divine liturgy? Are we working to make worship services that condemn and resist racism and homophobia in our society?

The PC(USA) denomination is mostly made up of small, struggling congregations in quite different conditions and circumstances. We have a huge economic gap between the "big-steeple" rich churches and the struggling churches. Is this condition of being church what marks our liturgical efforts to make a "common worship book"? We cannot hide inside "universal" liturgies when we live in such an unequal and diverse national situation. This situation presents us all with a tremendous challenge, overall, and in our liturgies.

Liturgical methodology must consider for whom and with whom we are doing this work. It must consider going from neutrality to clear choices and situated language and commitments, from the fiction of the purity of our faith and clear proper identity to the ongoing mixture of beliefs and multiple identities. The end result is often more attentive to "the tradition" than to the lives of the people. Can worship be the same in radically different locations? How can radically different churches pray the same prayer? How do we care deeply for poor, struggling churches and people under strenuous forms of oppression? How do we help create liturgical language to tackle racism, poverty, climate change, and economic inequality in our society? What does the grammar of our faith teach us to speak about?

Thus, finding better prayers—or just more choices of prayers—will not suffice if we refuse to tackle the national sins of our country. What we actually need is to find a new methodology, one that is contextual, one that comes out of living with people, so we can find the feelings, the hurts, the settings, the situations, the relationships, the power dynamics, the ideologies, meanings and challenges of our realities. A key point here is to realize that any liturgical methodology needs to know what kind of people we want to sit with to learn and to pray together.

If *leitourgia* is the work of the people with God, what kind of people are we talking about and whose God are we talking about? Who and where are they? What is the earth they are living on? Who owns that land?

The current prayer book methodology tries to respond to a metaphysical God, a white God who lives in and through purity, universality, a certain neutrality, and a-historicity. This "neutrality" can be seen, for example, in the eucharistic prayers. We tell the history of salvation as narrated in the Bible and then we stop. We do not allow God's action to be named within either older (than biblical history) or contemporary radical events of liberation/salvation. Once we land in the current history of our time, our liturgies become political in the sense of being actual living in the *polis*, the city, the world, something we try to avoid at all costs. As if our traditional liturgies were not political! We are certainly not trying to make liturgy a political act in the sense of political parties. Liturgy is the way we love God, and our common prayers intend to honor and give worth to God. However, we need to wrestle with a politics of the understanding of "common" in our tradition. This concerns what is at the heart of our reasoning.

A Detour: White Reasoning

There is indeed something called white reasoning. In the book *Critique of the Tupiniquim Reason* (which he also understands to mean "Brazilian reasoning"), the Brazilian writer Roberto Gomes says that Brazilian reasoning could only take place through fiction, a fiction that begins by negating and denouncing reasoning without color, reasoning supposedly grounded in neutrality and universality.[7] White reasoning invented the Western canon from a mythic place of purity, a zero point of thought where everything is born, a self-enclosed essence where everything that is strange to that essence is shoved aside and excluded, or simply ignored as non-existent. Everything else, according to this reasoning, is fiction. Our Indigenous peoples and their reasoning, which are considered mythical or fictional themselves, could never beat the historical Greeks.

In his *Critique of Black Reason*, Achille Mbembe, a thinker from Cameroon, also criticizes white reasoning.[8] White reasoning is inevitably related to a specific culture, the European culture descended from Greek-Hellenistic sources. White reasoning was created through the colonization process in the meeting of Europeans with Asian, African, and Indigenous peoples. These encounters troubled Europeans' awareness of their own identity. By encountering other people, they had to make a double movement to define themselves: they had to both distinguish and equalize themselves with the people they encountered, establishing a deep distinction from Indigenous and African peoples and establish some kind of sameness when encountering Asians, the "Orientals." The way to do this was not only to use power and brutal force to win over and subjugate these peoples, but also and

---

7. Gomes, *A Crítica da Razão Tupiniquim.*
8. Mbembe, *Critique of Black Reason.*

fundamentally, to create a sense of identity through a developing form of reasoning established by slavery, the trans-Atlantic slave trade, the plundering of lands, and the exchange of merchandise. Through this process, the Europeans' given sense of humanity had to be discussed, theorized, racialized, and composed through colonizing and modernity, the whitening of reason. In this process, the process of conquering was marked by a sense of civilization, purity, and salvation.

All non-whites became the source of European identity: European colonizers and their compatriots and coreligionists negated the other so as to affirm themselves. By establishing the lack of humanity in everyone else, the colonizers fulfilled their own sense of humanity. In other words, during the colonization process from the fifteenth century on, there occurred a racializing of the ones who were to be conquered, the strange, the foreign. "Neutrality" became a code for God's will driven by ferocious forms of power and dominance. As if the rulers of the faith were saying, "All we want to do is God's will."

After severing people's lives from their land, displacing the earth from knowledge, connection, cosmology, living, and survival, one of the tactics of this white European reasoning was to avoid the very relation to the earth, the soil, and where one lives. By abandoning local geography as the structuring of life, the unaware avoidance of one's own cultural, social, and historical context was translated into universal truths. Thus, from the small towns of Germany, Belgium, England, Switzerland, and Scotland, the premise was that the (European) Christian way of thinking was a universal way of thinking about humanity. The local thinking of these places crushed the local knowledges of other places by enforcing a universality of thinking (cosmologies), feelings and behaviors (civilization), and religion (Christianity). With the advent of colonization and the uprooting of the conquered, a focus on space gave way to a focus on time; a variety of spiritualities and forms of worship had to give way to one form of liturgy and spiritual practice, and a particular tradition was turned into God's desire. Anything that did not resemble this way of reasoning—and the related spiritual practices and understandings of God—was not proper Godly reasoning and was thus in need of correction, illumination, order, correction, and organization.

We can see three major aspects of this totalizing way of thinking: universality, neutrality, and purity. A socially and culturally unmarked white reasoning shaped the world and marked everything with a certain truth, with "universal" (though in fact particular) values. Its ethical demands are always shaped from within that reasoning. So too in the realm of theology. The continent of Africa could never be as wise or important as Greece, the purported cradle of humankind. Western and Eastern Asia—"the

Orient"—could never be the location of the most significant historical accomplishments and human creativity. Indigenous peoples could never be seen as bearers of foundational cosmologies and civilizations. White reasoning is neither naïve nor innocent, for it enforces the thinking of the appearance and behaviors that define—from the perspective of its own logic—what human life is about. For the purposes of our discussion here, we can say that precision of reason, historical authenticity, and coherent logic are European characteristics and that any form of reasoning that does not assume these characteristics, or reflect them as mirrors to oneself, must be considered less human, uncivilized, barbarian, or at least poorer, or not academic enough, or "popular," an offense to the tradition.

This colonial dominance continues today even under rubrics of niceness and openness to other cultural forms of worship. The central, centripetal, non-negotiable forms of believing and worshiping must always be the ones coming from the tree of white reasoning. If we look at our customary liturgical resources, what do we know or teach about theological, philosophical, or liturgical reasoning from Africa, Latin America, Asia, or Indigenous peoples of any continent, in our seminary courses? Their forms of knowledge were destroyed, what is now called epistemicide[9] or epistemological genocide. If they exist in that setting, they are present as adjunct knowledge in relation to the more enlightened fundamentals of white reasoning.

But let us go back to the historical forms of white reasoning. During the Enlightenment of the eighteenth century, says Mbembe, white reasoning was marked by "white thinkers' indifference to slave trafficking." There was little writing or fight against slavery, if any. This indifference was already shaping Black people's lives in relation to white Europeans'. Indifference, couched as neutrality, was a way of denying, diminishing, concealing, and killing Black people. This indifference was not neutral; instead, it created the contours of white reasoning, based on a racist core, dealing with anybody "other," in this way: the stranger was to be de-nigrated, turned Black.[10] Anyone who was not white was thrown into a Blackness that served to form and define its opposite, whiteness.

9. Santos, *Epistemologies of the South*.

10. Denigrate: "If you 'denigrate' someone, you attempt to blacken their reputation, with 'blacken' here in its commonly accepted pejorative meaning. It makes sense, therefore, that 'denigrate' can be traced back to the Latin verb *denigrare*, meaning 'to blacken.' When 'denigrate' was first used in English in the sixteenth century, it was meant to cast aspersions on someone's character or reputation. Eventually, it developed a second sense of 'to make black' ('factory smoke denigrated the sky'), but this sense is somewhat rare in modern usage. Nowadays, of course, 'denigrate' can also refer to belittling the worth or importance of someone or something." See https://www.merriam-webster.com/dictionary/denigrate.

In other words, it was now necessary to respond to the force of race, and the answer was to turn all those who were not white into the categories of impure, lower races and groups: Blacks, Jews, Muslims, Natives, women, children. Over against this Blackness, Mbembe talks about not only the presence of whiteness but the necessary *appearance* of whiteness. He writes,

> The work of racism consists in relegating it to the background or covering it with a veil. . . . Racism consists, most of all, in substituting what is with something else, with another reality. It has the power to distort the real and to fix affect, but it is also a form of psychic derangement, the mechanism through which the repressed suddenly surfaces. . . . I have emphasized that racism is a site of reality and truth—the truth of appearances. But it is also a site of rupture, of effervescence and effusion. The truth of individuals who are assigned a race is at once elsewhere and within the appearances assigned to them. They exist behind appearance, underneath what is perceived.[11]

This appearance of whiteness shows up as neutrality and universality, which can be understood as indifference and violence toward blackened races, working to dismantle their particularities. Its mythic purity serves to render everything else impure. All these dimensions of white "reality"—neutrality, universality, purity—must be enforced. Threatened by the Blackness of others, white reasoning had to deploy a whole complex of power dynamics to sustain its validity. Exploitation, control, and even annihilation of the newly blackened world was necessary. We see a "reasonable" movement of brutal forces moving throughout five hundred years of colonization of the Americas up until today, imposing structures and strictures of behavior and thought upon Indigenous, Black, and brown people.

Coloniality is the reasoning of white supremacy at work, conjuring up a complex plethora of forced activities, a network of violence that aims at control and domination. As Mbembe says, "Colonial violence is a network, 'a node of encounter between multiple, diverse, re-iterated and cumulative forms of violence,' experienced as much on the level of the spirit as in 'muscles, and blood.'"[12]

Major forms of control and annihilation of these three groups of people have included old and new forms of theft and occupation of lands, slavery, socio-economic apartheid, mass incarceration, elimination of opportunities and resources, material and psychological barriers, economic constraints, and deportation. Most of the wealth of the Americas today, including here in the

---

11. Mbembe, *Critique of Black Reason*, locs. 842, 850, Kindle.
12. Mbembe, *Critique of Black Reason*, loc. 2266, Kindle.

US, is in the hands of white people as a result of these centuries of theft and oppression. The private land in this country is stolen land, and now we all believe in a democracy that supports the rights of private land ownership. Despite color-blind rhetoric and the myth of shared public space, white dominant economic groups and private owners try to use media to shame Black people for "their" violence when they take to the streets, claiming that their intent is to riot and destroy "public common things."

White reasoning is not the privilege of white people only: colonized people of any color have participated in the same ways of thinking by adhering to orders, hopes of power, and acceptance by white masters. When properly "ideologized" and tamed, people of color are used to defend the white, hierarchical (and heteropatriarchal) establishment. The dominance of white reasoning has buried knowledge and weakened resistance by dark or blackened people.

Let me be clear that I do not write this chapter as a personal critique of my precious Christian brothers and sisters. There is truly nothing personal here. What I am trying to do is to show the systemic ways many Christian denominations, and not only Presbyterians, have used their books of common prayer as a particular book of experiences with God and turned these experiences into universal claims. People on the receiving end have used these books in different ways. Some have embraced these books; others have rejected them; many transformations have taken place.

I think, write, and perform from within as well as from outside of white reasoning. I understand my work as a counter-tradition, as resistance to and dismantling of a colonizing white reasoning that totalizes and neutralizes. I engage our worship and theology of worship as a Latinx, but a Latinx placed outside the dominant Latinx realm since I am a Brazilian-born American and Spanish is my third awfully broken language. In strange ways, I am also grateful for the faith I have received.

As we examine the methodology of the *Book of Common Worship* and work toward its renewal, I hope we will challenge white reasoning by building our foundation with other forms of reason—of wisdom, of beliefs, cosmologies, cultures, movements, performances, symbols, languages, rituals. In other words, I hope that we will consider and engage different ways of being human. I am concerned that this has not been done.

Expanding the Commonality of Liturgical-Theological Reasoning

Our reasoning must be expanded if we are to continue to be both Reformed and reformed. Without fear! We need a more concrete sense of the people we are serving and working with so that our God will make sense in our liturgies. Coming from liberation theology, I would say that the choice of our theologies should follow God's choice: the marginalized and oppressed. There, with the poor, where it hurts, is the place where we should start figuring out our prayers, confessions, sacraments, preaching, and praise.

This feels like a dangerous move. What happens to our tradition and identities if we commit to the poor? To loosen our tradition might be a way to lose our sense of white belonging, and I imagine this is the source of our fear and resistance to transformation of our liturgies. What is the judge of our present liturgies? Jaci Maraschin, one of the most important liturgical theologians in Latin America, delves into these questions:

> The liturgical moment is always a kind of center where the memory of the divine lives in the past, yet facing the challenges and the exigencies of what is to happen. If the gathering emerges from tradition, but does not close itself to this tradition, its very nature is to be open to what has not yet happened, and turns tradition into a model for the future with the clear presupposition of a critique. That is why *the judgment of the present* precedes the celebration of what happened in times of liberation, and it is animated by the hope of what might happen because of our commitment to this common decision. . . . However, what kind of gatherings do we have now? Assemblies eaten away by the commitment to the powers of this world and captive to the social, political, and economic system, in which we live. That is why, in general, liturgical gatherings become tiresome, devoid of the vital element that would make them interpreters of reality, exulting in joy.[13]

Thus the judgment of the present is fundamental for our task here and it puts tradition in a place of vibrant force, one of possibility of empowerment. The choice of which people we want to serve has also to do with the methodology of this renewal.

We participants in the consultation about the *Book of Common Worship* renewal received a survey about the prayer book. The survey was essentially technical, since it was concerned with form, structure, and order.

---

13. Maraschin, *A beleza da santidade*, 133–38. Emphasis mine. My translation.

The survey was intended to be expansive in trying to encompass a variety of liturgical resources, but it failed to hint at something else, perhaps a more fundamental move: the survey did not take into account a contextual and embodied reflection. In other words, it did not reflect the pain and hurts, racism, and economic hardships of poor people since we as a church are a white middle-class people. The survey imagines a world without racism and with a lot of entitlement.

I wonder, what is our understanding of "our people"? The formality and shape of our survey responses limit and define our work, a work somewhat detached from our bodies and any kind of real life. The survey comes before and after the body, never with it. What is expected in this survey is not a change in the ways we do the liturgical work of the people, as a possible way to become agents of our own histories with God, or how we live our prayers or check our confessions from harsh realities. The church of our survey is a church that has a clear sense of class—and a commitment to remaining of a particular class. The survey was a renewal of the (same) forms and (expansion of the same) contents of the book. If one looks at the previous *Book of Common Worship*, created twenty-five years ago (1993) and at the new one (2018), the only difference, it seems, is in more alternatives for prayers and greater ease of use. The main concern is with formality and not with the situation of our country and world.

Could we foster a movement of the church toward lower classes and the margins of society and be with them in praise and worship? If we fight for this to happen, then we might have a more just distribution of resources to our people, and we can understand better what "common prayer" might mean. If we can listen to the earth, we can start perceiving our deep belongings: common realities and symbols, materiality, and spirituality, money, and social conditions in the same breath as prayer.

For our prayer book to be fully accomplished in its commonality, it must be constituted of liturgies that would bring symbols and practices from beyond white churches and their theologies. A truly common worship book would have to have a diversity of expressions and forms. We need to have a variety of understandings of "decency and order" that go beyond a white reasoning imposing conformity, forms of understanding that would not only expand the understanding of time, of use of space, forms of worship and of cultural differences but would see racism as the utmost indecency, and social inequality as a fundamental worship disorder.

Back to *Leitourgia*

Let us go back to our sense of *leitourgia*. How do we understand the work of the people when we think about creating liturgies and liturgical spaces where the people of God can be reformed, by God? If we are to do liturgy as the work of the people for the common good, we may need to pay attention to what Ruth Meyers wrote in *Missional Worship, Worshipful Mission*:

> *Leitourgia* is formed not directly from *laos*, "people," but from *leitos*, which means "concerning the people or national community"—that is, "the public" or "the body politic." . . . When I use the term "liturgy," I have in mind *both* the structured ritual activity that involves texts and actions, using symbols, speech, song, and silence, *and* the assembly's work for the common good, its public service as a gathered community and as the people of God in the world. Liturgy as work for the common good is thus a form of participation in the mission of God.[14]

This definition, while still constrained by an unmarked sense of liturgical reasoning, an absence of pluralities and diversities of being with each other and in relation to the earth, is still a good understanding of *leitourgia* as it relates to the common good. Thus, I wonder if our group of liturgical experts has been working *on behalf of the people* and not *with* the people. If we understand liturgy as being with the poor, then, we must notice that we are mostly working in a safe environment telling people in dreadful situations what is common to our group and how to pray our way. But if our sense of liturgy is to serve mostly a middle-class community, then the understanding of "the people" might mean those currently counted in our formal statistics. There is something wrong with this scenario. "Our people" must include those whom we are called to join: the least of these, those outside the four walls of the church. Could we think about moving to the first theological choice: be with the ones abandoned by everyone? Then we could start a new way of revising the prayer book.

A group reforming the denomination's prayer book should begin by gathering its content, not by a new-old formal shaping of an already fixed source and understanding of liturgy, but rather, begin in reality, in specific places, in context, with issues that are killing our people and destroying the earth. From there we will shape our *lex orandi/vivendi/credendi*, or in other words, what is common, how to resist the forces of death and destruction, and how we can share a bit more in life as we say these prayers. Then a sense of universality could finally, miraculously, be achieved.

---

14. Meyers, *Missional Worship*, locs. 672–73, Kindle.

We need a new methodology for the creation of a book of common worship, a methodology that actually takes us to the places of pain, hurt, injustice, and death and that will help us pray and sing from these places.

If that is the task of the *Book of Common Worship* and other prayer books, we cannot avoid the very naming of places, situations, contexts from and with which we must work, and we must address this naming fully. If we look at reality, three major threads are shaping the United States that should shape our worship services as well: the patriarchal fascism that is taking over this country, the war against the poor, and the extractivism of the earth. Our worship book should not only offer prayers and instructions on what to pray, but also be a source of resistance for our communities to 1) gain consciousness about these issues, 2) gain new language to pray about these issues and respond to these realities, and 3) create forms of resistance and reciprocity. In this way, reformed Reformed worship services would be faithful to our tradition's core sense of constantly being reformed, but also assist in the undoing of the structures of evil that swallow our glorias and take away the breath of our praise to God.

It is safe to say that our predominantly white church does not feel the need to think much about racism. We are "safe" and determined to keep our spaces safe. Most of our white middle-class churches' members do not worry about their children arriving home safely or getting sick from working in unsafe conditions. Our church is one of the institutions that, when it does not consciously and vigorously denounce racism, contributes to social and racial injustices and divisions. How can the pain and despair of Black folks be in a book of prayer that wants to be "common" when these experiences are not common to most of this denomination?

Thus, if we speak the names of the devil in our worship to God, such as racism, patriarchalism, xenophobia, sexism, social exclusion, and depletion of the earth, in their local and broader contexts, we might gain a better sense of the hardships and the difficulties of the struggle for hope against these evil forces, both within and beyond ourselves.

Let me say that I am not advocating superpowers for liturgy, as if we could change the world from that one place. Our rituals of worship are just one aspect of our faith. Nonetheless, every part of our faith, and fundamentally our liturgy, where we learn so much of our Christian faith, should be a part of our bending with the arc of justice, a vision of our empowerment by the grace of God, through faith, hope, and love, to speak plainly and openly about God's reality in a way that names, and thus in some sense removes, the mystifying power of a racist agenda.

Subverting Our Liturgies: Naming Our Racism

Speaking to my class "Worship and the Arts," McCormick Professor David Daniels once said that we have to create "disruptive liturgies," liturgies that subvert white privilege by interjecting anti-racist forms of worshiping God." In the making of our liturgies, he said, "We should ask: does this liturgy mention the Black Jesus? From whose points of view is liturgy done? Is our white view privileged? Are the views of people of color privileged in the liturgy? Are races present? Does [the liturgy] deny despair?"

The white reasoning of which I spoke earlier is also mirrored in what Daniels calls white-Anglo liturgy. He defines a white-Anglo liturgy as "shaped by white concerns such as the white guilt, shame, culpability, alleged innocence, love without justice, peace on white terms, and/or bewilderment, a liturgy focused on ministering to white people. A liturgy tied to a progressive white frame of seeing as a frame of reference."

If a book of common worship is always a reflection of its time, what are we saying if our worship resources do not bring ways to undo racism and confront an evil that is literally exterminating the Black people of this country? Does our liturgy make us complicit? And let us not forget the Native Americans who are almost exterminated. Our *Book of Common Worship* should struggle against five hundred years of colonization, including its universal, white, unmarked worship services.

This means that the new *BCW* should help move us all towards places of hurt and exclusion and disaster. From these places—prisons, the wall between Mexico and the US, poor neighborhoods, failing school districts, neighborhoods controlled by drug dealers, modern slavery, racism, economic exclusion and poverty—we will create prayers, choose songs, frame our worship services, decide about our eucharistic food, and shape our liturgies, calling people to worship God. From places of violence and abandonment, we will confess at the baptismal font our complicity with the economic system, preaching against the hegemonic forces of the state against the poor. At the eucharistic table, we will announce that no one goes hungry, that everyone is the *imago Dei*, and that freedom, equality, and social justice are possible. The table of communion will be a table filled with food and reciprocity, where we learn with each other and are forever changed. From dirty rivers, we will confess to the waters our lack of care for God's Earth and commit to taking care of the rivers near our homes until they are alive again. This is what a liturgical methodology and a liturgical theology must consist of for our new worship book.

This methodology will foster and bring forth a mixture of several reasonings so that it can help undo the violence of a hidden white reasoning that is grounded in a certain cultural sense of order and decency. We need to add other forms of reasoning. David Daniels talks about African American liturgical reasoning's giving us "a liturgy shaped by African American concerns such as racial equality, justice, empowerment, anger, reconciliation, disillusionment, and despair. A liturgy focused on ministering to Black and non-Black people. A liturgy tied to a progressive 'Black' way of seeing as a frame of reference."

If we continue to add different frames of reference and a variety of cosmologies, we may start to dismantle white reasoning by infusing transformative liturgies that belong to other forms of reasoning. With this variety of non-white reasonings, with all their dangerous ways of being human, we can foster not only different liturgical theologies but different world-views and possibilities for life, living into different senses and forms of thinking, trusting God and each other until we develop a true priesthood of all believers in worship.

The priesthood of all believers is a whole community accountable to each other as its members break systems of poverty and all become equal before God and one another. This community will not turn worship into its own image, as another consumerist good to buy, but rather, its members will be challenged in their desires and in their actions, and will be able to search Christian history and find sources of empowerment, liberation, blessings, and solidarities.

I can only believe in a *Book of Common Worship* that is a garden with a variety of seeds for flowers and plants of all kinds and from various places. Perhaps we should visit congregations across the United States that are poor churches populated by undocumented people, talk to the Black Lives Matter Movement, visit Indigenous people and learn from them, do chaplaincy in prisons, listen to the birds. Perhaps our children should tell us what is common. That would finally be the common place, the common good, the common life for us all.

Only in this way can we learn from various peoples across the nation what they say and do, what feelings they have, what emotions they cherish or wrestle with, what local symbols they use or how they use the Christian symbols to survive, what songs they are singing to sustain their own faith and in what conditions they are living God's grace in and through their bodies. In this movement, we would develop a sustained sense of how our bodies live out, are marked, punched, moved, filled, transformed and trans-versed by this faith. Then we would come with our expertise and prayers and songs to perhaps expand the sources of liberation and offer something that is not already there. I am calling us to do what the philosopher Antonio Gramsci calls the work of the "organic intellectual." We the organic liturgists, preachers, theologians, Bible experts, adding our expertise to the expertise of the people and the wisdom of *la vida cotidiana*, the quotidian life.

Then we can begin to distribute the sources of our faith to the poor—and not only our prayers but the monetary resources of our institutions. In this way, we will have a worship book that carries the possibility of a common life. What if we go be with the people who are hurting, to early pick-up lines for day jobs, and stand there with them? Or go with undocumented immigrants working on tomato plantations, or stay with homeless people on the streets to understand what it means to be homeless? Or listen to Black communities always under vicious attacks and learn how racism is deeply woven into the threads of our society? Or go and listen to Native Americans and see and hear the ongoing violence against their lands and lives? From these places we can sit down to hear and cry together and learn prayers and songs that we can bring back to our communities.

Professor Daniels gave to my class the trajectory we must follow, an exceedingly difficult one. What should our liturgies do? He answered, "Expose, subvert, and transcend." And I add:

Liturgies will expose our racism and injustices and hatred and class struggles.

Liturgies will subvert economic disparities and will restore our prayers for equal distribution of wealth, within the church and in the world.

Liturgies will transcend the limitations of our situations, fomenting and creating places, contexts, relations, and power dynamics that will show the real work of the people with God and the commonality of our lives. In this way, we will learn that liturgies, as well as theologies, should always be a *second step*, to be done after being with people.

An Example: Pentecost 2020: Let it Burn![15]

One example of how to orient the liturgical calendar and our common resources is to read from a particular place, paying attention to the surroundings and the commitments our faith must make along the way. I wrote these words after the death of George Floyd and the fires burning around the country. The idea is to show how thinking of a liturgical time from the perspective of the margins, from perhaps another form of reasoning, can foster other forms of prayers, liturgical actions, preaching, and sacramental

---

15. I write this in the living memory of George Floyd and João Pedro and all the Black people across the world who are killed daily by white supremacy, simply for being Black. ¡PRESENTE!

emphasis. I wish to show a way we might orient our faith from real situations. From a local place, we say a prayer to the world.

George Floyd, a forty-six-year-old Black man, was mercilessly killed by the police in Minneapolis. João Pedro, a fourteen-year-old Black boy, was playing with his cousins at his house in Rio de Janeiro when the police shot his house seventy times and killed him.

The streets and buildings of Minneapolis and other cities are burning. Like previous burnings in Baltimore, the burnings are signs of power, resistance, and a deep awareness of Black people and what it means to live in a country dominated by a white elite ever since the invasion of the Americas by the white culture that permeates every inch of this country. Only Black mothers and fathers know the fears of not having their children back home at the end of the day. This white culture is spread through every street of the US and within the whole democratic system, including forms of legislation. It invades every single institution, from local political groups to local churches, gerrymandering, and voter regulations, from lack of workers' rights to wage disparity, from political party systems and legislative representatives to the Supreme Court and the White House. Everything is infused with forms of living, thinking, and organizing that come from white values and their forms of living, perceiving, and feeling. This structure trickles down in every form of local power dynamics, school districts, poisoned waters, state austerity budgets, male domination, military might, jail and prison systems, school access, and police forms of domination.

All of the historical processes that built this country have served only to fuel a fire that was already running underneath the social threads of this country and that is and will always be ready to explode. There is no way that this country, ruled by predatory capitalism, will not have its buildings burned and its fortunes and ways of ruling put at risk. It is part of the game. White supremacy and fascism are foundational parts of capitalism, and as long as we have capitalism as the system of organizing life together, there will be no way to dismantle racism, white supremacy, and fascism, or not to have buildings burned.

Since crisis is built into the capitalist system, crisis will always be necessary. The crisis of the neoliberal capitalist system tends to be economic, with the crashing of the market once in a while for more domination and stealing, but also by using natural disasters. Water spilling into New Orleans' Lower Ninth Ward gave way to the economic advantages of vultures sucking the blood of the poor. Along with a growing number of deaths caused by

COVID-19, especially of the poor, we see that the world's richest billionaires have continued to enrich themselves.[16]

Our hopes have been crushed. We all feel the closing in of public spaces, the shortening of resources, the destruction of the earth. The increasing pauperization of the world will grow exponentially, and crisis will continue—we just don't know to what point or extent. The earth is giving us ample signs that we are killing ourselves and there will be nothing left for us if we do not change. The burning of Minneapolis is also telling us that if we do not change, something else will happen that will be worse than we imagine.

The death of George Floyd in Minneapolis set the Black community on fire in a country where people go on with their lives pretending that everything is all right and this is the greatest country in the world. George Floyd's death shows us that this country is a nightmare for many of its own people.

The fires on the streets are signs of life from Black people putting themselves into re-existence, the loud "language of the unheard," as Martin Luther King Jr. put it. As I see it all, I join them with my heart and soul. I will never condemn them for doing what they are doing, for they are trying to survive in this country. I would rather condemn the politicians (be they Republicans or Democrats), the market, the banks, and financial corporations for what they do. They should be persecuted for what they have historically done to Black folks and Indigenous people and brown and yellow people with the stealing of the land, erecting of walls, and building of private jails and concentration camps. I will never condemn Black folks for their strength and bold courage for saying no, for saying "No more!" Theirs is the kingdom of God! They are my people! In fact, they are breathing the breath of God into us, the fire of the Holy Spirit. Pentecost! From the lives of Black people! A gift from God! The whole Gospel for Pentecost Day is in a speech by Martin Luther King:

> I think America must see that riots do not develop out of thin air. Certain conditions continue to exist in our society which must be condemned as vigorously as we condemn riots. But in the final analysis, a riot is the language of the unheard. And what is it that America has failed to hear? It has failed to hear that the plight of the Negro poor has worsened over the last few years. It has failed to hear that the promises of freedom and justice have not been met. And it has failed to hear that large segments of white society are more concerned about tranquility and the

---

16. Ponciano, "World's 25 Richest Billionaires."

status quo than about justice, equality, and humanity. And so in a real sense our nation's summers of riots are caused by our nation's winters of delay. And as long as America postpones justice, we stand in the position of having these recurrences of violence and riots over and over again. Social justice and progress are the absolute guarantors of riot prevention.[17]

In Acts 2:2–3, we read, "And suddenly from heaven there came a sound like the rush of a violent wind, and it filled the entire house where they were sitting. Divided tongues, as of fire, appeared among them, and a tongue rested on each of them" (NRSV).

Pentecost can be understood through three lenses in this year of 2020:

Fire

"... for indeed our God is a consuming fire."

—Hebrews 12:29

Fire! We need fire! Fire that will burn buildings, systems, oligarchies, "democratic" systems, pretensions of common life and fake mutual care. Fire that will burn religions, scholarships, spiritualities, forms of knowledge and financial exchange that contribute to the collective death of us all. Fire!

Our God is a consuming fire!

Consuming fire that puts down any human project made of injustice and the appearance of fairness.

Consuming fire whose uncontrollable choreography will dance around our protections and pretenses, order and decencies.

Consuming fire consuming every private property so we can finally understand that nothing is private but belongs to all. Then burning the privacy of excused treaties, secret changes in political offices taking away resources from the poor time and again and giving them to the rich.

Consuming fire that burns private ownership of anything.

Consuming fire burning false spiritualities of Christians who think that holding worship on Sundays will be enough to hold onto the name of Jesus.

Consuming fire burning every liturgy or sermon that does not say the name of George Floyd with a loud voice, churning stomach, and trembling heart.

Consuming fire to any rationalization of the protests that does not take a clear side with Black people.

17. King, "The Other America."

Consuming fire that compels our work around public gestures of change to local policies, police force, and demands that legislators change, listening to the voices of those abandoned.

Consuming fire to the nuanced and blunt entitlement of white folks, be they liberal, very liberal, conservative, or of any other political ideology.

Consuming fire to any church who does not start an anti-racist workshop and teach its folks about the history of African Americans in the US, Black theologies, Womanist theologies, and Black religions.

Consuming fire to any confession of sins that does not pause at the death of George Floyd. Consuming fire to any blessing that is not preceded by "woe to" those who are keeping racism in place.

May the fires of Baltimore, Minneapolis, and other places spread across the world so our that faith can be enflamed by the presence of a burning Spirit who is unruly and will not accept anything less than a life fully committed to all of the abandoned, enslaved, oppressed, jailed, poor people in this country and elsewhere.

Fire everywhere! So we can rebuild from ashes. Ashes not only from our Ash Wednesday evocation of ashes, but ashes that come from the fire of the Holy Spirit who burns works of injustice and white supremacy.

Ashes

The ashes of Minneapolis's burned buildings are clear signs that this time, our time, is over. Time cannot wait anymore. Nothing else is working. It did not matter that Black people used their music, art, knees, and protests, screaming "Black Lives Matter!" Nothing could change the minds, souls, and structures of a country living off the oppression of Black people. Ashes! Time is up! Time is over!

Ashes will tell us that a new time has arrived, a time that is uncountable and uncontrollable and cannot be narrated anymore, since time will be counted by the nobodies of the world. *They* are the agents of this new time. The nobodies of this country are saying to all, we are nobody for you, but in our communities we are somebody, and it is this somebodiness that will destroy the pretense of nobodiness that you threw us into. We are more! Look at your streets: the ashes of your buildings are the signatures of the nobodies! We are the nobodies whose names you cannot speak in your clubs, houses, churches because silence is what you have chosen. Now take a look here and see our names, nobodies!

We are the fire that turned your world into ashes so we can perhaps start in a different time with new narratives, new legislations, a new life together, mutual respect, and new forms of distribution of wealth. Your safety is not as safe as you thought. All of us, not only Black people but also all of the blackened people in this country, all who were made nobodies, we are back to terrorize your kindness and your niceness. We are coming and will be coming back again.

Remember the fears you have lived with your whole life but tried to deny time and again so it would not be embarrassing? The fears deep inside that used to flare up when we got close to you? You thought that controlling the fear would keep you safe, didn't you? I know you didn't want to live this way. But you didn't do much to change, right? So the nobodies—they are the very measure of life you thought never existed. We came back with a vengeance. We came back as the nightmares you have decided not to pay attention to. We are the ashes of your world.

Ashes upon ashes, the debris of a world that didn't work when organized just for a few, even though you thought it was for all. As we are taught, let the injustice be without making too much of a fuss, and things will find their way to oblivion and cultural structures of normalcy. Ah, you thought we were defeated, but you should never underestimate the power of those who have survived centuries and are still standing. We have seen wars of all kinds and we have survived. We are still standing. From Brazil, a country that also knows Black oppression, philosopher Vladimir Safatle writes:

> It is true, we lost several times, but we were never defeated. For our defeats are, in fact, the high fire that forges the steel of our victories. Every true victory is the result of a profound loss. It reverberates with the animal desire to never lose again. Therefore, only those who fell and patiently wait for a second chance will win. It will come sooner than we expect. That's what leads us to affirm that such losses are not defeats at all.[18]

We will multiply, we will resurrect! Our ancestors will come back for us and they are telling us that the time is over. Our memories, our songs, our ways of being will sustain us. We will use everything we can and want.

We have prayed over the ashes of our sons and daughters for too long. Now you will know what it means to face our strength. Not for revenge, for we have no business in revenge. But simply because of the law of circularity. We harvest what we plant. Roughness is the new harvest and our love will not be easy. In hope, the Spirit of ashes will resurrect all of those who enter into this new time, a time of the Spirit, a time unknown, a time for deep changes, a time to lose individually and gain collectively, a time not merely to change our prayers, but to change the world.

18. Safatle, *Quando as ruas queimam*, 12. My translation..

Breath/Spirit

This change can only happen if the breath of the Spirit is breathing our lives together. This breath is fundamental to our living. The coincidence of COVID-19 and the extinguishing of George Floyd's breath is stunning. In the pandemic, we have been attacked in the most precious thing we have: our breath. We have put our knee on the necks of animals, destroying their own spaces, we have invaded their habitats and used them for our own sake. Now we are living with the result of the overuse, abuse, and dominion of the earth. Capitalist white society has put its knee on the necks of Black and blackened people (Indigenous, brown, yellow, poor), stealing their resources, uprooting them from their lands, and then abusing them, displacing them through redlining, gerrymandering, throwing them into the corners of our cities and giving them the opportunity to come back to work for whites in the same cities.

In the US and in Brazil, there has been a genocide of Black people and Indigenous people. The structures of racism are murdering Black people everywhere. The lack of care for the most vulnerable during the onslaught of COVID-19 is taking its toll within the Indigenous, Latinx, and Black communities. Everywhere, people literally cannot breathe. Frantz Fanon has seen the difficulty of breathing in many cultures; he sees this not in one group but in an expansive "we" who cannot breathe. In *Black Skin, White Masks*, he writes, "When we revolt it's not for a particular culture. We revolt simply because, for a variety of reasons, we can no longer breathe."[19]

George Floyd couldn't breathe, Black people can't breathe, Indigenous people can't breathe, the brown people at the borders can't breathe, the earth can't breathe, a whole population of humans and species and plants and forests can't breathe either. If anything, this Pentecost has to remind us of our collective breathing: breathing life together into new worlds and other ways of living. For we either breathe together or no one will breathe at all.

The breathing of the Spirit is the breathing of life. This Pentecost, we are challenged to see the fire in the world and give thanks for it. We are challenged to see the ashes of a world that did not work. And we are challenged to see the possibility of breathing new life-giving breaths together. May the memory of George Floyd and João Pedro bring about new worlds for us to breathe together.

---

19. Fanon, *Black Skin, White Masks*, loc. 305, Kindle.

6

Praying with Black People for Darker Faith

Almost always, the creative, dedicated minority has made the world better.

—Martin Luther King Jr.[1]

Break any of these rules sooner than say anything outright barbarous.

—George Orwell[2]

The thief comes only to steal and kill and destroy.
I came that they may have life, and have it abundantly.

—Jesus in John 10:10

For more than five hundred years, Indigenous people have had their lands stolen, their culture appropriated, their people marginalized, exploited, jailed, killed.

For almost four hundred years, Black people have had their origins uprooted, their culture appropriated, their people kidnapped, pushed to the margins of society, exploited, jailed, killed.

For more than 180 years, the original Mexican people have had their lands stolen, and with other Latinx people in this country, they have had their culture appropriated and their people abused, pushed to the margins of society, exploited, jailed, killed.

---

1. King, "A Knock at Midnight."
2. Orwell, "Politics and the English Language."

For all of this country's history, the stranger and the non-white have been demoted, defaced, abused, ripped apart, thrown away, yet used as a resource for the building of the nation.

This chapter continues the work of the previous chapter, with examples of prayers to begin developing a language that can dismantle the silence of racism in Christian churches. With this chapter I have tried to follow what theologian Willie James Jennings writes in *The Christian Imagination: Theology and the Origins of Race*: "I yearn for a vision of Christian intellectual identity that is compelling and attractive, embodying not simply the cunning of reason but the power of love that gestures toward joining, toward the desire to hear, to know, and to embrace."[3]

I have also tried to follow womanist ethicist Emilie Townes's call for justice and peace and the words of Howard Thurman, whose work she values as I do. Townes writes, "Our world needs a new (or perhaps ancient) vision molded by justice and peace rather than winning and losing if we are to unhinge the cultural production of evil. Doing so is to respond to the call by the Black mystic and theologian Howard Thurman who joined others in encouraging us to blend head and heart."[4]

Since the invasion of the Americas, there has been a project of whitening the continent. This project has been made possible by the de-negrating (denigrating), blackening, turning "negro," of everybody who was not white.[5] The blackening of people was a way for the dominant, conquering cultures to organize non-whites into a lower caste of humankind by marking bodily features, composing sources of religion, forming culture, and defining how someone can be called human. Notions of white normalcy, control, and order, shaped through the images and concepts of light and darkness, were at the heart of this process.[6] The creation of race was necessary for the creation of whiteness as an uncontested form of superiority and power control.

Thus, the reality of life and also the appearance of that reality forged racist ideas that grounded the very foundation of this nation. The founders built a society with legislative and democratic views that would not be able to distinguish whiteness from moral virtues and Blackness from deviation, malfunction, and dubious origins. In other words, this historical racial process—really a process of *racializing*—has been organized by white reasoning,

---

3. Jennings, *Christian Imagination*, 8.
4. Townes, *Womanist Ethics and Cultural Production of Evil*, 164.
5. See my discussion of "denigrating" and "blackening" in chapter 5.
6. See Allen, *Invention of the White Race*, and Heng, "Invention of Race in the Middle Ages."

that is, the whitening of sources, forms of thinking, living, praying, worshiping, believing, and understanding of how to be human.

This whitening of the Americas has been accompanied by the stealing of the riches of this land. Europe and the US Empire still live off of the riches stolen from Africa, the Americas, and blackened people—and by blackened people I mean the denigrating process of make non-whites become colored.[7] Since the beginning of colonization, and for all these centuries, power has been in the hands of white individuals and families while blackened people have had to face all forces of death and struggle to survive. It has been the inner work of resistance and resilience, strategies and wisdom, strength, and faith of all the blackened people of this land that have brought them and all of their wisdom and sources this far, alive.

During all these years, Christianity has been a part of this creation of racial ideas. It has been part and parcel of the whitening of the American continent. The contours and content of the Christian faith have been built on white sources. Theology has mainly been a white project. Worship has been a white project built over the bodies of people of color to teach people to pray in white ways, whether ways of articulating the content of prayers or the ways of performing them. Historically, white churches have learned to discern faith and life in white terms—in other words, to sense with a bodily perception that is white, the whole world and God through white religious glasses.

During all these years, only a few people and groups have fought against the degrading and devaluing and disrespecting of Indigenous, Black, Latinx, and Asian people and all who fit the category of the stranger. All the strangers were thrown into the same exclusionary bus. Very few people prayed for people of color, with people of color, about people of color and their histories.

For more than five hundred years, this mighty project in the Americas also convinced we colored people that white people have always been the best thing that happened to this land. And to us! Civilization, progress, culture, manners, organization, order, sexual standards, were all proper forms of humanity wrapped in religious language. Civil religion was mixed with religious beliefs, conflating obedience to slave masters with obedience to God. Good and evil were established by the colors of religious ownership. The demonizing of forms of Black(ened) bodies was fundamental to the conquest of the Americas. In a play of values around what was to be considered human, what was worthy of honoring, and what was to be condemned,

---

7. See Galeano, *Open Veins of Latin America*.

there was a need for the demonic[8] actions of white slave owners that created racial-social-theological constructions to turn Black people (blackened bodies) into natural creations, social expressions, and cultural manifestations of the demonic. From there, the whole reasoning of the racial demonizing was set. Disobedience and lack of submission by blackened bodies was a sign of being occupied by the devil, and obedience, submission, proper (white) manners, lack of resistance, and acceptance of God's will were signs of being closest to the God and most obedient to the Bible. The formation of a white civilization came through the denial of the full humanity of blackened people, those who were not-white.

Colonization used liturgical sources such as prayer, hymns, orders of worship, liturgical moral and gestural codes wrapped up in white religious reasoning. However, even if Africans and other blackened people embraced Christianity, the Christian faith did not serve to give them their worth or full humanity. African American theologian and historian Gayraud S. Wilmore writes:

> The British rationalized the enslavement of both Africans and Indians because they were different in appearance to themselves and because they were heathens. When it became evident that Blacks were becoming believers despite widespread neglect by official church bodies, Virginia was the first of the colonies to make short shrift of the matter by declaring in 1667 that "the conferring of baptism doth not alter the condition of the person as to his bondage of freedom."[9]

The forms of colonization—its inward and outward brutality, its ugly and kinder forms of appearance, its angry faces and smiles, its passive-aggressive moral conducts—brought forth racist ideas that have shaped our societies, designated our common riches for only a few white people, and told us how and where we should live, how we should think—have molded our own feelings and established what is normal in our society. Five hundred years of heavy and violent colonial education and white European theology have deeply marked our universal and white religious understandings of God, our detachment from the earth, our perceptions of the sacred, our hymnody, our liturgical gestures, our orders of worship. Everything was covered by a divinely given understanding that kept the white faith dominating every heart, without even a need for explanation.

---

8. Throughout this chapter, the use of the word "demonic" has to do with breaking and ripping apart, with destruction and death. The intent here is not to demonize any person but to name the powers and forces of destruction as evil structures of death.

9. Wilmore, "Historical Perspective," 21.

The structural forms of dominance are marked in our historical documents. For example, the Declaration of Independence, the US sense of its own exceptionalism,[10] and the doctrine of Manifest Destiny created a necessary mass of critical symbolic and concrete materiality that established a forceful white ideology of conquering and expansion so as to secure its racist underpinnings. Grounded in an undeniable—but also idolatrous—faith, turning God into what was not God (that is, sanctifying civic actions into God's promises), this country was understood to be chosen to be great from its very beginning and apart from all others. The theological and civic privilege—the duty—to expand and conquer was given by God and protected by God. The moral superiority of those holding the power, be it political, economic, or religious has fed the formation of an Empire of demonic forces of destruction of people of color. At the heart of these events, there were rich white people thinking, believing, acting, leading, and using power—even against their own poor white folks, the "white trash." This white dominion was guarded by demonic power that had Indigenous, Blacks, and Latinxs either killed or enslaved so that the conquest could be established.

This conquering power created laws that fall under the sacred umbrella of "democracy." It allowed conquest to move on to the wastelands—land that was not under the control of white folks in some form of appropriation or progress—and to use blackened bodies in whatever way it was necessary to build the empire. In this way, the demonic, that which breaks and rips apart and steals, conducted the owning and privatizing of common natural resources and the free labor of Black people that were at the root of the savage system of capitalism that now rules this country.[11]

That demonic power is still at work today. The use of power to structure life and the very forms of thinking and being continues today with the ongoing killing and disenfranchising of Blacks, Indigenous people, Latinxs, immigrants, with the control of the economic market by the white private sector, and the necessary US engagement with endless wars across the globe in order to maintain the structure of the US economy and to protect, expand, and fulfill the call to continue being the American Empire.

Same Power Structure, New Forms of Disfigurement

The words of Jesus in the Gospel of John witness to us: "The thief comes only to steal and kill and destroy" (10:10 NRSV). The thieves that came more than five hundred years ago continue to lie, steal, destroy, and kill. Our politicians

10. See Douglas, *Stand Your Ground*.
11. Leiman, *Political Economy of Racism*.

lie, our economic structure destroys the poor, and the white reasoning of this country continues to kill our people daily.

Symptoms of this ongoing demonic structure have surfaced with the killings of Black people by the police across the US. The recent awareness of the deaths of Black people (Trayvon Martin, John Crawford III, Amadou Diallo, Manuel Loggins Jr., Ronald Madison, Kendra James, Sean Bell, Eric Garner, Michael Brown, Alton Sterling, Breonna Taylor, George Floyd, and so many others) has exposed patterns of policing that have existed since the era of slavery.[12] In the United States, young Black men were nine times more likely than other Americans to be killed by police officers in 2015.[13] These killings are fully associated with a demonic structure of living that was planned, organized, and enforced through a system that persists in whitening the country by disfiguring all that is not white. "The thief comes only to steal and kill and destroy."

The only reason we know about these recent killings is because of the power of phone cameras and social media used by common people on the streets who made videos go viral. The historical lack of information about police reports has now surfaced and police departments, often led by white people, had to start publicizing their reports.[14] Moreover, the erasure, denial, or approval of violence against Black people in the media (often owned by white people), the decisions by states to invest in prisons rather than schools, the ongoing cuts in social support for blackened communities often supported by white political representatives, the policies that replaced Jim Crow, continue to be the structures of death, even if that death is called democracy, an illusory system whose main task is to maintain the appearance of equality and justice.[15] Democratic systems, education, churches, economic systems, prison, police, and housing are all institutions of the same form of racism, supporting a white system of control of power and riches. Public policies are thieves, killing systems majorly sanctioned by demonic laws that continue this control locally and nationally. The thieves are in the highest places stealing from the poor and giving to the rich. For example, from 1934 to 1962 the US government backed 120 billion dollars worth of home loans that were given only to white people as a result of what came to be called "redlining," the systematic drawing of red lines around certain neighborhoods, not coincidentally inhabited by people of color, especially

---

12. In Brazil, a Black person is killed every twenty-three minutes. See, for example, http://www.bbc.com/portuguese/brasil-36461295.

13. Swaine et al., "Young Black Men Killed by US Police."

14. Lowery, *They Can't Kill Us All*.

15. Alexander, *The New Jim Crow*.

African Americans. Redlining created a ripple effect of white people with rising assets and Black people continuing to live in poverty, in the "ghetto," without investment by the state or the banks, and consequently a lack of good schools, job opportunities, and social expansion.

The thieves are everywhere. Along with public policies, the stereotyping of Black people as lazy, not wanting to work, and abusing federal resources lies deeply seated in white people's consciousness, spread as truth, and affecting the feelings and worldviews of both white and Black people, in very different ways. The psychological effect of five hundred years of colonization and the daily manifestations of racist ideas, gestures, relations, and power dynamics have had immense reverberations in the ways Black people live their lives.

The thieves are deeply invested in the institutions of this country. Politically, neither political party has ever fully served the racial-ethnic minorities—soon to be the majority—of this country. The best they have done is to mend parts of the system in order to keep the structure of exclusion running. The disease of racism plagues this country and has kept Black people as second-class citizens for our entire history, away from the wealth of the country and its social sources of sustenance.

The Same Power Structure in the White Christian Churches

The thieves have stolen Christianity. They have stolen the revolutionary kernel of the Christian faith, have destroyed its promises of equality and justice, and have killed the central idea of God's option for the poor. In a game of appearances and platitudes, the thieves and all their related demons have made a failed Christianity look as if it were alive through the performance of perfunctory religious rituals.

The system of white reasoning has caused white Christian churches to hide under a gospel of "unconditional love," an unmarked sense of love that in reality hides the markers of racism and the exclusion of people of color. The structures of white Christian churches and their theological and liturgical resources are often produced or constructed by white people for white people of a certain class.[16] This has immediate consequences for our prayers and how we pray. If prayer is the grammar of our faith and the white church has never created a deep religious language to engage with Black people, Indigenous

---

16. See my critique of the creation of liturgical sources in the Presbyterian Church (USA) in chapter 5 of this volume and an earlier, shorter version in Carvalhaes, "White Reasoning," 19–27.

people, Latinx, Asian-Pacific, or immigrant communities of any race or culture, then the content of the Christian faith has never had a grammar where prayers could be spoken as a means to enter into solidarity with non-white communities. The results are that faith continues to have a fully white vocabulary that offers scripts and scriptures of life in a specific format. When white churches deal with non-white people and their concerns, the response is often muted, for there is no vocabulary to help address them. I have seen white people who are willing to engage in solidarity with Black people, but they lack a vocabulary to do so, which prevents them from acting and from making mistakes, from saying something wrong.

The larger result in the public arena is that white churches end up supporting white Christians or white people in most political circumstances. In the 2016 presidential election, eight in ten white evangelical Protestants voted for Donald Trump, and the majority of white Roman Catholics and mainline Protestants also supported a candidate who has publicly shown his racist views. These numbers show not only the inadequacy to engage non-white people but a visceral rejection of "blackened" people, a rejection mixed with fear, anger, and resentment. In this vein, Donald Trump becomes the white man who "gets it," the one who will correct the wrongs of a government that has put blackened people ahead of white people with social assistance, against white people who are suffering and did not receive help from their government. The favorite candidate, his supporters believe, will get rid of the blackened people and bring the country back to a mythical and imaginary time when this country was great.

This is only possible because white churches have almost always had pastors and theologians who have never engaged blackened people, their ways of living, their sufferings, and their resources. The grammar of prayer has not moved us toward blackened people. I wonder how many prayer books contain prayers referring to Black people, prayers composed by Black people, that raise their concerns, their history, and their pain and openly speak against the violence of racism and white supremacy.

It is a demand and not an option for Christians to pray with Black people for the dismantling of the racist structures of liturgies. Prayers can shift our worldviews, our desires, call for change and offer seeds of change. Perhaps it is wishful thinking, but I do believe prayers can offer seeds of change. Prayers can shift our feelings, move our ideas, transform our behaviors, invent new ecclesiologies and concrete forms of mission, create new practices, and bring about forms of concrete love for people we never knew we could love or even had to love in a real way. Prayers inspire us and empower us to engage in ways of living that can help to restore humanity to blackened people. Providing a new grammar and vocabulary for our faith, prayer can shift the form of our thinking; it can open for a new kind of anthropology, one that is beyond our present concept of white superiority over people of color. Beyond that, as we see elsewhere in this book, prayer can also shift our view that humans are above animals and that we have the earth to exploit for our own desires.

Praying with Dr. Martin Luther King Jr.

Liturgically, the church cannot be silent either! It has to confess its ideological liturgical silences and universalized colonial supremacies, its uncomfortable feelings, its theological "forgetting," and its liturgical vocabulary of faith. In a word: its vicious sins. We must start a new vocabulary of prayer. I propose these prayers to start breaking the white vocabulary of Christian liturgies. What follows is an exercise of prayer along with some writings of Martin Luther King Jr. To do so, in this section I am using several sources. I quote from two of King's works: "A Tough Mind and a Tender Heart," the first sermon in King's book *Strength to Love*,[17] and the well-known "Letter from Birmingham Jail," written in 1963. (The first three quotations are from "A Tough Mind and a Tender Heart," and the remaining quotations that follow are from his "Letter.")[18] I also have in mind the work of artist Daniel Rarela, who "designed a series of memes to stop the late civil right leader from getting whitewashed."[19]

From "A Tough Mind and a Tender Heart"

> Let us consider the need for a tough mind, characterized by incisive thinking, realistic appraisal, and decisive judgment. The tough mind is sharp and penetrating, breaking through the crust of legends and myths and sifting the true from the false. . . . This prevalent tendency toward softmindedness is found in man's unbelievable gullibility. . . . This undue gullibility is also seen in the tendency of many readers to accept

---

17. King, *Strength to Love*.

18. Because of this litany's length, worship leaders may wish to use it in sections in different parts of the worship service. I am highlighting passages of my own choosing, but also following the highlights chosen by artists who have illustrated those excerpts to highlight the power of King's work.

19. My hope is that the reader will read the whole letter several times and view the images on the website: "Artist creates 'Letter from a Birmingham Jail' memes to stop people from whitewashing ML." https://www.mic.com/articles/165598/artist-createsletters-from-birmingham-jail-memes-to-stop-people-from-whitewashing-mlk.

the printed word of the press as final truth. Few people realize that even our authentic channels of information—the press, the platform, and in many instances the pulpit—do not give us objective and unbiased truth. Few people have the toughness of mind to judge critically and to discern the true from the false, the fact from the fiction. Our minds are constantly being invaded by legions of half-truths, prejudices, and false facts. One of the great needs of mankind is to be lifted above the morass of false propaganda. . . . Softminded persons have revised the Beatitudes to read, "Blessed are the pure in ignorance: for they shall see God." . . . There is little hope for us until we become toughminded enough to break loose from the shackles of prejudice, half-truths, and downright ignorance.

Prayer

God of our thinking,

give us a tough mind to be with Black folks all the way.

Help us think with them and not against them.

Help us understand their historical pain.

Help us know the difference between them and the people who call them thugs.

For our weary times are filled with half-truths.

We know people are paid to misrepresent the truth

so that we cannot find a way to oppose and resist.

We continue to be confused,

so we pray for wisdom!

Wisdom to know the sources of news.

Wisdom to choose the better forms of knowledge.

For we know where there is wisdom, there is happiness. There is justice.

Help us see the difference between truths and half-truths,

structural violence and localized violence,

and deliver us from ignorance and fear.

God of wisdom,

more than anything we need wisdom

and the desire to learn

to read

to engage

to listen to those who suffer.

So we can have our minds changed, our hearts moved.

So we can be transformed.

In Christ the truth, we pray.

Amen!

From "A Tough Mind and a Tender Heart"

But we must not stop with the cultivation of a tough mind. The gospel also demands a tender heart. Toughmindedness without tenderheartedness is cold and detached, leaving one's life in a perpetual winter devoid of the warmth of spring and the gentle heat of summer. What is more tragic than to see a person who has risen to the disciplined heights of toughmindedness but has at the same time sunk to the passionless depths of hardheartedness?

Prayer

God who sees us all,

we pray for these two gifts:

a tough mind and a tender heart.

May we gain a tough mind

to face those who live near us who are filled with hatred

and see Black lives matter as a threat.

May we gain a tender heart

so we can trust that goodness and love

will trump racism.

Teach us to be disciplined

and relentless in the struggle for racial justice.

May we discern that only when our Black friends are safe and have a full life.

Our minds and hearts can finally rest in you.

Again we pray: give us tough minds and tender hearts

so we can live with Black folks in justice and equality

like a bird that needs two wings to fly.

In your mercy!

From "A Tough Mind and a Tender Heart"

I am thankful that we worship a God who is both toughminded and tenderhearted. If God were only toughminded, he would be a cold, passionless despot sitting in some far-off heaven "contemplating all," as Tennyson puts it in "The Palace of Art." He would be Aristotle's "unmoved mover," self-knowing, but not other-loving. But if God were only tenderhearted, he would be too soft and sentimental to function when things go wrong and incapable of controlling what he has made.

Prayer

We all praise you God

because from your tough mind and tender heart

you have looked upon us equally.

But we have made your love look more favorably on some white people.

We who have everything

have not looked at those who don't have.

We even think that the have-nots are where they are

because it is their fault!

We have learned to contemplate you and you alone

without contemplating those who have been wronged by history.

We pray that in our worship together

you may help us to see how some have benefited

from a certain sense of your love while others have not.

Help us see how we have naturalized your love

just for those who are from the same class, race, sex and health.

Discipline us to see racial structures of love and hate everywhere.

To see that our society

is only made for some to live

while others are sentenced to prison and death.

Judge us and give us another chance.

We praise you for helping us deal with our fears

and helping us approach blackened brothers and sisters.

May your tough mind and soft heart

help us in our racism.

Help us find courage to hear what we need to hear

and engage with one another

and repent

help us to be transformed, become better people to one another.

We praise and worship you o God of all Blackness!

In your blackened name we pray!

From the "Letter"

> You deplore the demonstrations taking place.... But your statement fails to express a similar concern for the condition that brought about the demonstrations. I am sure that none of you would want to rest content with the superficial kind of social analysis that deals merely with the effects and does not grapple with the underlying causes.

Prayer:

We confess

that we are afraid of street demonstrations and protestors.

We confess that we are fearful.

We confess that we are angry

that they don't follow proper order and laws that we follow

in order to make changes.

We confess

it has to either be our way or no way

because we think we are the ones who understand

the more democratic ways to behave.

To behave properly.

We confess

that we feel we built this country and they came later.

We confess

they are destroying things that we consider sacred: the US flag, private properties, public symbols.

We confess

that we do not know how to handle it and feel safer when they are put to jail.

We confess

we cannot see the perspective of the marginalized

and are content to believe major news reporting.

We confess

that we tried to settle the case of Black people as quickly as possible,

turning our racism into personal issues,

blaming the Black folks for violence

without looking at the violence of our racialized systems of oppression.

We confess

that we blamed Black people for their violence against each other

without understanding that it is the lack of basic conditions of life

that creates violence and dysfunction.

We confess

we don't know the basics of the history of racism in this country and how this country was built on the backs of Indigenous, Black, brown and other marginalized people.

That is why we cannot understand "their" situation.

We have no clue how it is to be a Black person in this country.

In your mercy!

From the "Letter"

You may well ask, "Why direct action? Why sit-ins, marches and so forth? Isn't negotiation a better path?" You are quite right in calling for negotiation. Indeed, this is the very purpose of direct action. Nonviolent direct action seeks to foster such a tension that a community which has constantly refused to negotiate is forced to confront the issue.

Prayer

God of our abysses

We do indeed ask why we need direct action, sit-ins, marches, and civil disobedience.

We cannot understand why they can't talk, calmly, in the order that makes us comfortable.

Why can't they kindly ask for change? And wait for due process?

We think we have always wanted to negotiate

but now they invade public and private places and make demands.

Why oh my soul do I think that way?

What is it in me that I cannot grasp the fact

that their rights are bigger than my fears?

That their time is not my time?

That my fulfilled needs allow me to wait through longer transformation?

That my entitlement cannot keep me from processing

the immediacy of their complaints?

Give us darkness!

So we can see their light!

Give us light to understand the extent of our racism and the extent of white supremacy.

Help me God to rid my soul of the thinking

that only my life, family, and property are important.

With your help, I will understand that we have refused to wrestle with the difficult issues related to Black people.

With your help, we will be able to see

that Blacks or Indigenous or Latinxs or immigrants

are no less than your children.

In your mercy!

From the "Letter"

> We have not made a single gain in civil rights without determined . . . nonviolent pressure. Lamentably, it is an historical fact that privileged groups seldom give up their privileges

voluntarily. . . . We know through painful experience that freedom is never voluntarily given by the oppressor; it must be demanded by the oppressed.

Prayer

God who can change us,

help us go through conversion.

May your Spirit create in us a true change, conversion, metanoia.

For we cannot see we have so many privileges

and instead we have called it blessings

that you bestowed upon us!

We know that the place we have now was given to us by our fathers and fathers' fathers

who worked hard for it!

And we now work hard to keep it.

Why now do we have to give anything?

God of change

we cannot really see this.

We cannot change

but we pray

help us change

and see that power is not voluntarily shared.

Help us see that!

In your mercy!

From the "Letter"

Justice too long delayed is justice denied.

Prayer

O God,

why do we see this sense of justice only when it has to do with us and our needs?

Why do I believe in long democratic processes for justice when it is for others

and am so impatient when I need justice for myself?

Why don't I go out to the streets and demand justice for Black people right now?

Help us, O God, to join the fight!

May we learn the justices and injustices of our country!

May we go to the streets with Black Lives Matter!

May we listen to members of this movement

see what is needed to support them in love, care, and sustenance.

Help us go to the streets where communities of color, now my people,

are fighting for justice!

Help us O God!

From the "Letter"

When you have seen hate-filled policemen curse, kick and even kill your Black brothers and sisters; . . . when you have to concoct an answer for a five-year-old son who is asking: "Daddy, why do white people treat people of color so mean?" . . . Then you will understand why we find it difficult to wait.

Prayer

Merciful God,

when a child asks, we often listen.

But when our children ask about race or Black people,

we silence and deny racism exists in our household

in us and in our country.

Yes we have mistreated Black people,

yes we have enslaved them,

yes we have created laws to impede them from living full lives.

Help us, O God, to be honest with our children

even when they don't ask.

Help us to speak up and be honest

with you

with our children

and with the blackened people.

So we can be attuned to your own voice and your own love!

In your mercy!

From the "Letter"

One has a moral responsibility to disobey unjust laws. I would agree with St. Augustine that "an unjust law is no at all." . . . Any law that uplifts human personality is just. Any law that degrades human personality is unjust.

Prayer

God of truthful laws,

we are learning with our brothers and sisters that the law is not sacred,

that laws are a human creation and not sanctified by you.

Give us strength to fight the laws that privilege some people

and dismiss others.

Give us strength to fight the state when it creates laws that support the lives of a few people and put many others in jail.

Help us go after the local policies of our communities and see how racism is so fully present here.

Help us dismantle the unjust system of laws,

so we can create legislative equality for all.

In your mercy!

From the "Letter"

I have been gravely disappointed with the white moderate. . . . The Negro's great stumbling block in his stride toward freedom is not . . . the Ku Klux Klanner, but the white moderate, who is more devoted to "order" than to justice; who prefers a negative peace which is the absence of tension to a positive peace which is the presence of justice; who constantly says: "I agree with you in the goal you seek, but I cannot agree with your methods of direct action"; who paternalistically believes he can set the timetable for another man's freedom. . . . Shallow understanding from people of good will is more frustrating than absolute misunderstanding from people of ill will.

Prayer

We confess

that all we've attempted to be

is moderate

to uphold order

to find a common ground

to foster positive peace

so we wouldn't need to change anything, much less ourselves.

Help us to move away from that place,

where order and decency

is a facade for the protection of white people.

Give us courage

for we are weak and slow in making up our minds.

May we finally see that we are not free

unless our brothers and sisters are free.

Our churches have not necessarily associated themselves with the KKK,

but we have been silent, we have not spoken up.

So we pray you give us voices and words to speak,

to you, to each other, to our congregations, and to those in power.

Help us sit with and listen to those who are suffering.

Help us change O God, help us change!

In your mercy!

From the "Letter"

One who breaks an unjust law must do so openly, lovingly, and with a willingness to accept the penalty. I submit that an individual who breaks a law that conscience tells him is unjust, and who willingly accepts the penalty of imprisonment in order to arouse the conscience of the community over its injustice, is in reality expressing the highest respect for the law.

Prayer

God of love,

in your name we will go to the streets.

We will disobey the human laws that trap the poor so we can obey you!

From you, we have learned that when we are fighting for those suffering,

we discover where Jesus actually is.

Help us always commit to stand alongside the poor.

Help us see that your love is given to all,

but preferentially to the poor

and those who are at the margins of history,

at the margin of our communities.

In your mercy!

From the "Letter"

We who engage in nonviolent direct action are not the creators of tension. We merely bring to the surface the hidden tension that is already alive. . . . Injustice must be exposed, with all the tension its exposure creates, to the light of human conscience and the air of national opinion before it can be cured.

Prayer

God of solidarity,

we will join our Black brothers and sisters.

We will go where they are.

We will eat a common meal.

We will ask what it is to live the lives they live.

We will listen.

Our communities have people who are sick

Help us visit each other,

our communities have families who have beloved ones in jail.

Help us visit each other

and fight against homelessness,

the incarceration of blackened people.

Help us find places, organizations, and people so we can fight together!

May our community cry out loud: Black Lives Matter!

May our local church be chapters of justice, making a grassroots revolution.

In your mercy!

From the "Letter"

I should have realized that few members of the oppressor race can understand the deep groans and passionate yearnings of the oppressed race, and still fewer have the vision to see that injustice must be rooted out by strong, persistent and determined action.

Prayer

May we be those who can understand the deep groans and passionate yearnings of the oppressed race. May we see, hear, and sense the anxiety, fears and all the challenges of growing up as Black and colored people in this country!

May we engage in deep listening! Now and for the days to come!

In your mercy!

From the "Letter"

We will have to repent in this generation not merely for the hateful words and actions of the bad people but for the appalling silence of the good people. Human progress never rolls in on the wheels of inevitability; it comes through the tireless efforts of men willing to be co-workers with God, and without this hard work, time itself becomes an ally of the forces of social stagnation.

Prayer

We repent, O God,

for we have run this race without paying attention to those who run

with much more weight on their bodies.

Dealing with centuries of trauma, with a deeply colonized history, and destitute of land, of honor, of possibilities.

May we have our minds and our hearts transformed.

Help us see that we have also created and supported systems of injustices.

Help us create innovative structures of peace, redistribution of money, sharing of resources, health care for all, free college tuitions, and an egalitarian education system.

Remind us that we are each other's keepers.

May we fight all of the forces of social stagnation, including the ones inside of us! Now and forever!

We pray that by your grace and mercy, our world will grow darker

by the blessed presence of colored people!

May we see the gift of darkness

against the illusion of a self-made light

that only shines our own!

In your mercy!

Amen.

Conclusion

Professor Stephen Ray once reminded me of how the blackening was meant as evil and how, as with all things, God brought good out of it. So many of us found freedom in the Christian faith. Christ has become our liberator! Now we can have a church that is talking over its historical failures and moving toward justice and the true love of God by dismantling the work of the thieves. While Jesus says in the first part of John 10:10, "The thief comes only to steal and kill and destroy," in the second part Jesus says, "I came that they may have life, and have it abundantly." Together, whites and all blackened people, by the grace of God in Jesus Christ, will turn lies into truth, restitute what was stolen from oppressed people, bring life where there was death, and rebuild what was destroyed. Together, we will show this abundant life we live in Jesus by building and defending together the beloved community, which has people of all colors. "The beloved community," originally coined by US pragmatist philosopher Josiah Royce, is a term developed and popularized by Martin Luther King Jr. and Howard Thurman. King wanted to use this metaphor as a springboard, a symbol, and also a concrete arrival of our society, a place where love, peace, and justice could live together. Dr. King's hopes for this beloved community were grounded in non-violence, but also as a place with generative conflicts, where justice should be a constant struggle with the belief that through our common *agape* love we could make it happen.

We can also build, defend, and expand the beloved community through its liturgical structures, orders, and rituals of transformation. For liturgy is always a call to conversion! The "liturgy's danger," says liturgical theologian Nathan D. Mitchell, "is to resist or ignore its call to conversion."[20]

To pray with a blackened faith in a darker context begs us to consider the relationship between *lex orandi, lex credendi, lex vivendi,* and *lex agendi,* that is, the intertwining of the *rule of prayer,* the *rule of belief,* the *rule of life,* and the *rule of action.* This is because when we pray, all vulnerable life is at stake, especially Black lives. When we pray, our very breathing, our hunger, our limitations, our desires, our social systems, everything enters into a movement of circulation of feelings, energies and thinking. When we pray, our own breathing reminds us that we are made of the air, the sun, the soil, the birds, and all God's creation. When we utter words in prayer we are disclosing not only our hearts to God but also our biased heart is exposed, our racist upbringing becomes clear. When we give our offerings in prayer we are also showing the systems to which we are connected, where we live, what kind of health insurance we have, what culture we are part of, and what and with whom we have our deepest commitments. Thus, prayer is always prayed in some deep context, which includes the race and ecological systems in which we are immersed and help to sustain.

Thus, to pray is to weave together the liturgy of the church, the liturgy of the world, and the liturgy of the neighbor against forms of racism and exclusion. To pray is to make an option for the poor. To pray is to turn our hearts into a darker faith, because we are now unequivocally inhabited by all people of color. With faith, hope is also turned Black! Love is turned Black! For to pray is to enter the darker side of all those disfranchised, of all colored people, which surely included "darkened" whites, where the number of disposable people across the globe grow every day. Darker ethics and darker creeds, darker social actions and darker prayers, all shaping desires, giving contours to hurts, establishing ways of living, creating economic mechanisms of control, forming joys, elaborating concerns, relating us to

---

20. Mitchell, *Meeting Mystery,* 42.

the earth, defining pain, making us sing some songs, and throwing us into living in certain ways with our local communities and our plural world. All of these things together compose every prayer we pray.

Our ever-expanding Christian identity calls us into new and constant metanoias, changes our ways of thinking, shifts our views of the world, embodies individual and communal prayers of justice so we can create a praxis of solidarity and transformation with the poor and the earth. And we can only do that if we engage our prayers into breaking the potencies of racism. In order to do that, we must embody Christ as our full prayer.

7

Praying with the People of Axé

An Interreligious Dialogue[1]

THE CHRISTIAN FAITH CANNOT be understood without its many ways of praying. Prayer is the very grammar of our faith, the way in which we Christians hear, speak, and understand. As human beings, we cannot escape language, and as Christians we cannot escape prayer. Prayer gives shape to who and what we are. The philosopher Ludwig Wittgenstein wrote that "the limits of my language mean the limits of my world."[2] In the same way, the limits of our prayers are the limits of our faith. Faith is a complex and interconnected web of personal and collective struggles, hybridisms, behavior codes, voices, random gestures, historical developments, political battles, and the movements of the Spirit of God.

Christians stand between Babel and Pentecost, both in Christianity's biblical accounts and its contemporary engagements and enactments across the globe, building societies, and organizing differences between Christians and people of other faiths and wisdom paths. From these ancient and contemporary places we create and recreate our prayers and our identities. In this endless becoming, we are called to expand the traditions of prayers in the history of the church just as we are to expand the limits of our faith and our world.

Traditioning Our Prayers

Our prayers are a result of many people's traditions wrestling with the Christian faith in their own times and spaces. Tradition comes from the Latin

---

1. An earlier version of this essay was published in Carvalhaes, *Eucharist and Globalization*, 203–41. A version was also published as Carvalhaes, "Praying Each Other's Prayers."

2. Wittgenstein, *Tractatus Logico-Philosophicus*, 68.

traditio, "to hand on." (The Greek *paradosis* has the same meaning.) Having received our faith from our ancestors, we are now in charge of shaping it in accordance with our challenges and needs. Frederick Van Fleteren writes that "texts from the tradition can legitimately be used as an occasion for entirely new thought."[3] Thus, it is our task, from the location in which we are placed, to engage the sources of our traditions, honor these traditions as they offer possibilities for justice and mercy, and reshape these traditions according to a new perspective, one that entails both new and old thinking and that aims to engage in actions from a place of love. The purpose is not to make tradition what we want, but rather to bear witness to our people about how people of faith have responded to past challenges and to see the ways in which God's love helps us respond to the situations in which we now live.

The pattern of the church's prayer can help us as we connect Earth, life, ethics, and belief. We also need prayers that will orient us towards other religions. We need to learn their prayers and to offer our own prayers of supplication for those who are not Christians with blessings and healings. Our prayers for these people and communities would be also prayers of thanksgiving to God for their existence, their wisdom, and their ways of living. Our supplication for today should be for a world without violence, for lives to have a fundamental value regardless of any religious categorization or affiliation. At the same time, our prayer should be for the protection and restoration of ecosystems. Our prayers of supplication and thanksgiving must help us to realize that we are all the *imago Dei* (image of God), and that we are responsible for each other and for our daughters and sons. In our time, our prayers of supplication and thanksgiving must be prayers for the survival of every person, especially those persons who are poor. In this way, our prayers of supplication and thanksgiving offered every Sunday and every day must say, "Black lives matter! We offer supplications for them!" Our prayers must say, "We are killing the earth and we need to restore its sources and rhythms of life! We pray for this." Our prayers must say, "There are people exploiting and subjugating other people, oppressing and killing people of other faiths, and we need salvation for all!"

When we pray these prayers of supplication, we are generating the mutual learning and social sustenance of hope. This work of hope is also a way of engaging our Christian traditions. Orlando Espín, using "tradition" as a verb, writes about traditioning and hope:

> How can Christians tradition their hope without adulterating its subversive challenge? A hope that subverts all that humans regard as definitive has been one of the crucial forces driving the

---

3. Van Fleteren, "Interpretation, Assimilation, Appropriation," 270–85.

complex of traditioning processes that create and have sustained the religion we call Christianity.⁴

Against what Espín calls "Christianity's historical inclination to 'doctrinify' the subversive hope," he proposes that "Christian traditioning can (even as it liberates)—witness interculturally to the subversive hope that lies at the heart of Christianity."⁵

Our commitment is thus not to doctrines, but to our brothers and sisters in need, to the care of the earth, and to brothers and sisters of different faiths living in destitution and fear. Our prayers are a commitment to our neighborhoods, our villages and cities, and our communities. Our commitment is to create networks of hope, through prayer, belief, and ethical actions, combining the laws of *orandi*, *credendi*, and *vivendi*.

Our contexts beg for us to create ecumenical connections and relationships, moving away from the model of denominational self-sufficiency and distinctive cultural identities to a model of ecclesio-interconnectedness and intersectionality of identities. We must see other religions as distinct from ours, yet we can be involved with them on different levels. We cannot afford to live with only one worship book, one prayer book, and one hymnal. We are called to tradition our worship, prayers, songs, and lives in and through a vast array of identities and sources, so as to be empowered by the Spirit in a multiplicity of God's revelations. We are called to connect with our brothers and sisters from different faith and religious traditions, and this chapter seeks to engage the possibilities of that connection.

Expanding the Circles of Tradition: Interreligious Prayers

The Dalai Lama was once invited to Riverside Church in New York City for a conversation, and I was part of the group from Union Theological Seminary that created a ritual on the occasion of his talk. We had art and artists, symbols and music, but none of them was religious, perhaps because of the fear of superimposing Christian sources upon an already Christian worship space and thus being inhospitable to our Buddhist guest. On his way to the pulpit to speak, the Dalai Lama bowed down to the cross and made a sign of reverence. That was a powerful gesture with deep meaning.

On another occasion at Union Theological Seminary, Farid Esack, a Muslim scholar and liberation theologian, recited his Muslim prayers in St.

---

4. Espín, *Idol and Grace*, xv.
5. Espín, *Idol and Grace*.

James Chapel in Arabic, in the presence of people of different faiths and religious traditions. Were we only watching? Were we praying with him by praying through him?

We must ask again: Can we pray each other's prayers? Prayers are the containers of our innermost desires, the treasures of our communication with God, and the beliefs that we hold onto as the source of our identity as Christians. If we are to say somebody else's prayers, are we uttering somebody else's desires and speaking a new tongue? The potentially frightening and unsettling feeling in and among people praying somebody else's prayers is a reality, and the risks are high. Why don't we just leave those prayers alone, so that each tradition can say their own prayers for themselves? This connection, one fears, could cause more harm than healing.

Nonetheless, a possible "yes" filled with challenges is also laden with apparent impossibilities. In some ways, it might seem impossible to pray the prayers of others, and it might not even be the right thing to do. The main problem for this conversation can be summed up in one word: appropriation. We must be aware of the interconnection of power, history, and colonization, and the continuing appropriation and misappropriations of colonized people's theologies, celebrations, and traditions. We must be aware that when we are borrowing prayers, or even making somebody else's prayers our own, we might be continuing this practice of colonial appropriation. So the dangers of my proposal may be insurmountable, and the perils ever present.

Thus, at the onset of our trajectory of praying together, we must announce in a loud prayer voice (in symbolic and other concrete ways) that when we stand before somebody else from a different religion, we are marked by our inherent inability to access this other religion. Not only are we likely unfamiliar with the core of a particular religion, but we also do not have the particular practice or life of another religion, steeped in its blessings, gifts, and demands. The irreducibility of somebody else's religion, the unavoidable appropriation of my sister's and brother's prayers and meaning, are always at stake. We must be aware of all of the colonial traces inside of us that want to repeat the trauma, as well as the control, of the colonizing conscious and unconscious process. To avoid this danger, we should search for social gatherings and rituals that will help us pray each other's prayers in each other's presence. Appropriation is the use of somebody else's prayers and stories without the presence of the other, without care for the other, without commitment to the life of somebody else, without engagement in each other's lives. What I am exploring here is the possibility of *living together through our prayers*.

We must begin by considering that when religious people utter a prayer, they have in mind some sense of their deity, their gods, and they are often loyal to this God and to this God alone. To pray somebody else's prayer could mean offering ourselves to a different god, being entangled in other religious practices devoted to that other God, and this offer and practice could signify betrayal for some religious people. It could also lead some to a diminishment or lack of strong faith and even to a commitment to a God and a community not their own. That is because the logic of prayer is often marked by an exclusionary commitment to one's own God. Thus, in order to pray each other's prayers, we must assume that there is indeed some sense of disruption, or to use a better word, an expansion of our commitments. Therefore we must ask: can we keep our oath to Jesus Christ if we pray to Buddha, or Allah, or an *Orixa*?[6] Is the other totally other? Are there possible intersection points between our language about and gestures towards the divine?

In my Christian upbringing, I was taught to consider people of other religions as the targets of my evangelism. They were all going to hell without knowing it, and I was chosen by God to save them. They were also an obstacle to the conquering Christianity in which I believed, a Christianity that caused me to live in a jumble of compassion, fear, and anger. The binary they-versus-us provided me with poles that shaped my thinking. It was much later that I learned that people of other religions could also be my brothers and sisters, and that their way of worshipping God and their God were to be respected. I even learned that I needed to engage in dialogue with them. However, it was only within the last decade that I realized that this dialogue entailed a much deeper commitment on my part. In order to engage in dialogue, I had to go a step further and venture into a conversation that demanded not only respect and acceptance, but also presence and a willingness to turn what was foreign to me into something familiar. But how could I do that?

Timothy Wright's book *No Peace without Prayer: Encouraging Muslims and Christians to Pray Together; a Benedictine Approach* can help us here.[7] Wright starts from a Benedictine understanding of spirituality and

---

6. Reginaldo Prandi writes of the *Orixas*, "For traditional Yoruba and Yoruba followers in the Americas, Orixás are gods who received from Olodumare or Olorum, also called Olofim in Cuba, the Supreme Being, the task of creating and governing the world, each one of them responsible for specific aspects of nature and certain dimensions of life in society as well as the understating of the human condition. In Africa, most Orixas are circumscribed to a certain city or region, while a few receive worship mostly throughout the entire extension of the Yoruba lands. Many Orixás are forgotten, others appear in new cults." Prandi, *Mitologia dos Orixás*, 20. My translation.

7. Wright, *No Peace without Prayer*.

engages a Muslim spiritual perspective in order to find common ground between the two. A deep connection emerges out of this dialogue because the author is not afraid to learn about the Muslim tradition while also exploring a deeper understanding of his own tradition. In this double commitment, Wright brings forth common issues such as healing, remembering God, living in the presence of God, spiritually experiencing God, understanding God's revelation and human responses to it, and finding ways that communities can experience and support each other through a dialogue on spirituality. One simple way in which he engages these two religions is through daily prayers. In this model he offers, Christians and Muslims pray several times during the day, and each prayer has specific requirements to be remembered for the saying of each prayer.

Pairing the daily prayers of Christians and Muslims shows that these two forms of faithful practice can be done in such a way that each religion can enlighten, empower, and enrich the other. After describing the practice, Wright notes, "This advice offered here from the Christian and Muslim viewpoints is helpful: it starts to build bridges before any dialogue can start. . . . At one level, it is the commitment of faith by the participants that will take the dialogue forward."[8]

The key aspect of any interreligious conversation is open engagement with the specificities of each faith. Fear is a monster that keeps us disconnected from each other. We are bombarded daily with news that portrays people who do not look like us as frightening and as potential destroyers not only of our faith, but of ourselves and our world. Thus, in order to engage with someone else's faith, we need to have a more mature personal faith, trusting that God's love is bigger than our differences with our neighbors. For Christians, this involves trust that we are so loved by God that we can engage in any interreligious dialogue. Also, because this love of God demands that we love our neighbor, we lose the fear of approaching, getting closer, and offering ourselves in love and care. This unwavering love and this precious grace received are the ground from which we can go out into the world and work and hope for the restoration of the earth and the empowerment of our neighbors. Love is what sets us free, giving us freedom to see and acknowledge similarities and differences between our faith and that of others.

Any good interreligious dialogue must start with the full affirmation of one's faith. From there, we must find space between us for a(n) un/common ground, a moveable place where we might kneel or dance, praying together.

---

8. Wright, *No Peace without Prayer*, 312.

From this place, we can either pray our own prayers with somebody else, or, if we are able to venture a little further, we might be taught how to pray someone else's prayers. As I try to pray somebody else's prayer, my challenge has to do more with my own trust in my God in this process than the fear that somebody else's prayer will do something to me, my relationships, and my commitments. In the economy of my community's faith, would God still relate to me if I prayed to a God who does not have the name of the one to whom I usually pray? The *ecos/oikos*/household of God in the Christian faith contains a *nomos*, a law, that embraces everything. Nothing and nobody is outside of the love—the house—and the *nomos* of God. In this loving house, we have to strive for peace and mutual dignity and recognize that in this space, the name of our utmost desire will be blessed and anointed.

In this house, my supplications that once were for the salvation of other religious people now include myself. We need each other, and our common prayers of supplication are a sustaining part of this "inescapable network of mutuality," as Martin Luther King Jr. wrote.[9] Mutual salvation, collective redemption, common solidarity, one world house for all? Perhaps! We can indeed look at our Christian faith for help in creating the conditions that would allow this sharing of prayers to happen.

My Experience with Candomblé and the Christian-African Religious Dialogue

In order to wear this garment of mutuality, in order to tradition the hope of the Christian faith, I want to pray with Afro-Brazilians. By doing that, I believe that I, along with others, will be able to honor, love, and restore a word of justice to the Black people of my country. Candomblé is a religion that came with Africans to Brazil and continued to be practiced by them throughout the era of slavery and colonialism. As an oral religion, it was able to survive and continue its practices, even though it has changed and become an indigenous Brazilian religion.

The history of Brazil cannot be told without remembering the history of slavery and the white manufacturing of the racism so rampant in that country's society today. That history is embedded in the daily lives of people in myriad ways. For instance, I grew up thinking that every African religion—surely made up by Black people—was a creation of the devil, and that every one of its practices was infested by demons. I was taught to evangelize its practitioners and cast away their demons. Along with my white Christian religious education from the United States, there was a racist underpinning

---

9. Wright, *No Peace without Prayer*, xvi.

that gave support to my hatred and deepest fear (of what or of whom?). This same hatred and fear has been institutionalized in exclusionary ways within Brazilian society, and the new Pentecostal churches' mission goals include the destruction of a certain number of African American houses of worship.

It was in the city of Salvador, in Bahia, the Brazilian state with the country's largest Black population, that I discovered that this hatred and fear lives in my body, a realization by which I have been forever transformed. While I was there, I acted as the interpreter for Professor Emilie Townes's class from Union Theological Seminary. During our visit, we were supposed to engage with and meet practitioners of Afro-Brazilian religions, and in one of these visits we were scheduled to go to a Candomblé worship service. There, the *mãe de santo* (the mother of the saint), who is the pastor and leader of the religious community, was supposed to throw beads and bring the voices of the *Orixas* to each student, and I was in charge of translating what the *Orixas* wanted to tell the person. However, as we were getting into the van, my body froze, and I could not move. For a couple of minutes, I had no control over my body. A friend who was with us, a Brazilian Methodist pastor who was also a member of Candomblé, told me that I was going to be all right. Slowly, my body went back to normal, and I was able to get into the van and go to the place of worship. Wondering why my body froze unexpectedly, I realized that while my mind had made the journey from wanting to save this group to desiring to learn with and from them, my body was still dominated by a narrative of fear. My body had learned for so many years that I should fear these people, that they were possessed by demons, and that I could die in their presence, that it was telling me, "I am not going to expose us to this danger!" This experience changed my life, my scholarship, and my way of thinking about interreligious dialogue.

From that day on, I have been challenged to think about interreligious dialogue from the perspective of religious rituals and of presence in practices, and not just from a sociological, theological, or even scriptural viewpoint. It is exceedingly difficult to engage varying religious practices, for the spaces in which they occur can be dangerous due to their religious codes and specificities. For example, in some Candomblé festivities, if I wear anything Black, I can disrupt the movement of the *Orixas*.

For me to engage in this internal and external dialogue is to recover what I have destroyed and to engage in a national movement of recovering the Brazilian soul, honoring African Brazilians, and protecting not only the *Axé* people—the people who belong to the Afro-Brazilian religions—but also the imperiled lives of Afro-Brazilians in general, who make up more than half of the Brazilian population. The elimination of Black people in Brazil continues. Black boys are being killed every day throughout Brazil, just because they are Black in a deeply racist country. Thus to engage in an interreligious dialogue has a more expansive way of being in solidarity with Black people.

From a more theoretical perspective, the Chilean-Peruvian theologian Diego Irarrázaval offers Christians four main points of dialogue between Christian and Afro-Brazilian religions:

1. to celebrate and to think with an understanding that the celebratory ways of African religions are ways of thinking, of constructing the lives of their members, and of re-creating the world;

2. to identify ourselves and our continent as African-American, calling ourselves Africans so as to help us embrace the life, history, and depth of African religion as common to us all;

3. to celebrate the mystery of the African way, which is the celebration of the sacred in our bodies, and to realize that the body is a privileged place for the revelation of the sacred; and

4. to wrestle with syncretism and belongings.[10]

Given Brazil's history of slavery and its pervasive racism, can we provide a space of reconciliation and hospitality through common prayers? We might think about that by reflecting on a certain common pneumatology.

It Is the Spirit That Makes Us Pray: Holy Spirit/*Axé*

Every beginning depends upon the Spirit, both for Candomblé and for many Christians. It is the Holy Spirit that initiates God's love in us and prepares and empowers us to live this love in the world. Communal acts of praise and work dedicated to God are always a response to God's love, generosity, and demands. For Candomblé, the *Orixas* and other entities move the world's energies and make us respond to their calls and demands.

Thus, the very reason for worship in both the Christian and Candomblé faiths is the movement and call of the Spirit/*Axé* in people's lives. Prayer is an act of praise and gratitude. Because people of both religions depend on the work of the *Axé*/Holy Spirit, it is to God that they go with petitions.

In both religions, there is common food and common good for the people, in Eucharist and in food offering, and under the power of the Holy Spirit and *Axé*, people gather as strangers and become a family. The presence of the Holy Spirit offers forgiveness, healing, and reconciliation through common worship, meal, and bath, even if they are continuously interrupted by

---

10. Irarrázaval, "Salvação Indígena y Afro-Americana," 69.

fear, hatred, anxiety, injustice, death, and the perils and conflicts of the world. For Candomblé, the presence of *Axé* also balances the level of bad and good energies in the local communities through offerings and dances.

Since God is the one who manifests Godself where God wants, and makes a covenant with whomever God wants, we are the ones, inspired by the Holy Spirit, who can create channels for God's grace to be experienced in ways that we may not yet have been able to experience. Thus, we are trying to find ways in which the covenant of God can be expanded and in which we can offer hospitality to people of other faiths. We can become channels of God's incarnation.

For practitioners of Candomblé, the communal living out of the faith involves channels of blessings and healings to the community. The dances and offerings are forms of sacrament where the *Orixas* organize the world of the living, protecting those who are searching to balance their energy and making others pay for the unbalance of the energies brought about by their actions.

In worship, Christians have their Bibles, sing their songs, and pray their prayers, praying "Come, Spirit, Come." However, in this dangerous prayer the coming of the Spirit might do something we do not want or like, and the Spirit can arrive as the coming of a stranger, a guest, one whom we were not expecting or even desiring. Once we pray "Come, Spirit, Come," the movement of the Spirit can no longer be controlled. After our prayer, we might have to welcome members of the Candomblé faithful dressed in their white dresses, dancing and singing, asking for the *Orixas* to come and move energies through the primal energy, *Axé*.[11] Once the Holy Spirit takes over, we must follow.

The Holy Spirit and the *Axé* are the moving forces that establish, shift, and balance the world and all of our respective universes. The Holy Spirit and *Axé* can transform whatever they want and are the very source of life. Christians and Yoruba are totally dependent on the movements of Spirit and *Axé*, and they are the sources we tap into so that we can engage each other around the table and be able to expand our religious horizons.

The engagement with *Axé* and the Holy Spirit can become a vital theological response to the globalized world we live in. The increasing sense of dislocation marked by the growing flow of people around the globe, the hybridity of immigration, the accumulation of capital in the hands of fewer

---

11. "Axé is the primal force, life principle, sacred force of the Orixás . . . it is power, it is charisma, it is the root that comes from the ancestors; we can gain and lose Axé, Axé is a gift from the gods . . . it is above all, the very house of the Candomblé, the temple, the roça (place where you plant for and with your family) the whole tradition." Prandi, *Os Candomblés de São Paulo*, 103–4. My translation.

than five hundred people around the world, the trafficking of people, brutality against women, the shifting of labor markets, and the growing diversity of local neighborhoods are just some of the signs demanding that our theologies and communities deal with the constant flow of identities and "mobile personalities"[12] that characterize our era. The force, potency, and agency of the Holy Spirit/*Axé* can help us engage these challenges and dismantle deadly world realities. The Holy Spirit/*Axé* can also help us find plural identities, not in the de-ritualizing of our own religious rituals, but rather, in the renewing processes of the ritualization of our beliefs (the expansion of our rituals) as we encounter others along the way.

The Spirit of God shows itself through movements of unfolding openness and alterity, movements marked by dis/placements of generosities. The Spirit of God must be seen in my responsibility to myself, but always in relation to *some-body-else*, even if this some-body-else throws me into an abyss of inescapable inner and outer challenges. The presence of some-body-else at the table of Jesus Christ connects me to unexpected obligations toward this other and to that person's people, a people that I might not have paid attention to until that moment. Thus, the movement of the Spirit in us can be a call to us to pay attention to some-body-else.

From this place of unexpected openness given by the Spirit, Christians can find common ground to welcome practitioners of Candomblé. Common elements for a theology of the Spirit in Christianity and Candomblé include: (1) the Holy Spirit/*Axé* has a deep connection with the body, and without our bodies there is no community. In both religions, the Spirit/*Orixas* can possess bodies. (2) The Holy Spirit and *Axé* and the *Orixas* help us not only to deal with our daily life, our struggles, and our wounds, but also give us strength, wisdom, and vision to go through life. (3) The Holy Spirit/*Axé* always engages with a guest or visitor. (4) The Holy Spirit/*Axé* is deeply connected with creation. (5) It is the Holy Spirit/*Axé* who creates and sustains the gathered communities. And (6) the presence of the Spirit/*Axé* is manifested in both worship and work.

Candomblé and Christian believers pray to the Holy Spirit and to *Orixas* for guidance and wisdom in their daily lives. Both groups of believers bless the Spirit and endeavor to walk in their daily life in ways pleasing to the Holy Spirit/*Orixas*. Both religions have a deep commitment to the transformation of society through their beliefs and practices. For both religions, God is always doing something through us. Or, to use J. Edgar Bruns's words, "God is the doing of something"[13] in our religions.

---

12. See Betcher, "Take My Yoga upon You," 58.
13. Cited by Betcher, "Take My Yoga upon You," 72.

It is in, under, through, and around the Spirit/*Orixas* in our diverse bodies and rituals that we can recreate our daily and common life within and among ourselves. In both religions, God/the *Orixas* are doing something in and through us, and we are also doing something in and through our worship, recreating the world, recreating life. As Jaci Maraschin says, "It is in the body that we are spirit especially when our bodies are ready to recreate life. Let us, then, make of our bodies our main instrument of worship."[14] Open to the unknown movements of the Spirit and *Axé*, we move along together.

In order to pray with people of *Axé*, Christians first need to walk towards adherents of Candomblé, combat the racism that formed most of Brazil, and undo the demonization of the *Axé* people. This movement is what Derrida calls *un certain pas*, a certain step (or "a particular step," "a given step") moving from one place to another. The movement forward entails working within a given context. In general, in Brazil, depending on the specificities of each local context, this work would entail:

1. Christians starting to pray for *Axé* people in their own worship services: Christians praying not for the salvation of the people of *Axé* but for the continuation of their long history of gifts and blessings to Brazil. Everything starts in the body, praying as a way to cast away from our bodies the prejudices, bigotry, fear, and racism that live in our bodies. To pray with and for Yoruba people is to undo centuries of hatred and fear in our bodies. Our bodies, along with our minds and hearts, have to learn to pray in a very different way.

2. Christians encircling places of *Axé* worship to protect those inside from other Christians who see them as the devil.

3. Christians visiting the worship places of people of *Axé*, learning how practitioners of Candomblé pray and dance and what their offerings mean. Being with them, staying with them when possible, learning to see the power, beauty, and glory of the Yoruba people, *Orixas* and *Olorun*.

4. Christians inviting *Axé* people into their worship spaces to share prayers and common celebrations.

5. Christians and *Axé* getting together for a meal and to share stories.

6. Christians and *Axé* teaching each other daily prayers for comfort and protection, blessings for the house, a new job, a birth, an illness, and other life events.

14. Maraschin, "The Transient Body."

By loving the *Axé* people, Christians will learn that love can cast away fear. By loving and creating bridges of connections, dismantling our racism, decolonizing our faith, disrupting our theologies, and undoing our fears, we might be able to pray together. Or, by praying together, we might be better equipped to love, and thus, to dismantle our racism, disrupt our theologies, and undo our fears. This interreligious dialogue is not for the sake of the dialogue itself. Rather, it must be done for the sake of life together!

Conclusion: Worship Comes After

If we are to think, form, and practice a ministry that can create possibilities for people to pray the prayers of others and to live interreligiously through rituals, we must know that rituals and liturgies never stand alone. Often, rituals are a secondary event in the life of a community. People gather because of friendship, because of a particular issue, because they need to find small forms of social organization. A community gathers because of a need for a place to be, to relate, to search for meaning, to help, and to be protected. In the same way, it is our mutual responsibility to each other that brings us together. After that come our rituals and worship, our shared prayers and singing.

In order to pray together, we need to dance and eat together and get to know each other's lives and faith. We must enter into a common interreligious mystagogical place where we teach and learn together how and what and where to pray. By expanding our religious education, and decolonizing our faith, we will be able to shift the places of trust, and thus the place of God, away from structures of power that set us apart to places of mutual confidence in local structures. This can be accomplished through the resources we have received and with those we already have in our communities.

Prayer is about getting to know who we are and what our common situation is so that we can offer supplications for each other. What Paulo Freire writes about education—"Things to know, how to know, what to know, for what and whom to know and therefore against whom and what to know"[15]—can also be said about prayer: "Things to pray, how to pray, what to pray, for what and whom to pray and therefore against whom and what to pray." This is our mission as people of faith.

Releasing our fear, we might begin to see that there are not only points of connection between these two religions, but also significantly different views of the world and gifts of life. Perhaps the Christian catechumenal process could include the stories and the dances and songs of those

---

15. Freire, *Cartas à Guiné-Bissau*, loc. 271, Apple Books.

who practice Candomblé. Perhaps adherents of Candomblé could learn some of the Christian prayers.

Everything starts with the praxis of the people, its challenges, and its needs. We start with life and friendships. From there, people engage cultural and faith traditions, other important sources, and then move, or step, beyond themselves towards each other. The place to meet is in the middle, where nobody owns anything and where our prayers can then become a common place of sharing and learning. We are called to cross borders and limits. There must be "a certain step" beyond ourselves towards somebody else. This step beyond ourselves is a Christian demand, a step that embodies our faith, a movement towards the world and its people.

What Jacques Derrida calls "the step beyond and not beyond"[16] is both a step toward somebody and a step of the other toward me. Both are movements toward my life to which I must respond. Alterity is all around us when we pray. My prayers of supplication can be this very step "beyond and not beyond," a movement that invites my neighbor and exposes me to a situation where I am prohibited from shutting down, from living in my own bubble. My prayers are a way to care for the world and all that is in it. Shall we pray?

---

16. Derrida defines this step: "The crossing of borders always announces itself according to the movement of a certain step [Fr. *un certain pas*]" (*Aporias*, 11). This step entails a step beyond and not beyond. John Caputo explains it: "The step not beyond is the necessity and impossibility of approaching the other; it means to approach the inappropriable, to approach without appropriation" (*Prayers and Tears of Jacques Derrida*, 84). See also Derrida, *Psyche*, and Derrida, *Parages*.

8

Praying with the Earth

A reLent Practice—Praying with a Plant

—Virginia Cover[1] and Cláudio Carvalhaes

> Believe me, you will find more lessons in the woods than in books. Trees and stones will teach you what you cannot learn from masters.
>
> —Bernard of Clairvaux[2]

IN THIS CHAPTER WE will begin to relate to the earth with small gestures: reading, praying, talking to plants. These gestures create a language that hopes to help us shift the ways we relate to the earth. How so? The hope is that we will begin to relate more closely to the earth and move from a certain distance, a utilitarian relation, or even a sense of human dominion over nature, to a relationship that is based on care, responsibility, and reciprocity. From small gestures at home, we hope to move to a place where the earth and its ecosystems and biodiversity, along with the whole human, animal, and vegetal worlds, can coexist in a relation of mutual attention, provision, and equal participation.

The earth, Gaia, Pachamama, is our home and without this home we all die. Alas, our earthly condition right now is disastrous. The earth is dying before our eyes and we are dying with it too. We must awaken and start to think about the planet, countries, cities, and back yards from the perspective of the earth: we need to respond to the earth's pain caused by

---

1. Rev. Virginia Cover is Senior Pastor at Grace Lutheran Church in Camp Hill, Pennsylvania.

2. Bernard of Clairvaux, Letter 106, 2, quoted in Churton, *Early English Church*, 333.

the over-use of nature for our own desires and the consequent degradation of human life due to the climate calamity. To pray with the earth is to pay close attention to God's creation and to its suffering. We must *learn how to be with the earth* in a more conscious, compassionate, and fair way. We must listen to the earth, talk to plants, and relate to them as living creatures who need care just as we humans do.

How can we turn away from exacerbating the growing climate calamity? The earth is working to expel us due to our abusive ways of exploiting every form of life. If we Christians are called to be deacons in service to God's creation, we must change our ways of living and praying. Here are a few moves with which we can begin.

First, we must learn that we cannot escape the web of interrelated beings, that we are all interconnected and interdependent in complex, reciprocal ways. We are responsible for the well-being of humans, non-humans, the animal, vegetal, and mineral world.

Second, we need to acknowledge that we are NOT masters of nature, that we have no dominion over it, that we do not rule the earth.[3]

Third, we must begin to think about the ways in which our local communities are being affected by climate calamity. While we must keep in mind what is happening around the world and fight for the whole earth, we must push our federal and state governments to create laws that protect the earth. In our villages and towns and cities, we must care for the soil and rivers and ecosystems around us: to attend to local farmers, the poisoning of grass, the death of birds, the destruction of wildlife, and lack of care for parks. We must study what provokes such calamities. We must pay attention to what we eat. We are believers in and followers of the incarnation of God in Jesus Christ. Jesus's incarnation demands attention to our own bioregions, to the voices of ancestors in this land, to the history of the place we live and how we are collectively responsible for the many forms of life on Earth.

Fourth, we must relate to what other religions besides our own say about the earth and how we must relate to the earth. Indigenous knowledges will also transform our ways of thinking and relating to the earth. Professor Robin Kimmerer, in particular, shows this through her work.[4]

Fifth, the work of the Holy Spirit, coming upon Jesus like a dove, can also come to us, perhaps, through the plants near us. In the same way the body of God comes to us through the grain of wheat and the blood of Jesus in the pressed grapes. How can the whole earth be lifted up in these ways by

---

3. Listen to Bob Dylan's song about our relation to the earth, "License to Kill." See https://www.youtube.com/watch?v=4zP9OUNuUk4.

4. See Kimmerer, *Braiding Sweetgrass*, and Kimmerer, *Gathering Moss*. Also see her many videos on YouTube.

the Holy Spirit? God in flesh, seeds, leaves, trunks, feather, fish skin, rock, wood, air, water, matter.

In order to illustrate and embody some of these shifts in perspective and action, Pastor Virginia Cover has created the following devotional guide, which is to be used during Lent and puts a focus on plants. This resource can also be adapted to other seasons of the church year.

ReLent: A Devotional Guide

This devotional uses Cláudio Carvalhaes's written work and the lectures of Robin Kimmerer, Distinguished Teaching Professor and founding Director of the Center for Native Peoples and the Environment at the SUNY College of Environmental Science and Forestry in Syracuse, New York. Virginia Cover, Pastor of Grace Lutheran Church in Camp Hill, Pennsylvania, has put together biblical verses and stories as a pastoral resource for the people of her congregation. This resource can be used during Lent by any congregation or individual. You can adapt or expand it according to your own visions and local needs.

A Word about This Devotional

Like many devotional booklets, this one engages the reader in spiritual practice and discipline. Like many Lenten devotionals, this one engages the appointed worship readings throughout the season of Lent. Quite possibly unlike other devotional guides for Lent, this one asks you to engage in a spiritual and physical practice you might never have engaged in before. That is a part of its design. While you may feel uncomfortable with this new practice, we encourage you to continue on throughout each day's discipline, in the hopes that your comfort level and understanding will increase on your Lenten journey to Easter.

Setting up Your Devotional Space

This devotional is designed with the reader(s) and a live plant together. At Grace Lutheran Church's Lent Event, every household is given a bulb, planted that day, in the hopes it will grow and bloom around Easter. Whether you received a bulb at this event or not, consider positioning your devotional area with a live plant. (If your bulb fails to sprout, use another live plant in place of it at that point in the weeks of Lent.)

Set up your devotional area based on the growing needs of your plant or bulb. Consider a window where the sun can warm the plant and you can see out into the world beyond yourself. Pick a comfortable chair to place in your space, if possible. Perhaps you like to have a candle near when praying, so add that as well. Another ancient practice of prayer involves mindfully gazing into an icon, a visual picture or "window" into God's activity in the world. Consider how your plant and the actual window could function in the same way for this devotional.

Often we use devotionals to read or pray in our hearts (silently). While that is a wonderful practice, this devotional asks you to broaden your discipline to include praying, reading, or speaking out loud. This is the case whether there is another human around to hear you or not. This may be a practice that takes you away from your comfort zone, or at first makes you feel "silly," but we encourage you to stay with it and see how it changes you over the journey of these forty days.

Sunday, the First Sunday in Lent

> By the sweat of your face you shall eat bread, until you return to the ground, for out of it you were taken; for you are dust, and to dust you shall return.
>
> —Genesis 3:1[5]

Many of us have a disconnected relationship with nature and we relate to nature as "outside things," as "it," as "commodities" or "resources" for our use. Is that the only purpose of nature? When God created the heavens and the earth, the plants and animals, trees, and oceans, they were created out of the same ground we were. We are dirt kin, family members held together by the blood of the earth, by the dust to which we will one day return. Over this Lenten journey, we will embark on reconnecting with our long-forgotten earthly brothers and sisters. You will be asked to talk with your plant, with rocks and soil, and to listen to them. It may be very uncomfortable at first, but do not let that discourage you. After all, there was a time when we conversed with these things on a daily basis, ages ago; the Scriptures have captured Eve having a full conversation with a snake! Imagine! There are peoples even now who practice this as a way of life—and they have something to teach us about ourselves that we, to our detriment, have forgotten.

---

5. All Scripture epigraphs/quotes in this devotional are taken from the New Revised Standard Version (NRSV).

> *Prayer (pray out loud)*
>
> Holy God, we give you thanks that you breathe life into all living things, though we are but dust. Sustain and renew us, as you sustain and renew the earth, and watch over us all, plants, waters, animals, forests, as we grow. Amen.

Monday

> See, I am doing a new thing! Now it springs up; do you not perceive it?
>
> —ISAIAH 43:19

Every Monday this devotional will lift up the practice of *attentiveness*: of noticing something you did not notice before. Let us begin with looking out your window: what do you see outside that is full of life? Take a moment to jot that list down, and keep it nearby. We will pick it up later.

> *Prayer (pray out loud)*
>
> Creating God, you have made all living things, and take delight in them. You call everything good. Teach us how to do the same. Amen.

Tuesday

> Then the Lord God formed humankind from the dust of the ground, and breathed into their nostrils the breath of life . . . and out of the ground the Lord God made to grow every tree that is pleasant to the sight and good for food . . . and out of the ground the Lord God formed every animal of the field and every bird of the air.
>
> —GENESIS 2:7, 9, 19

As creatures ourselves, in and of the earth, we are inextricably bound together in a web of life, as organisms deeply entangled in ecological community. Consider that you and your plant are a community—which at its root means you "hold things in common." We share the air we breathe, the ground from whence we came, the One who gave us life. We share a death, a returning to the ground, and a resurrection. Without coral reefs, we cannot breathe. Without seeds, we cannot eat. Without rocks stable under our feet, we collapse. Without trees, we cannot have water. Without the miraculous balance of the interconnectedness of life, we cannot survive. This is how it was made from the beginning; this is how it still is now. We worship the God who made all things, and gave us the gift of community within creation.

Prayer (pray out loud)

God of all the earth, you have given us each other to journey with—not only people, but also trees, fish, animals, oceans, and even this plant. This plant is present with me on this Lenten journey. Show me how to be present with this plant on its journey too. Amen.

Wednesday

> Let the heavens rejoice, let the earth be glad; let the sea resound, and all that is in it. Let the fields be jubilant, and everything in them; let all the trees of the forest sing for joy.
>
> —PSALM 96:11

I knew a pastor who would practice his sermons by walking in the woods. He would preach to the trees. Someone once asked him, "Why don't you practice your sermons by speaking to someone who can listen to them?" He replied, "But they are listening." Trees are the oldest citizens of the world. We can only stand in life because they stand for us, purifying the air and cleansing the waters that we drink. The Scriptures are full of trees, from beginning to end—the word of God is the "tree of life" from Genesis to Revelation. The Psalms have the most interesting lines of all about trees. They call for the trees to give God praise, as if they have on other occasions. Perhaps they have, and we just didn't notice.

Prayer (pray out loud)

Gracious God, may we be like tall trees planted by streams of water, who give their fruit in due season, praising you each day. Amen.

Thursday

> Jesus said, "I am the vine; you are the branches."
>
> —JOHN 15:5

One of our greatest gifts is technology. You can be connected to a person on the other side of the world in seconds; you can see national and international events unfold in real time. My cousin, a Naval doctor, was stationed in Afghanistan as part of his rotation. He is an orthopedic surgeon by training; he was stationed with two other doctors to serve a large and medically diverse population of service personnel, who came in to his operating room with injuries that were beyond his orthopedic specialty. Technology enabled him to talk with a brain surgeon halfway around the world, and in real time, he could video conference the surgery procedure, saving lives. Technology is also a great curse, because it separates us from our natural family members, our dirt kin. We have fallen into the trap of relating to things and not people, our phones rather than our children, our screens rather than the fields and parks right outside our doors. Our food, our water, are technologically brought to us, such that we do not even think about their sources, or how we depend on their earthiness so that we, who are of the earth, can survive. In an ironic twist, we call this "advancement."

> *Prayer (pray out loud)*
>
> We bless you, great God, for the gifts of ingenuity and invention that connect us to so many things. May we never lose sight of what we are truly connected to—the good creation, each other, and you. Amen.

Friday

> When the Lamb opened the seventh seal, there was silence in heaven for about half an hour.
>
> —REVELATION 8:1

The church in Lent has often marked off Fridays as a way to observe, in a small way, the realities of Good Friday—the death of Christ. Catholics refrain from eating meat as a way of fasting. Others fast the whole day, breaking the fast at dawn. Silence is often kept in some form, as a way of remembering that even the sun would not give its light and those who witnessed the crucifixion stood by at a distance, silent. Sit in silence with your plant for a period of time. Begin with five minutes. Set a timer because this will feel long to you at first. Let your mind and heart be attentive to how it is growing—what might be happening under the surface, that is active but not yet seen?

Prayer (pray out loud)

Holy God, you are active in ways we cannot always see. You bring life from what appears to be dead. We give you thanks for life in Christ Jesus. Amen.

Saturday

> And should I not be concerned about Nineveh, that great city, in which there are more than a hundred and twenty thousand persons who do not know their right hand from their left, and also many animals?
>
> —JONAH 4:11

Do dogs go to heaven? Many of us wonder about this question after burying a beloved pet, a near-son or near-daughter in many households. The fact that we wonder about this question, consider it as a possibility that God through Jesus Christ has redeemed the life of even an animal, should tell us something. We long to be connected to every living thing, not only while we have the breath of life, but even when we return to the ground. And yet, we do not live as if this were the deepest truth about ourselves. We treat animals as if they exist only for our consumption, or our entertainment, or our pleasure. What if we relented of this mindset, and turned instead to see animals as co-occupants of this world God so loves?

Prayer (pray out loud)

God, thank you for the gift of animals. Show me how to live with them and learn from them as you intended. Amen.

Sunday, the Second Sunday in Lent

> Praise the Lord from the earth, you great sea creatures and all ocean depths, lightning and hail, snow and clouds, stormy winds . . . you mountains and all hills, fruit trees and all cedars, wild animals and all cattle, small creatures and flying birds.
>
> —Psalm 148:7

Robin Kimmerer, a respected forester, botanist, and member of the Potawatomi Nation, joins science's ability to "polish the art of seeing" with her personal, civilizational lineage of "listening" to plant life—heeding the languages of the natural world. Her bringing together of two worlds opens a new way for us to reimagine a natural reciprocity with the world around us as "a generative and creative way to be a human in the world."

She writes about how humans have forgotten that all living things are our kin. She says we need to relate to plants differently. They are living creatures that deserve to be treated with honor; they are not here only to please us or give us something. They are not only for sale, a commodity or a resource. She suggests calling them a "he" or "she" instead of an "it."

Today, give your plant a name. Decide if you will refer to your plant as a he or a she.

Prayer (pray out loud)

> Gracious God, thank you for the gift of all living things. Thank you for the gift of _____ (your plant's name). Move your Spirit in both of our lives, renewing us each day. Amen.

Monday

> A shoot shall come out from the stump of Jesse, and a branch shall grow out of his roots.
>
> —Isaiah 11:1

We have returned to another Monday, and it is time to practice our discipline of attentiveness once again. Look closely at your plant. Do you notice a sprout, or any other sign of new growth? Do you think your plant needs anything at this point in the journey? More or different light? Water? Something else?

Prayer (pray out loud)

Thank you, God, for my plant _____ (name). Help me to care for him/her in the best way possible, as you care for every living thing on Earth. Amen.

Tuesday

> Let each of you look not to your own interests, but to the interests of others. Let the same mind be in you that was in Christ Jesus, who, though he was in the form of God, did not regard equality with God as something to be exploited, but emptied himself.
>
> —PHILIPPIANS 2:4

Professor Kimmerer calls attention to the "economy of gifts" that exists in nature. Nature offers us gifts, and we are responsible for the gifts we receive. They are not to be used for profit or to be exploited; they are not ours to take exclusively and as often as we desire, demanding more and more. With the gifts from the earth, we share, we give away, we honor the giver and embrace our responsibility for the earth's richness and beauty. We return the gifts by respecting, protecting, and caring for the earth just as God cares for us. This is a posture of gratitude, a humbling of ourselves, so that we can bend low and see the life at our feet and all around us.

Prayer (pray out loud)

Gracious God, I thank you for _____ (your plant's name). Keep us both in your loving care on our journeys. Amen.

Wednesday

> It is God who sits above the circle of the earth, and its inhabitants are like grasshoppers; who stretches out the heavens like a curtain, and spreads them like a tent to live in.
>
> —ISAIAH 40:22

This beautiful earth seems like it will be hanging around within this universe forever. Within this earth, we humans live as if we can live and invent life all on our own. Our problem is that we have lived in our world as if the earth were the backdrop of our world, serving this world, making it possible for our world to exist. Many of us humans have lived as if the earth were just a support system for our world. We have seen the earth as a natural resource for our desires, animals as creatures ordained to our appetite or amusement, mountains for our buildings, oceans for our food, the soil for our movement around the world. However, this disconnected way of living cannot be supported anymore. We are coming to a time where the earth is going from the backdrop of our adventure to taking over the central stage of our world. We are coming to a time when the earth will continue but our world will disappear. So we might have an earth without a world.

Prayer (pray out loud)

Gracious God, I thank you for _____ (your plant's name). Keep us both in your loving care on our journeys. Amen.

Thursday

> Jesus said to them, "Take care! Be on your guard against all kinds of greed; for one's life does not consist in the abundance of possessions."
>
> —LUKE 12:15

A word for our times is "extractivism": everything you can think of has been or is being extracted—fossil fuels, minerals, trees, diverse biomes, waters, ocean species, mammals, and more. Everything in creation has been turned into profit. Landscapes are good if they can be used for profit, for development, for tourism (which means development). Animals are good inasmuch as they can give us something. And yet our way of being in the world, our constant need for development and growth cannot be sustained by the earth. We see this in an unimaginable rate of species extinction, glacier melting, and an unprecedented phenomenon of forced migration. We need a new way of thinking and being in this world, one not derived from endless development and a search for profits, but one derived from our kinship with the earth—from solidarity with every living thing.

Prayer (pray out loud)

Gracious God, I thank you for _____ (your plant's name). Keep us both in your loving care on our journeys. Amen.

Friday

Be still, and know that I am God!

—Psalm 46:10

Sit in silence with your plant for a period of time. Set a timer and mark five minutes. Let your mind and heart be attentive to how your plant is growing—are there things you can see above the surface, at this point?

Prayer (pray out loud)

Holy God, you are with us, even in the silence. You are with us even in death. We give you thanks for Christ Jesus our Lord. Amen.

Saturday

I know all the birds of the air, and all that moves in the field is mine.

—Psalm 50:11

I know many of our homebound church members who cannot move easily about their home or apartment; they do not have the ability to come and go as they please any longer, having given up the privilege of driving or lost the ability altogether. They spend much of their day in the same chair, or at least the same room. Many of these same folks find a sense of purpose and life in bird-watching. They secure food or housing for the birds through their family members who come to visit. When I sit with them, they tell me stories about them—what they like to do, with whom they interact, what their best features are. And when one of them is missing, they worry and wonder when they will return. For this pastor, the similarities to the stories they tell me of their own children and grandchildren are striking.

Prayer (pray out loud)

> Gracious God, I thank you for _____ (your plant's name).
> Keep us both in your loving care on our journeys. Amen.

Sunday, the Third Sunday in Lent

> A gentle tongue is a tree of life, but perverseness in it breaks the spirit.
>
> —PROVERBS 15:4

Using Professor Kimmerer's view of the natural life around us, from this point on, you are encouraged to speak to your plant, using his or her name. As she says in a recent interview, "We don't call anything we love and want to protect and would work to protect 'it.' That language distances us." Today, an introduction is where we begin. Here is a sample of what you might say:

> "Hello _____ (your plant's name). My name is _____, and today I am trying something very new and different. I thought I would introduce myself to you. I feel a bit odd talking to you, but I want to relate to you differently and see you as a fellow member of the creation of God. **Let us pray together:**
>
> God of all life, I give you thanks for _____ (your plant's name). I thank you for giving him/her life. Help me to see _____ in a new way, as part of your good creation. Amen."

Monday

> Blessed are the pure in heart, for they shall see God.
>
> —MATTHEW 5:8

Today we return again to the spiritual and physical practice of attentiveness. Look closely at your plant. Is it getting enough light? Does it need to be turned slightly to aid the light warming it? Is it moving toward the light on its own?

Do you think your plant needs anything at this point in the journey? Water? Something else?

Close with this prayer, and pray it out loud next to your plant:

God of all life, you have given _____ to me, and me to _____. Thank you. Amen.

Tuesday

> Praise God, sun and moon; praise him, all you shining stars! Praise him, you highest heavens, and you waters above the heavens! Let them praise the name of the Lord, for he commanded and they were created.
>
> —Psalm 148:3

Many saints and forebears in the church spoke of the earth differently than we do; they claimed a deep connection with creation, and they wrote and taught its way as life-giving. St. Francis of Assisi is the saint most fondly remembered for his love of animals (his feast day is when churches often hold a "Blessing of the Animals"). He wrote a beautiful canticle—a sung prayer celebrating a world fully interconnected:

> Most High, all-powerful, all-good Lord, all praise is Yours, all glory, all honor, and all blessings. To you alone, Most High, do they belong, and no mortal lips are worthy to pronounce Your Name.
>
> Praised be You, my Lord, with all Your creatures, especially Sir Brother Sun, Who is the day through whom You give us light. And he is beautiful and radiant with great splendor, of You Most High, he bears the likeness.
>
> Praised be You, my Lord, through Sister Moon and the stars; in the heavens you have made them bright, precious, and fair.
>
> Praised be You, my Lord, through Brother Wind and Air, and fair and stormy, all weather's moods, by which You cherish all that You have made.
>
> Praised be You, my Lord, through Sister Water, so useful, humble, precious and pure.
>
> Praised be You, my Lord, through Brother Fire, through whom You light the night. And he is beautiful and playful and robust and strong.
>
> Praised be You, my Lord, through our Sister, Mother Earth, who sustains and governs us, producing varied fruits with colored flowers and herbs. Praised be You, my Lord, through those who grant pardon for love of You and bear sickness and trial.

Blessed are those who endure in peace; by You, Most High, they will be crowned.

Praised be You, my Lord, through Sister Death, from whom no one living can escape. Woe to those who die in mortal sin! Blessed are they She finds doing Your Will. No second death can do them harm. Praise and bless my Lord and give Him thanks, and serve Him with great humility.[6]

Speak to your plant again, and tell your plant something about your day. Use the paragraph from Sunday, if needed, to get you started.

Close with this prayer

God of all life, you have given _____ to me, and me to _____. Thank you. Amen.

Wednesday

> Then God said, "Let us make humankind in our image, according to our likeness; and let them have dominion over the fish of the sea."
>
> —GENESIS 1:26

Dominion has become a dangerous word. We do not understand the word *dominion* the way our Scriptures reveal its meaning; we think only of the way the use of the word is in our time today, in a world that has borne witness to colonization and slavery, to human trafficking and poaching. We see dominion as "rule over," as take what we want, as dominate what is not human, such as the animal and vegetal world, as please only ourselves, as the purview of a harsh master. And yet, when God granted the first humans the task of *dominion,* it was about service, relation, to relate to every living thing in creation as God relates to us (according to our likeness). The task of giving names to animals was a way to learn with them, be with them, relate with them in a mutuality of mutual living and survival. The Scriptures reveal that God relates to us not in a harsh "ruling over," but in a nurturing, protecting way—even when we deserve otherwise. In Lent we recall a verse from Joel to reflect God's character throughout all of Scripture: gracious and merciful, slow to anger, and abounding in steadfast love. We have to move away

---

6. There are several translations of Francis of Assisi's "Canticle of the Creatures." This classic one may be found in Toole, *Handbook for Chaplains,* 13.

from *dominion* and move to relatedness and service, as guarding, protecting, restoring, reciprocating, and caring for what God has called good. Speak to your plant, say you are sorry for the way we have dominated what we were not supposed to dominate. Tell your plant something about your day. Use the paragraph from Sunday if needed to get you started.

> *Close with this prayer*
>
> God of all life, you have given _____ to me, and me to _____. Thank you. Amen.

Thursday

> Then the Lord answered Job out of the whirlwind: "Where were you when I laid the foundation of the earth? ... Who shut in the sea with doors when it burst out from the womb? ... Do you give the horse its might? Do you clothe its neck with mane? ... Is it by your wisdom that the hawk soars, and spreads its wings toward the south?"
>
> —Job 38:4, 8; 39:19, 26

An Indigenous leader once said, "What you call natural resources, we call our parents." Many people, of various religious groups and spiritual affiliations, call the earth Mother Earth. In our tradition, this conversation God has with Job richly points to the great attention and care with which God formed everything—and still does. God is our ancestor, and Christ Jesus our closest kin. The earth and everything therein belongs to God, and so it belongs to us—as a gift on our journey here. Speak to your plant, and tell your plant something about your day. Use the paragraph from Sunday, if needed, to get you started.

> *Close with this prayer*
>
> God of all life, you have given _____ to me, and me to _____. Thank you. Amen.

Friday

> The Lord is in his holy temple; let all the earth keep silence before him!
>
> —HABAKKUK 2:20

Sit in silence with your plant for a period of time. Set a timer and mark seven minutes. Let your mind and heart be attentive to how your plant is growing. What is changing with your plant? What is changing with you?

> *Prayer (pray out loud)*
>
> Holy God, you are with us, throughout our lives. Though we change, you are a constant companion. We give you thanks through Christ Jesus our Lord. Amen.

Saturday

> I lift up my eyes to the hills—from where will my help come? My help comes from the Lord, who made heaven and earth.
>
> —PSALM 121:1

The mountains are immemorial beings of time. They carry the markers of our cosmic life and are witnesses of our history. They are the elders of all of our lives, holders of wisdom and bearers of our stories. Once, a company wanted to extract from a mountain and they asked an Indigenous man. He said, "You cannot just go take things from there. You have to ask the mountain if the mountain agrees with it." Mountains are the witnesses of biblical history. As I teach my confirmation classes, in a kind of biblical shorthand, "Everything important in the Bible happens on a mountain!" Moses receives the Ten Commandments at Mount Sinai, his face shining like the sun; Jesus is transfigured on a mountaintop, shining bright as God's Son; the disciples are gathered together on a mountaintop and sent into the world to go and baptize and teach everyone about Jesus. Here in Pennsylvania, we are blessed: We can lift up our eyes to the hills and behold the beautiful gift of mountains with the Appalachian Mountains, the Allegheny and Pocono Mountains. Consider all they have witnessed.

Speak to your plant, and tell your plant something about your day. Use the paragraph from Sunday, if needed, to get you started.

Close with this prayer

God of all life, you have given _____ to me, and me to _____. Thank you. Amen.

Sunday, the Fourth Sunday in Lent

> Though I walk through the valley of the shadow of death, I shall fear no evil; for you are with me; your rod and your staff, they comfort me.
>
> —Psalm 23:4

The appointed psalm for today's worship is Psalm 23, a beloved scripture for many. The number of times this psalm has been chosen for funerals is too many to count, largely because it is so familiar to the population as a whole, but also because it is incredibly comforting. In these times that are upon us—as some of us shelter-in-place from a virus we cannot readily see, and others hurry off to work, fighting against time and an enemy hardly understood—this psalm offers us words of hope.

Pray the whole psalm with your plant. Give thanks that even in this time of anxiety and fear, God's still waters provide for you both. God is with us all, and God will comfort us, as the psalmist bravely sings:

> The Lord is my shepherd; I shall not be in want.
>
> The Lord makes me lie down in green pastures and leads me beside still waters.
>
> You restore my soul, O Lord, and guide me along right pathways for your name's sake.
>
> Though I walk through the valley of the shadow of death, I shall fear no evil; for you are with me; your rod and your staff, they comfort me.
>
> You prepare a table before me in the presence of my enemies; you anoint my head with oil, and my cup is running over.
>
> Surely goodness and mercy shall follow me all the days of my life, and I will dwell in the house of the Lord forever. Amen.

Monday

> And my God will fully satisfy every need of yours according to his riches in glory in Christ Jesus.
>
> —PHILIPPIANS 4:19

We have returned to another Monday, and it is time to practice our discipline of attentiveness once again. Look closely at your plant. Do you see buds or blossoms? Do you think your plant needs anything at this point in the journey—more or different light, water, something else? How do those needs differ from your own? Given our shelter-in-place these days, do these needs differ from our own?

Pray with your plant

> God, you are our provider. Open wide your hand and satisfy every living being. Amen.

Tuesday

> Do you not know that you are God's temple and that God's Spirit dwells in you?
>
> —1 CORINTHIANS 3:16

For a few years, a group of pastors in the area would get together every month or so, and participate in a workshop called "Spirit Café." It was unlike any workshop I had ever been to before, because rather than bringing in a "expert" in a certain field, we relied on the wisdom already present in each of us in the room—and especially the collective wisdom that emerged through our mutual conversation and prayer together. Together we would find creative ways to solve problems, to think differently about worship or Sunday School, or to dream new ways of serving our community. At the end of our time together, we each took a turn offering one word to honor our time together. "Energizing," "thought-provoking," "wisdom," and "bold" were among those regular one-word offerings. Consider the mutual conversations and prayer time you and your plant have shared together. Offer a word now for your plant—a way to honor his/her presence with you all these days.

Pray with your plant

Holy God, dwell in us, and teach us to honor your presence in all creation. Amen.

Wednesday

Jesus said, "The water that I will give will become in them a spring of water gushing up to eternal life."

—JOHN 4:14

The day my daughter was born, a water main in Harrisburg broke, contaminating the water supply to the hospital. All who came to visit her—grandparents and friends—were so conscientious about hygiene, always stopping at the sink in the room to wash their hands, before asking to hold her. Every time this happened, however, we tried to tell them to stop. "That's not clean!" we said. They thought we were just sleep-deprived! (Which we were!) Everything was so complicated after that water main broke. Her first bath, taken in the hospital, was a boiled one. We take our access to water for granted, don't we? We take whole bodies of water for granted, really—like our Susquehanna River, a water source for many, which feeds into the Chesapeake Bay, a body of water that sustains everything from marine life to livelihoods. The watershed area for the Chesapeake Bay extends five hundred miles from upstate New York to Virginia. The decisions we make in the entire watershed area—about where we build, where we dump our waste, and whether or not we control run-off (which carries nitrogen, phosphorus, and sediment, just to name a few)—all impact the river, which impacts the Bay, which impacts the ocean and impacts our life and so on.

Pour yourself a glass of water. Consider where it came from, and how it made its way to you. If you pour it down the drain in your kitchen, where is it going next?

Pray with your plant

Holy God, you give us to drink the well that is you. May we embody your love for all creation, until it springs up as living water, accessible to all. Amen.

Thursday

> Then the angel showed me the river of the water of life, bright as crystal, flowing from the throne of God and of the Lamb, through the middle of the street of the city. On either side of the river is the tree of life.
>
> —REVELATION 22:1

There is a beautiful hymn in our hymnal called "There in God's Garden" (*ELW* #342).[7] The verses recount how this passage from Revelation, a book thought by many scholars to be about the practice of worship, describes the tree of life—Jesus Christ—being offered to us at the Communion table, the fruit of life its gift to us in bread and wine, while we stand in the waters of our baptism—the same waters the author of Revelation terms "the river of the water of life."

On more than one occasion, the Scriptures capture a deep connection between water and trees. Psalm 1 praises the people of God, saying they are "like trees planted by streams of water." It's a beautiful image to our ears, but also a reference to the interconnected way trees and water interact. As the "Ten Million Trees" project in Pennsylvania describes it, the landscape can either be a gray funnel or a green filter. Buildings and highways are the gray funnel, that pushes rainwater and toxic run-off directly into creeks and rivers. Trees are a powerful green filter, their roots acting as streamside buffers, holding back pollution from our waterways.

Turn on the faucet so you can hear running water, like a river. Creeks and rivers near us like the big Susquehanna River and the Yellow Breeches and Conodoguinet Creeks. If you live near a creek or water source, step outside so you can hear it moving. Offer a word to honor the water—consider its source, vulnerability, and purpose in your life.

Prayer

Holy God, bless the waters above and below us, and the waters that surround us. Amen.

Friday

> Jesus said, "Let anyone with ears to hear listen!"
>
> —MARK 4:9

---

7. Evangelical Lutheran Church in America, *Evangelical Lutheran Worship*.

Sit in silence with your plant for a period of time. Set a timer and mark off seven minutes. Let your mind and heart be attentive to how it is growing. Is your plant loaded with buds and full of life? Has it already bloomed? What parts of your life or heart are eager to burst with joy? Think back over your whole day (or yesterday if this is a morning devotional for you). Offer a word now for your plant—a way to honor his/her presence with you in that time and place.

Pray with your plant

Teach us to quiet ourselves and listen for your voice, O God, that we may hear you speaking through all creation. Amen.

Saturday

> Does not wisdom call, and does not understanding raise her voice? . . . She cries out, "The Lord created me as the beginning of his work, the first of his acts long ago. Ages ago I was set up, at the first, before the beginning of the earth. . . . When God marked out the foundations of the earth, then I was beside him, like a master worker.
>
> —PROVERBS 8:1, 22, 29

Wisdom, or *Sophia* in Greek, is a personified female in the Scriptures. Often in Christian circles she is closely associated with the Holy Spirit, such that some scholars call her Spirit-Sophia. Proverbs 8 reminds us that Wisdom is God's master worker, elemental in forming creation, delighting in all God's creatures—even the humans. Wisdom and wisdom literature, such as the book of Job, remind us God's ways are not our ways and are beyond human knowledge. Our wisdom is not God's wisdom; and while Job longs for an answer to his suffering, the truth is that no answer will do. God's "answer" to Job is a first-class passage with Wisdom herself, on a tour of the creation—a world much bigger than ourselves, a world where we are not the center of the universe any longer; the universe is its actual center. God is the center, not us. Does that give us "understanding," or perhaps, comfort? I can't say. I can only say that like many others I know, when I am faced with difficult challenges or overwhelmed by the pain and hurt in the world, standing next to the ocean, with its widening boundaries too far to see; or hiking into the mountains, with their grandeur and size too big to measure against my own,

I feel differently about things. Perhaps you can relate. (Take a virtual dive into the ocean with NOAA.[8]) Think back over your whole day (or yesterday if this is a morning devotional for you). Offer a word now for your plant—a way to honor his/her presence with you in that time and place.

Pray with your plant

> Give us your wisdom, O God, that we may behold the majesty and magnificence of creation, and our place in it. Amen.

Sunday, the Fifth Sunday in Lent

> The dead man came out, his hands and feet bound with strips of cloth, and his face wrapped in a cloth. Jesus said to them, "Unbind him, and let him go."
>
> —JOHN 11:44

In Jewish tradition, the rabbis write comments or notes to "fill in the gaps" of the Scriptures, and they call it Midrash. According to a nineteenth-century rabbi, Samson Hirsch, who wrote many such notes on the Torah, God gave the Sabbath "so that the people should not grow haughty in their dominion of God's creation. For on the Sabbath you should refrain from exercising human sway over the things of the earth. . . . You should return the borrowed world to its Divine Owner in order to realize that it is but lent to you." Many who follow this teaching of Sabbath see it as a day each week on which they do not transform nature at all; anything that has an effect on nature is not performed—plucking fruit or leaves, planting seeds, anything that transforms the environment. It has the effect, they say, of altering a person's feelings about holding control over nature. It makes them remember: it is truly only God who does this. The rabbi continues: "Imagine! Sabbath in our time! [This is the nineteenth century, mind you.] To cease for a whole day from all business, from all work, in the frenzied hurry-scurry of our time! To close the exchanges, factories, workshops, to stop all railway services—great heavens! How would it be possible! The pulse of life would stop beating and the world would perish! But would the world perish? On the contrary, it would be saved."

There is an unbinding that happens when we practice Sabbath. It is like the unbinding Jesus calls all those around Lazarus to participate in to remove

8. See https://sanctuaries.noaa.gov/vr/.

the signs of death and destruction that still cover him. There is a freedom in pausing to remember who we belong to and who is really in charge of this world—our God, who made us and everything that lives from mere dust. It is life-giving to reconnect with our own beating hearts in the moments of silence, and to consider that our hearts only beat because God's breath is in us, because God is that much a part of us. It is a resurrection of sorts to reflect, if only for a moment, that God is that much a part of every living being in all creation—even those plants and trees, and those people, who have returned to the ground. Celebrate the Sabbath today by taking up a practice that will remind you to seek balance with the natural world. Unplug electrical appliances you won't use today, wear clothes made of Earth-friendly materials; instead of driving, take a walk; and so on.

> *Pray with your plant*
>
> Unbind us, Gracious God, and free us from ourselves, that we may unbind the earth. Amen.

Monday

> The flowers appear on the earth, the time of singing has come.
>
> —SONG OF SONGS 2:12

We have returned to another Monday, and it is time to practice our discipline of attentiveness once again. Look closely at your plant. Is it full of life and blooming?

Is there any other living being coexisting with your plant? A microorganism, a moss? What gift might it be giving to your plant at this time?

> *Pray with your plant*
>
> Thank you God for my plant, _____ (name). Help me to care for him/her in the best way possible, as you care for every living being on Earth. Amen.

Tuesday

> Now John wore a garment of camel's hair and a leather belt around his waist, and his food was locusts and wild honey.
>
> —MATTHEW 3:4

Insects are fascinating and fundamental to our living; without them we would perish. Among other things insects are vital as pollinators, and almost all plants rely on them for reproduction; insects are also food for other animals, especially for birds. Insects control pests and maintain the exact balance to our necessary biodiversity. Insects also aerate soil with their droppings, folding nutrients into it, and opening tunnels for water to irrigate it. Many decompose garbage, carrion, and other dead matter. Insects also serve as antibacterials, analgesics, anticoagulants, diuretics, and antirheumatics. We are made of the same dirt they are, and we praise the same God who gives life and breath to each of us. They are as important to the circle and sustenance of life as we are.

Explore an insect-friendly activity in your yard. Maybe you catch and release bugs using a butterfly net; or, on a sunny day, place an open umbrella upside-down under a leafy, low-hanging branch. Shake the branch like you mean it—then identify what lands in your umbrella with an insect book or online. Pause to look at these precious beings. Give each a name and say a prayer of gratitude for their work among us.

Prayer

God of unending creativity and love, you have created all these insects, those we know and don't know, those we love and those we are afraid of. Thank you for every little creature: spiders, worms, crickets, locusts, ants, beetles, bees, and butterflies. May we never take them for granted. Amen.

Wednesday

> When you enter the land that I am giving you, the land shall observe a sabbath for the Lord.
>
> —LEVITICUS 25:2

Here's a mind-blowing fact: there's more carbon in soil than in the atmosphere and all plant life combined. That's not a big deal when left to its own devices. But when soil gets disturbed—like it does when you convert a forest into cropland—all that stored carbon gets released into the atmosphere as carbon dioxide. That's one reason why deforestation alone is responsible for eleven percent of all global greenhouse gas emissions. (Another reason is that forests and grasslands are natural carbon sinks. Clearing them reduces the planet's capacity to remove carbon dioxide from the air.) The microbes in soil can also create greenhouse gases when they come into contact with fertilizer. Synthetic fertilizers revolutionized how we feed the world, but they release a powerful greenhouse gas called nitrous oxide when broken down by those microbes. Natural fertilizers like manure aren't any better because they release greenhouse gases as they decompose. Ecological agricultural practices need more attention and support in our world. Many such practices are well-known at this point, but many markets do not support or subsidize the changes needed, or the additional products produced using varying crop rotations. The buy-local movement, supporting a CSA,[9] and visiting your farmer's market are important ways you can support small-scale growers right here!

Go outside and take a scoop of soil. Hold it in your hands. Consider the life it holds, the microorganisms at work every second, and consider how much we have disturbed and misused this part of God's good creation over the centuries.

> *Say this prayer with the soil*
>
> Lord, let our hearts be good soil, open to caring for this precious gift. Amen.

Thursday

> The birds of the sky nest by the waters; they sing among the branches.
>
> —Psalm 104:12

I used to think I could hear music well. When practicing the piano, for instance, I used to think I could hear all the notes and whether I played them correctly. That was until I went to college in music, and learned about ear training, the practice of listening attentively to something over and over until you hear tones and overtones you never "heard" before. By the time of my senior recital, I could hear subtleties in piano performance I could barely describe. And yet, the farther I move away from that time of regular ear training, the less I can "hear." I thought of this when reading a recent post from

---

9. Community-supported agriculture (CSA) is a food production and distribution system that directly connects farmers and consumers. In short: people buy "shares" of a farm's harvest in advance and then receive a portion of the crops as they're harvested. See, for example, https://www.thespruceeats.com/community-supported-agriculture-csa-2216594.

a friend of a friend under quarantine in Wuhan, China. She writes, on day forty-eight, "Right now, I hear the birds outside my window on the twenty-fifth floor. I used to think there weren't really birds in Wuhan, because you rarely saw them and never heard them. I now know, they were just muted and crowded out by the traffic and people. All day long now, I hear birds singing. It stops me in my tracks to hear the sound of their wings."

Go outside or open a window and listen for the birds. It may take a few minutes to focus your hearing on their sounds, depending on where you live, and depending on how trained you are to hear their singing.

> *Pray with your plant*
>
> Incline our ears to hear your voice, Holy God, through the music of the birds. Amen.

Friday

> Jesus said to them, "Come away to a deserted place all by yourselves and rest awhile."
>
> —MARK 6:31

Sit in silence with your plant for a period of time. Set a timer, and mark seven minutes. Let your mind and heart be attentive to how your plant is growing. As your plant is blooming and changing, what is blooming or changing in you? Offer one word as an answer to this question, even if it is "unknown." Say it out loud to your plant. Offer a space of silence for your plant to answer as well.

> *Pray with your plant*
>
> Holy God, you are with us, in the silence, in the changes of our lives—both now and far into the unknown future. Amen.

Saturday

> Let my prayer rise up as incense before you, a lifting up of my hands, as the evening sacrifice.
>
> —PSALM 141:2 (TAKEN FROM OUR EVENING PRAYER SERVICE)

Smell is one of our senses, one that serves for so many reasons. Our smell attracts, repulses, creates memories, relations, and marks our culture. Smells are everywhere. Plants and flowers have a whole array of aromatic scents. There is no scent that is the same among the flowers, and there can be sweet, musty, spicy, or fruity odors that serve as signals for pollinators, offering them rewards. Plant scents attract some insects and repel others so they can survive in a chain of relations and cross-pollinations. Paul writes in 2 Corinthians that believers are the "aroma of Christ to God" for each other—a fragrance of "life to life," as he describes it. As all four Gospels tell it, when Mary anointed Jesus's feet at Bethany, a fragrance of the perfume (and of his impending death) filled the whole house. Perhaps the aroma of living beings in creation, and their diversity of fragrance, can remind us of God's gift of life for each and every one of us. Pick one thing in your kitchen to smell. (Take turns smelling its aroma.) Then offer a word to honor the scent.

Prayer

Holy God, we give thanks for the fragrance of Jesus's love and mercy to us all. Help us to learn the smells and scents of your Earth, that we may be the aroma of love to the world. Amen.

Sunday, Palm Sunday

Some of the Pharisees in the crowd said to Jesus, "Teacher, order your disciples to stop." He answered, "I tell you, if these were silent, the stones would shout out."

—LUKE 19:39–40

As the Gospel writers describe it, Jesus's triumphal entry into Jerusalem on this day had everyone shouting. And not just everyone, but every living being—apparently, even the rocks joined in the praise of the one who comes in the name of the Lord. "Hosanna!" they shouted. When I was around twenty years old, I attended the retirement service for the beloved senior pastor in the congregation. He had served for many years; he was a faithful preacher and teacher and well-respected by the community. I don't remember his sermon in its entirety, but I remember clear as a bell him saying, "I believe Jesus died for every person under heaven. I believe Jesus died for every rock, every tree, and every stream." At first I thought: oh, I'm glad he's retiring, because he's losing it. How could Jesus have died for the trees and rocks? What could they possibly need? But there was something about his confession of faith that I could not easily dismiss; that had me thinking about it twenty years later. Perhaps it was this passage from Luke's Gospel. Perhaps it was asking the question in these times, with this ecological and energy crisis: Who is it that longs for redemption, restoration, and renewal? Who is it that would boldly shout "Hosanna!" (which means, "Save us!") that day as Jesus rode a donkey into Jerusalem? Perhaps even the rocks would shout out.

Go outside and get a rock. Bring it in and set it with your plant as a companion.

Pray with your plant and rock

God you are our rock of ages. I give thanks for this rock, a timeless witness to your majesty, and a companion to us all. Amen.

Monday in Holy Week

Blessed are the pure in heart, for they shall see God.

—Matthew 5:8

This is our last Monday together in Lent, when we have taken up the practice of attentiveness. By now I imagine your own practice of attentiveness toward your plant is regular and heightened. Go outside and practice attentiveness with the nearest tree or shrub. Look closely. What do you see there?

Pray with this tree or shrub

Holy God, open the eyes of our hearts, that we may see you, alive and renewing all creation. Amen.

Tuesday in Holy Week

Blessed are those who mourn, for they shall be comforted.

—Matthew 5:4

Our time is filled with loss. Many of us who have been or are still sheltering in place have endured many recent losses. Holy Week is appropriately named for us because it is a holy time set apart to grieve our loss and to look expectantly for resurrection to come among us.

The earth has suffered loss at our hands. The way award-winning author Dr. Seuss describes the cutting of the last tree in his book *The Lorax*[10] captures the poignancy of the loss we create: "From outside the fields came a sickening smack of an axe on a tree. Then we heard the tree fall. The very last Truffula Tree of them all." A sickening smack. What this children's book does so well—and even more so, the recent movie version—is to give us permission to mourn these losses at our hands: to grieve as a people, to grieve with the earth itself.

(Watch this portion of the movie, a scene of grief, and discuss it.)

Go to any part of the landscape near you that has been altered by human hands: a tree that has been cut off, a house that has been erected, a road that has been paved. Offer a blessing for loss.

Pray with this place

Into your hands, O merciful Savior, we commend this place. Acknowledge, we humbly beseech you, a _____ (name of the landscape or planting) of your own making, an integral part of your good creation, a place of your merciful redemption. Amen.

Wednesday in Holy Week

By the breath of God ice is given, and the broad waters are frozen fast.

—Job 37:10

When President Taft created Glacier National Park in 1910, it was home to an estimated 150 glaciers. Since then the number has decreased to fewer than thirty, and most of those remaining have shrunk in area by two-thirds. Research scientists predict that within thirty years most if not all of the park's namesake glaciers will disappear. "Things that normally happen in geologic time are happening during the span of a human lifetime," says Daniel Fagre. "It's like watching the Statue of Liberty melt." Everywhere on Earth ice is changing. The famed snows of Kilimanjaro have melted more than 80 percent since 1912. Glaciers in the Garhwal Himalaya in India are retreating so fast that researchers believe that most central and eastern Himalayan glaciers could virtually disappear by 2035. Arctic sea ice has thinned significantly over the past half-century, and its extent has

---

10. Seuss, *The Lorax*.

declined by about 10 percent in the past thirty years. NASA's repeated laser altimeter readings show the edges of Greenland's ice sheet shrinking. Spring freshwater ice breakup in the Northern Hemisphere now occurs nine days earlier than it did 150 years ago, and autumn freeze-up ten days later. Thawing permafrost has caused the ground to subside more than fifteen feet in parts of Alaska. All over the world massive ice fields, monstrous glaciers, and sea ice are disappearing, fast.[11]

Place two or three ice cubes on a plate or bowl near your plant. Sit in silence as they melt. As you witness the melting, keep silence. Give yourself permission to grieve this death—it is a part of the earth, a part of God, and a part of you.

Close with this prayer

Gracious God, we grieve what we have become, and how we have wounded the frozen waters in this world. Teach us to heed these warnings, and show us a new way to live. Amen.

Maundy Thursday

And when Jesus had given thanks, he broke it and said, "This is my body that is for you. Do this in remembrance of me."

—1 CORINTHIANS 11:24

The Words of Institution, as we practice them, do not come from the Gospel witness, but from Paul's letter to the church at Corinth. Every time we eat the bread and drink the wine, we "proclaim the Lord's death until he comes." This is important, when we consider that Jesus's meal with his disciples took place in the course of a regular meal, using regular everyday table food. The bread was passed around first, as the Synoptic Gospels recount it, and then they ate the bulk of dinner. "After supper, he took the cup," and passed around the table wine—the cheap, everyday wine his disciples had with every dinner, that their neighbors had with every dinner, that everyone in Galilee and Jerusalem who did not live in a palace had with every dinner. In this same way we can make every meal we eat—every ordinary, regular meal—holy. Do we consider the food we receive on a daily basis holy? Do we treat it as such, giving thanks for the fields and the animals that gave their lives for

---

11. See Glick, "The Big Thaw."

our sustenance; giving thanks for the workers—mostly migrants in our country—who brought the food to our table? Do we consider the source of our food, whether it is at the Communion table or our dinner table—and do we measure our food production practices, our treatment of the fields, our privatization of seeds, our blindness to the humanity of workers—to be "in remembrance of me"? How would that change things?

Plant a seed today. Give thanks for the power it has to teach you about rebirth—for the way it proclaims our Lord's death as a way to life.

Close with this Buddhist practice:

Look at your own plate of food and repeat these phrases:

> In this food
>
> I see clearly
>
> the entire universe
>
> supporting my existence.
>
> Amen.

Good Friday

> When it was noon, darkness came over the whole land until three in the afternoon. . . . Then Jesus gave a loud cry and breathed his last.
>
> —MARK 15:33, 37

We have come to the last Friday in our devotional, a Friday we call "Good." In ancient times this day was called the "Triumph of the Cross." English speakers now call the day Good (originally "God's" Friday) because we know the end of the story. This Friday will carry us through every graveyard we know to resurrection. But first, we will walk through the darkness. Darkness in our racist culture is akin to evil. We associate Black and Blackness with sinister things; we are taught to fear the night and the shadows. The Scriptures have a completely different perspective. The psalmists ask God to "hide [us] in the shadow of your wings," for only there we can live in safety. God tends to show up at night, working literal miracles—whether that is blessing Jacob to be Israel, or bringing tidings of great joy to shepherds out in a field. Christ gives his life for us in the darkness, and rises on an early Easter morning, in the darkness—before the dawn. Darkness is a blessing, enfolding us like the very arms of God, bearing promise and blessing all at once.[12]

---

12. See Taylor, *Learning to Walk in the Dark*.

Turn down the lights, and sit in the darkness with your plant for a period of time. Keep silence.

Close with this prayer:

Holy God, we give you thanks for the darkness. May we behold its goodness and blessing upon us. Amen.

Holy Saturday

He will baptize you with the Holy Spirit and fire.

—MATTHEW 3:11

The pinnacle of the church's year is the Great Vigil of Easter. As all the light is extinguished from the church's worship on Good Friday, the service of Vigil begins outside, with what is called the "new fire"—a live fire in a fire pit. We light the Paschal Candle from this fire, marking a new beginning, quite literally, with the new year's numbers (this year 2020). We bring that fire, that new life, into the worship space again, among the people, and start again.

This devotional and theme of *reLent* has been a time for us to look at how we are living in the world, how we are living with each other, and how we are living with the earth. We have walked a path of self-examination; we have begun to learn how to see and hear all living beings—from butterflies to soil to trees to rocks to rivers—as belonging to God, and as speaking God's truth to us that we desperately need to hear. When we light the new fire this year for the Vigil, may we covenant to start again in all kinds of ways. May we mark a new beginning for ourselves and the earth, asking the question with Saint Augustine, "What do I love when I love my God?" And providing answers we never considered before.

If possible, light a fire outside and gather around it. (If not possible, light a large candle inside or one with multiple wicks.) Share what you and your family have learned these past weeks. Share your hopes for the year ahead.

Close with this prayer:

Great God, on this night you brought all creation from death to life. Bring us from the ways of our past to your ways of life, for our future. Amen.

Resurrection of Jesus, Easter Sunday

> Supposing Jesus to be the gardener, Mary said to him, "Sir, if you have carried him away, tell me where you have laid him, and I will take him away." Jesus said to her, "Mary!"
>
> —John 20:15

Isn't it interesting that of all things in this world, the resurrected Christ would be mistaken for a gardener? That Christ Jesus, who overcame death and hell, who freed us all from sin and the grave, would be found walking among us, talking with us, in the garden of all places?

We recently had to cut down a tree in our yard, a beloved English Walnut, probably a hundred years old or more, because of disease. The stories that tree had; the things it had witnessed—I can't even begin to imagine. It was a sad day when it came down, when the wood was chopped and hauled away, when even the stump was ground up. But it was not the end of the tree—it is mulch now, holding in water for another tree or plant; and as it decomposes, it will fertilize the ground on which it sits, and it will change the makeup of that soil, and it will nurture another plant that springs forth. Perhaps your resurrection project might lead you to plant a garden.[13] It reminds me of an article I read about a pastor who helped his congregation move to natural burial—laying their dead to rest, without intervention and chemicals, in the woods behind the church. While many resisted at first, over time they told just how much they learned about the connection between death and rebirth from the experience; about resurrection now, and in the time to come. But who they learned from, really, was the earth itself; from the trees under which their beloved dead were planted. From the wind that rustled the branches, as they lowered loved ones into the ground, the wind inviting them to lean into it, holding them up in their grief. And it was from the master gardener—Christ Jesus—who so loves even the dew on the roses, even us, even beyond the grave.[14]

Remember our exercise back on Monday of the first week in Lent. You looked out the window where your plant resides and jotted down anything you saw outside that was full of life. Look again out the same window. Consult your old list. Would you add anything you did not see before? Was it because it was not there before, or because you did not consider it to be full of life until now?

---

13. See the video "How to Start a Regenerative Garden at Home": https://www.youtube.com/watch?v=eNcSkb8uR-s.

14. See the Mormon Tabernacle Choir singing C. Miles Austin's hymn "In the Garden": https://www.youtube.com/watch?v=OcRCa7SDhxA.

Prayer:

Continue, O God, to create in us a new heart and a new way to see your world. Amen.

Here is a prayer to the earth that I, Cláudio, continue to pray:
Dear Earth, Gaia, Pachamama,
You who are and have always been my home, my solace, my ground.
I am made of you and of the stars.
Your water that runs in my body runs in your rivers and oceans.
I have grown up because of you. I have eaten what you gave me to eat. I have drunk what you gave me to drink.
I am now dressed in clothes that just the other day were a flower in the field.
I must confess that I have been estranged from you. I never paid attention to you. I have never talked to plants as if they mattered, I have never listened to the birds as if they were singing my song, I never paid attention to your pace and movements, I never stopped to hear the relation between you, the oceans, the moon, and the planets.
How can I teach my children to care for you if I don't know how to care?
How can I tell them to listen to you if I don't even know where to start?
Ah, I learned that I had to listen to God, but God was never in you, fully. So I always went elsewhere. For God was always elsewhere. Only partially in you. And now I can't hear either God or you. Perhaps I hear you asking me who we are as humanity without you. How much humus of that humus-humanity are we? The "we" of my theology was always the "we" of myself and God and other humans. The philosophy behind my theology was a Greek one establishing a duality between transcendence and immanence. Descartes made me think that I am what I can think. Kant distinguished things and beings from the imprecision of thinking itself. I think that I am a being and that whatever does not think is a thing—and therefore just a resource. I remember that Indigenous leader saying to us non-Indigenous people: "What you call natural resources, we call parents." The duality of transcendence and immanence, culture and nature, human and animal-vegetal, it all must die. Death to humanism! Death to modernity! Death to development and any economics of growth! Death to everything that tells us that we need something that cannot be found where we live.

Dear Pachamama, I have been in confessional mode here. But I am trying to find a subjectivity that implodes the objectivity of our thinking. When I wondered about my subjectivity, I learned that I had to go to therapy to listen to my own voice, which was truly important, but I never imagined that I could also listen to the mountains, the zebras, the worms, the butterflies, the trees, the bluebirds, the bees, the sunflowers, and the squirrels as if I were also listening to myself.

So now I wonder with a sense of subjectivity that is foreign to my own being. If 25 percent of myself is made of trees, 90 percent is made of water, and 100 percent made of stars, I feel now that these many new universes, pluriverses, are waking me up to write new verses in my body. And my heart rejoices. But I have so many questions to you, dear Gaia:

How do I learn to hear the undercurrent of waters within you?

How can I see the rivers that run above me between the trees?

How can I learn to hear your desires and your hopes?

How can I learn to mend and restore where you are hurting?

How can I make you be a fundamental voice to the constitution of myself but also of the constitution of every nation?

I must confess that I have lived as if you almost did not exist, as if you were there just to give me everything and my job was to develop, grow, expand, conquer, dominate. But now that we are destroying everything and our future is going to be completely compromised, we cannot not perceive you anymore.

So I want to have a heart that is near yours. I want to have a heart that can hear your heartbeat as the heartbeat of the body of God. I pray I learn to see the Holy Spirit in the quaternity of the air, earth, wind, and fire! May I learn that everything is in you and that my work is to wonder.

May the brilliance of the stars, the worlds and universes without ends make me wonder and exclaim "Wooowww! Aaaahhh! Wow! My goodness! Look at that, listen to it!" Every day.

May every plant be my family that I love and live for in reciprocity and care. My sacred text will be:

> Our vegetable love should grow
>
> Vaster than empires, and more slow.[15]

So please, dear Earth, help me listen to you. Teach me about you and your ways. I want to live and die with you. For as the Scriptures say, "From the dust we come and to dust we shall return." May my own dust be worthy

---

15. Marvell, "To His Coy Mistress," 51.

of your ongoing gift of life and care. May who I am be a gift of reciprocity to you. May the work of my hands be of ongoing restoration and regeneration.

May your wilderness be protected, and I become a shield. May I shield you as if I were protecting myself.

May your fields go back to full diversity and all the pollinators come and go and flourish throughout the whole earth. May I feel you as I feel myself. No need to be more than myself once I realize that you live everywhere in me, in every cell of my body. You are the deepest kinship I have.

May we bee like a bee.[16] I want to be like a bee dancing my way around the flowers.

May the oceans be resurrected and the fish live in peace.

May the trees live as long as they can.

May all of the extinguished species be honored and remembered.

May the birds never go without singing.

And may I learn their songs so I can sing to you their songs, my songs, our songs.

May I learn to listen to you as I learn to listen to God.

May I learn to listen to you as I learn to listen to my children.

May I learn to listen to you as I learn to listen to myself.

May I learn to listen to you as I learn to listen to you.

Amen.

---

16. The first "bee" is intentional. See https://www.youtube.com/watch?v=bFBobAX6RGA.

9

Praying with Each Other during Infected Holy Week

COVID-19 and the Possibilities of Our Resurrection

As I write, we—all of us, around the globe—have become immersed in the novel coronavirus pandemic and the ravages and upheavals brought about by COVID-19. As it happens, the pandemic's initial spread around the planet nearly coincided with the beginning of Lent. As we found our bearings and rethought our religious practices, hoping to stay faithful to the gospel and attentive to this new situation, Holy Week loomed. What then, of that holiest of weeks, the heart of the Christian liturgical year, in this destabilizing new era? This chapter is a prayerful way of revisiting Holy Week in the presence of COVID-19, a meditation from a theological, social, and ecological perspective. How can we be more aware of the ways we must live in this time and the ways in which we can and must pray? This is a time for praying a prayer that has not yet been prayed before, yet in the setting and spirit of our eternal truths and ancient liturgies.

Holy Week is a time of intensified prayer. Holy Week begins like every birth, with a prayer that has exclamations of joy and shouts: Hosanna! The utopia of a new time has arrived! As we approach this heightened liturgical period, we prepare the way with palm for what is coming. As a Latin American liberation theology song says: "God calls us to a new moment . . . alone, isolated, nobody can move." And here we are: alone, isolated, not able to move. This Holy Week is infected by COVID-19 and is drastically changing our ways of being in the world. It also is a call to us to change our prayers and the ways we pray.

As humanity, it seems that we have entered into the weeks and years of our last days. "Our house is on fire,"[1] the young Norwegian climate activist Greta Thunberg keeps telling us. The ecosystems are becoming

---

1. Thunberg et al., *Our House Is on Fire*.

disrupted and their many forms of equilibrium being destroyed. The ways in which the virus is accelerating, shifting, hiding, creating strange effects, and throwing us for a loop clearly shows how little we can control it. The presence of COVID-19 is like the arrival of Palm Sunday, but they appear to have two different outcomes: one—for we know the end of that story—can signal resurrection. The other may be preparing us for a calamity without redemption. Is this new infection a way into life, or should we ask, like the anthropologist and sociologist Bruno Latour, "Is this a dress rehearsal?"[2] If we do not stop our collective march toward death, what is coming after this is worse: frightening, unprecedented, and totally unknown. Just like COVID-19, the disarray of all ecosystems will be uncontrolled, and we will have to cope with Good Fridays and Holy Saturdays without end, without an Easter Sunday.

This infected Holy Week can be a parable of our time right now. In the gospel story, what we now call Holy Week starts with people preparing the way for Jesus to come. Then Jesus gathers with his friends, washes their feet, and shares with them a full meal. And then something starts to go really wrong. Jesus goes to Gethsemane. He is scared of death and scared to death. The story goes into a spiral of death and decomposition, not just of a human body, but of dreams and social threads. Jesus is betrayed, given over to the state, which mercilessly kills him. He descends into hell—and then a different life begins to take shape. Jesus's resurrection resurrects others; angels appear to the women who went to take care of Jesus's body; Jesus appears to some disciples. He is risen! The rest, as we know, is in us under the power of the Holy Spirit.

Our present Holy Week is fully infected with the coronavirus, which historian and psychoanalyst Phillipe Sansonetti called "the sickness of the Anthropocene,"[3] the presence of humans encroaching on nature and ripping it apart. Why on earth did this happen to us? We thought that we were celebrating life as always. Nothing was going terribly wrong until everything went wrong. We were thrown off our tracks and we are now in astounding disarray. The social filaments holding our life together are unraveling and we can see more clearly their already existing weaknesses. The limitations of our power are glaring. Our patterns of life were already sick; their forms of production were killing fish in the seas and animals on the earth. It has long been this way, but now we cannot avoid seeing it. We can even smell it. We can feel it. We are realizing that we have betrayed our own selves by

---

2. Latour, "Is This a Dress Rehearsal?"
3. Sansonetti, cited in Baschet, "COVID-19: O século XXI Começa Agora."

destroying the earth. The social, economic, cultural, and political apparatus of death cannot hide any more.

We are encountering a pain hitherto unknown, a numbness we cannot control, and many sincere questions within ourselves and around us about why all of this is happening. The main image and theological idea I carry into this infected week is that the earth was put on the cross, the animals were placed on the cross, the vegetable and mineral world were all placed on the cross, along with the bodies taken away by COVID-19, especially the people of marginalized communities, the poorest ones. The difference in this infected Holy Week is that we are not assured of resurrection anymore. We might all descend into hell without the hope of seeing the light of the new day. Unless we rise early in the day like the women and prepare the way to see a new life, we will miss the possibility of resurrection and will not be able to listen to the angel announcing to us that a new way of life is possible. There will be only a perfunctory repetition of rituals without justice. Marc Ellis asks, "Should we put our rituals on permanent suspension until there is justice? Will we hold on to a piety that does not relate to the pain of the world?"[4] What are our prayers for? So here it is: a possible journey through Holy Week with COVID-19.

Palm Sunday

The palm branches—which, in some countries and regions, are from other types of trees or shrubs—should be an exterior sign of an inner prayer. They are also sign and signal of the inbreaking of the love of God into the world, the perennial flowering or greening plants announcing that the realm of growing things is there for us if we live in reciprocity with them: they give us what we need to live and we give them space, care, freedom. On Palm Sunday we must walk outside of churches in procession, not as a perfunctory ritual but to see that what is outside our church buildings is not detached from the inside. If we want a new world to emerge, we cannot just stay inside.

As we process, we enter with Jesus into a new Jerusalem, a place where Palestinians, along with Israelis and sojourners from other lands, flourish like green trees, where Jews, Christians, Muslims, Druze, and others grow together. The problem is that we never know what to do when we are in Jerusalem. We stop short. We celebrate the idea of Jerusalem, we pray about it, and we even move towards it, but we are still so attached to the old Jerusalem of our thoughts—which still houses the ethnic cleansing

---

4. Ellis has asked this in conversation with me as well as in social media posts.

of Palestinians atop decades and centuries of violence and trauma—that we cannot imagine a new world and its demands. If we are to keep going in the direction of change, we will need to be broken open so we can find the ideas and means to actually live in a new Jerusalem. This new world as a utopia, a new time, comes to us in disguise from those who come from below. Not from a Messiah full of power but a poor prophet trying to tell us that we must change our ways.

Perhaps the story of Jesus needs to be recounted in conversation with the stories of Indigenous people and their multiple stories of relations with the earth. But we fall short: we imagine a new world, but then we cannot muster the demands of change that we need to comply with the demands of a new era. For Jesus's demands are much too high. Who would give everything away in order to follow Jesus? Jesus's demands present us with a dilemma: Jesus's sayings are mere platitudes or our ways of living our Christianity are cheap discipleship, sugar-coated religion, empty rituals, psychologized messages, and rationalized beliefs crafted to *our* demands and possibilities.

To follow Jesus is to hold on to the palm branches and break with what we can in order and move forward with what we must, giving up the old worlds in which we lived and our former ways of being. Otherwise, any utopia we sing or proclaim will mostly be a projection of what we want and a mirror of our desires. Palm Sunday should be the announcement of the outbreak of what we truly need, even if it is painful. Palm Sunday is a call to think about and express our joy, yes, but not the entitlement of personal happiness, happiness captured in the forms of individual expansiveness demanded by the Declaration of Independence. Palm Sunday is about how we will live our happiness when we get down to Jerusalem where everybody lives. This is a different happiness: a joy that comes from putting the call of Jesus first and from accommodating our desires to a collective sense of responsibility—a happiness in which everyone has the right to a life with dignity, in a democracy that takes into account not only human beings but the worlds of vegetable, mineral, and animal beings. Our prayers are a celebration, a work, a call for a collective democracy of Earth to come, not only for ourselves but especially for others: for the healing and well-being of all people and of animals, plants, water, mountains, and trees. Even if infected, can we pray for this new world?

Tenebrae

As we go down into the night, we do not know well how to stay with darkness and pray with the night. It seems that we cannot face our worst fears or listen to our dreams, which makes us play out these fears and not-knowing into destruction and sabotage of our own capabilities and possibilities for transformation. Our prayers do not seem to change us much. We have confused a life of prayer with a life of self-fulfillment. We have confused the desire of God in our prayers with the desires of the world in the form of prayers. We are so confused about who we are and what we truly want that we end up disguising our desires as forms of social demands. These forms of social demand are organized around neoliberal politics and economics that shape our feelings and affections, and we already realize that it is not working. We are sick, depressed, half-employed, unemployed, underemployed, riddled with anxiety, dying without health care. In our confusion, we have never known the limits between the human and the non-human or other-human worlds, and that is the source of our plagues: the entering into a world that does not belong to us. While these spaces are all part of us, we must also have limits and know that many natural places are biomes of other living species and not for us. COVID-19 is yet another sign of our having moved beyond our limit for consumption, control, and domain.

We are descending into heavy darkness. This is not the luminous darkness that Howard Thurman talks about[5] and that is glorious, but a space where there is a thickness of loss, fear, and confusion. So, we arrive at the Tenebrae Service, often celebrated on Wednesday of Holy Week. On that day, the ritual signals that something is going awry. A mixture of light, darkness, and something else is falling upon us and we do not know fully what it is. This Tenebrae Service says that we are in a place of descent that we can't quite figure out. In this infected era, some of us stay home, some of us will work. Some of us will be hit hard and will die. Others will survive. And many will starve. The wind of life is now filled with something we can't quite hear.

The earth has been changing for a while now. Indigenous people are saying that the skies are different, the trees are responding in weird ways, and the animals are receding. In the service of Tenebrae, what my Brazilian communities call *trevas*, we are overwhelmed by a thousand laments, not all of which we understand. We could, in this worship service, read Bruno Latour, anthropologist and sociologist, who points us to a certain why of this time in a form of a collective prayer: "Is this a dress rehearsal?"[6] Latour asks. We could add: Are we getting ready for what is coming? A global warming catastrophic series of events is already happening everywhere. Will we continue to be slaves of extractivist corporations

---

5. Thurman, *The Luminous Darkness*.
6. Latour, "Is This a Dress Rehearsal?"

everywhere that eat up everything that is Earth: mountains, rivers, soil, underground soil, even the moon?

Can we hear it? Can we hear the earth praying? It could be that the earth is telling us: You either go into silence and slowness or "I am about to spit you out of my mouth," as God said to the church in Laodicea in Revelation 3:16—which in this case means we will be kicked out of the earth. Sooner than we imagine, perhaps. So in this service of Tenebrae, we still read the *Lamentations* of Jeremiah and his offers of consolation without redemption.

The lights go dim and the candles are blown out. At the end of the ritual, there is only one candle lit, and then even that one is taken away. There is silence. A long silence. Silence is a profound form of prayer, perhaps the most important—or rather, the most necessary. Perhaps, if we can hear the silence, we may be able to see the luminous darkness within us. We might be able to leave our houses when it is still dark to wait for the first rays of the sun, and in prayer greet both the darkness and the light within us: the darkness within us brightened by the light that also lives within us and the light within darkened by the darkness of who we are.

In the Tenebrae Service, we go to a place where the thickness of the unknown will show up, and we will have no idea of the where or who or how of anything. There we will pray: God, I give everything up to you! So we will learn that we cannot control anything. And from there, a beam of responsibility, light and darkness leading the way into the night/light.

Maundy Thursday

The next day we gather for more prayers, carrying the thickness of this time within us. All we know now is that we need to help those who are suffering, those who are caught in the vortex of demands and exploitations by landlords and CEOs. We remember the poorer ones who cannot hide in their homes, the ones who are suffering domestic violence by partners enraged by their own violence and by the violence of this time, health workers putting their lives on the line for other human beings, fast-food workers who live with the upper classes' demand for service even though they are exposed to the virus every day, farm workers exposed to the coronavirus and COVID-19 illness without any protection, harvesting the fields for our nourishment, elderly people who are afraid of being alone and dying alone.

All we know today, Maundy Thursday, is that we must turn on the siren of our inner ambulance and go serve somebody. This is our innermost and outward prayer. Today is the day we learn from Jesus that the main symbol of

Christianity might not be the cross but the towel, the towel of service. When Jesus washes the feet of his disciples, he is taking the position of the slave who used to wash the feet of the guests at the door before they entered the house for dinner. Today we must serve those who were not invited to dinner. We serve those who do not belong to the list of invitees. Today we soothe hearts filled with anxiety and consumed by fear.

Some churches will follow the service with the ancient ritual of stripping the altar. This year we learn that our lives are already stripped: that which was there before was just an illusion of protection, order, and security. We are stripped bare naked, and our hearts are pumping as if outside our bodies, feeling all of the elements, afraid of what is coming. The dinner with Jesus's disciples was already a place where somebody was going to betray him, as our humanity, in our daily meals and actions, endlessly betrays the love of plants, animals, oceans, fish, rocks, fields, and soil. We are constantly betraying the love of the earth for thirty pieces of silver, for "economic progress." We say we love the earth, just as Judas loved Jesus. Judas did not actually want to betray Jesus. We do not want to betray the earth. And yet this is what we do. After the betrayal, Judas killed himself and we say a prayer for him, as we must say a prayer for all of us who are destroying our home, our planet. We must change before we also commit collective suicide with our ways of living. We must turn away from our betrayal and say, "No more! We do not want to give away Jesus, or the poor, or the earth!"

But we should expect that the state police will come after us and, countering our prayers, proclaim: "Go buy! Keep working! Keep the economy going! You will regret it if you don't! We will take away your jobs, we will crush your families, you will be desperate, and you will die! We control you! Go now and do what we are telling you! Go kiss the earth goodbye! We will take care of the earth later!" So this Maundy Thursday we leave the service torn between our faithfulness to God, who created the earth and demanded us to care for it, and the demands of politicians and economic corporations who threaten us. Before I left the church this year, I could hear within me Eliane Brum admonishing us: "Capitalism has already stolen our present, it cannot steal our future."[7] As we continue to pray, still infected, we will continue to pray and find ways to serve those who are infected and in need. *Ora et labora*!

---

7. Brum, "O futuro *pós*-coronavírus."

Holy ("Good") Friday

We failed. In everything. Miserably! Our prayers couldn't do a thing. Our fear of losing the immediate prevented us from caring for the future. Our future was overconsumed by the fear of scarcity. We prayed so much for our individual selves and families that we forgot that our life is much larger than that. We had to betray Jesus, for the police were breathing heavily down our necks. The police state had its boots on our face. It was either Jesus or us. We just couldn't. It was not our fault. The power system knew too well that Jesus was dangerous and had to use us, those who knew him, to enforce its deadly ways. Jesus also knew all too well our ways of being and would say, "Father, forgive them, for they know not what they do."

The violent state knew our weaknesses but could see what Jesus was doing with and for us. People started to believe; they were getting ready to change, and to change too much. We could actually break into a new life! We even saw a glimpse of the future in our living prayers! The Empire had to stop Jesus altogether.

That is why the spectacle of Jesus's death was, for the Empire, a necessary and merciless show of pain and violence. With this public act of violence, we are threatened and become afraid of what can happen to us. Jesus's death points to our death today. It was, as it continues to be, a clear message of the state, alerting people with a different set of civic, patriotic prayers, a different allegiance: "See this? If you do this, if you don't follow the demands of our economy and the rules of order and progress, this is what is going to happen to you. You have to believe we will care for you. Don't be foolish!"

And the feeling of shame, embarrassment, defeat, ruin, disaster. The cross of Jesus is the death of all of the wretched who also are put on the many crosses around the world. All of the poor, those discarded as things, as trash, all of those who have to work for others to live, all those who cause fear just by existing.[8] They are the threat to dominant elites, the upper classes, the ones with money, chosen by the biopolitics of the state to live well.

The cross of Jesus today is found in the jails and walls that are everywhere, in youth put in jail, the stealing of common resources, sick people dying without access to health systems, students without access to education and students carrying massive debts, expensive treatments only given to some by the pharmaceutical companies. Everybody who was abandoned was there with Jesus and everything that came upon Jesus for his death is the death of the world. Jesus cried out in one of his last prayers: "My God, my God, why have you forsaken me?" Abandoned by God, he died. No answer to the prayer was heard. He, and we, were left alone.

---

8. See the Korean movie *Parasite*.

In the same way, the earth is on the cross right now. We are mercilessly killing the earth and its forms of life. We do not care for the earth in our prayers. We brutalize animals for consumption, we empty the oceans of fish for our consumption, we throw gallons of pesticides into the soil, killing the earth slowly so that we can eat whatever we want in any season of the year, we plant monocultures of soy and corn to feed animals and turn forests into pasture for them and then consume them. We poison the air until we cannot breathe anymore, we pollute the rivers with trash from factories, we pour tons of plastic into the ocean. We decimate wildlife, we extinguish three hundred species every day, we poison grass for the pleasure of our manicured lawns. We need, we want, we desire, we demand! And then, all is dead or dying. Nothing will be left for us humans.

There is not going to be enough Earth for all of our greed and desires and demands. If we do not stop, the earth herself will come back to us with a vengeance, showing what we have done and without any chance of forgiveness. We have destroyed all that could give us some possiblity to begin again. Yet politicians and economic corporations do not care. They are building bunkers for themselves and even thinking about how to create conditions of life on Mars when what we have here is extinguished. There is no hope whatsoever. Everything is dead. We are truly infected, more than we ever imagined. Not even prayers are worth anything. *It is finished*, Jesus prayed. So are we!

Holy Saturday: The Great Vigil of Easter

We go home—to what, we are not sure. We keep praying as we breathe. But our lives seem to be over. Everything we had was taken away. We cannot hear the birds. The animals have left us. We are bereft, alone, isolated, like a plague that demands us to stay within, both indoors and inside of ourselves. And within is the most difficult place to stay. Jesus our North, South, East, and West is dead and there is no compass to measure our loss, our grief, our displacement. No prayer can console us. We don't anticipate anything anymore besides the lingering of death in its bitterness and emptiness within us. We lean on our numbness. Perhaps our task now is to find a place where we can be comfortably numb.

We compose a symphony of crashed dreams, empty pockets, a drawer filled with torn clothes, a bare kitchen sink, and some leftovers in the fridge that don't stay cold. Imagine that not long ago we were coming into a new world holding palm branches for new beginnings. Our future, we felt, was such a given. We even believed that we could change the ways of the world, starting with ourselves. We should have known better.

The revolution only comes from a place we cannot imagine. Where did it begin? All we know is that it ended and there is nothing on the horizon. We now spend the nights and days not knowing what to do or where to go. Everything we say to each other is muted, or even cancelled as if we must shut down anything that doesn't look like us. We fear. What is it coming our way? An even worse catastrophe? Our fear is now universalized, even though the politicians are prophesying their words of death towards us as prayers of illuminations: *You lost nothing; we are here for you. We will globalize our safety and no pandemic can defeat us. Don't worry: we have more power to destroy the world than a tiny arrogant virus. Fear not, my flock, fear not. Your president is here for you. I just need a little bit more of power for a time of crisis and we will go back to normal. I promise you! What do you have to lose? The world is already in a mess that we didn't create. We can't be responsible for that. But now we are here for you. Trust us! There will be a glorious future for us, one that nobody has ever seen, I promise you.*

While this proclamation is enticing, and it feels like we have no choice but to follow its invitation or else to remain in our state of abandonment, we are again very confused. We tend toward our old ways of prayer. Perhaps it is at this juncture, the one where the old prayers don't work, that a possibility lies, our very resurrection. If we follow the Spirit of God who comes from the future to say, "Do not trust any government, but demand a new pathway to a new life." If we hear that prophetic voice that literally comes from the wind matching the breath within us, we cannot solve problems, but we can create patterns for different ways of creating and producing. We can transform behaviors and give conditions for life to continue where it exists, and new life to appear where it no longer is.

But how can we muster the energy to go after our enemies without fear? How do we conquer our fear of the enemy if the fear of death is a sting still infesting our hearts? Who will pray for our strength? We sit down and light a fire for the evening, for it is cold, very cold. The Brazilian Presbyterian liberation theologian Rubem Alves once said that religion is about lighting a fire to keep us warm. With the hope that it won't burn us, I would respond. Instead, may it just keep us warm, so that we find the strength to change what needs to be changed.

At night, the demons come out, fears run loose, and we are afraid of the creatures of night. We are alone and when somebody who can warm our hearts gets closer, in fear we pray: "Stay with us, because it is almost evening and the day is now nearly over" (Luke 24:29 NRSV). And in the midst of the warmth, something can always happen. That is the beautiful thing about our collectivity, the human spirit, the power of prayer, that there is always somebody who will pray, a collective of people who will lead the way towards life, even amidst those who push us towards death upon death.

Thank God there were the women: Mary Magdalene, Mary the mother of James, and Salome. They were consumed by the emptiness of their loss, but they did what they had to do: care for the body of the deceased. "On the first day of the week, at early dawn, they came to the tomb, taking the spices that they had prepared" (Luke 24:1 NRSV). They had prepared the spices for Jesus's body and off they went. What they did not know is that they would find an empty tomb and an angel saying something like "What prayers have you prayed?" Or "What are you looking for? Your precious Jesus is alive."

The women go back and tell everyone the good news of a new world, of a new prayer they had never heard. This prayer was announcing a world too glorious to believe; such news was too much happiness to bear. This is the way of our times right now. We are in the midst of death: who would believe that a new form of life is possible from a world drenched in death and dying? Who would believe that a new form of prayer could create a whole new world? Or that a whole new world would create a whole new prayer?

Perhaps this virus is Earth-sent, a prayer from God for us. God's angel might be telling us that we are destroying ourselves, that we are going beyond our limits, that we are upsetting the delicate balance that took millions of years to happen. The angel might be suggesting that we are not praying well. The angel is telling us that COVID-19 can be a new way into our future if we pay attention and change our ways. The angel is trying to tell us that COVID-19 is teaching us that we can live as a community in ways that stop the engine of death, productivity, and progress that drives us. Perhaps COVID-19 is also telling us that if we pay attention and care, a new way of being may be possible. If we have already destroyed our present, perhaps COVID-19 will teach us to save our future—by changing now. If we look at the earth on the cross, at our collective death, maybe we can find an opportunity of resurrection given to us. Prayers are still possible and needed. Even if we are still fully infected. Can we hear the prayer of the angel of life and death?

Easter Sunday

Sunday morning comes and Jesus appears to the disciples: first the women, then others. Later, Thomas, like most of us, doubts, but he is invited to touch the woundedness of Jesus. He is transformed. He has a new prayer in his heart. Now everyone is paying attention. The *unthought,* that which has not been thought before, has given way to new thinking, the dead have given way to life. Prayer can resurrect and create new worlds! With the Argentine singer Mercedes Sosa, we sing,

> So many times they killed me
>
> So many times I died
>
> However, I am here resurrecting
>
> Thanks I give to misfortune and to the hand with a dagger
>
> Because it didn't know how to properly kill me
>
> So many times they erased me
>
> So many disappeared
>
> To my own funeral I went alone and crying
>
> I tied a kerchief knot but forgot later
>
> That it wasn't time yet
>
> And I kept singing
>
> So many times they killed you
>
> So many more you will resurrect
>
> How many nights will you spend despairing
>
> And at the time of the shipwreck and at the time of darkness
>
> Someone will rescue you
>
> To go singing
>
> Singing to the sun like the cicada
>
> After a year underground
>
> As a survivor
>
> Who returns from the war.[9]

And yet, while we hold this belief because of the resurrection of Jesus, we cannot know for sure that we will resurrect if we continue to kill the earth the way we are doing. For we are killing ourselves. We cannot control anything, not even the resurrection, much less the resurrection of Jesus; but in these times the resurrection is not a given anymore, which means that we won't necessarily resurrect. Nonetheless, even if we don't resurrect, the earth and other forms of life will resurrect and continue!

We need to *desire to resurrect* and to work on it with all our strength and will so that this can be fulfilled. And every desire that is life-giving

---

9. Sosa, "Como la Cigarra." My translation.

demands that other desires die, the ones that have the most difficulty dying. If we desire resurrection, many other desires must die. The desire to have possessions, the desire to be happy by ourselves, to have a life fulfilled with personal properties. All of these desires must turn into a desire for a collective life including the earth. We have no possession, the earth is nobody's property, and desire for happiness is only possible if everyone else is included in this desire. Can we say a prayer in that form of mutual desires? Are we ready for the resurrection we truly need?

Thus, against many forms of Christian theologies, we need to work for our resurrection, and work hard. Grace alone won't work because it hasn't worked. Grace alone will work when there is deep work related to it and as a response to God's grace. If we do not restore destroyed lands, grace alone is nothing. If we do not protect biomes and wild life, grace alone is fluffy stuff. If we do not see animals and the natural world as fundamental to our living, God's grace is an aberration. We can only see grace afterwards, in our ways of living. As Jesus said, "You will know them by their fruits" (Matt 7:16 NRSV). We are called today to be transformers of our own ways of feeling, thinking, believing, being, calling forth the arrival of a new time when a new form of economy—*oikonomia*, the ordering of our (common) household—can be organized. Not with large corporations, but around communities. We will fight for collective land; we will make health insurance universal and will have a universal salary. We will not allow anyone to become extremely rich and we will all share our gifts.[10]

Moreover, like the women, we must believe the signs that God is giving us everywhere if we see one coming our way. Then we realize that the spices we prepared are not needed anymore. We need other spices: other forms of thinking and feeling and organizing, both with and against religion. When religion does not serve to change our ways of relating with the earth, it is not worth it; we must throw it out. Anything that is interior or personal or private, that does not come with a sense of belonging with the whole and our responsibilities to the earth, is not worth it. We can throw it out. If we hear the angel of life and resurrection, we will touch the woundedness of the earth and begin to heal our hurts and to restore the earth. Bruno Latour calls us to pray that we can become what he calls "interrupters of globalization,"[11] creating actions, gestures that can eliminate modes of being that are deadly to our present and our future.

---

10. See Tamez, *Scandalous Message of James*.
11. Latour, *Imaginar Gestos*.

Thus we will come to know that the earth in all its complexity and diversity is always a sacrament. If Jesus is not resurrecting in and through the earth, the seeds, the oceans, and the trees, is Jesus resurrecting anywhere?

How can we give the earth space and time to resurrect herself? How can the advent of COVID-19 help us to create new rituals that envision new forms of life in reciprocity with the earth? How can our rituals—in this case the ones of the holiest week of the Christian year, but our other religious rituals as well—give us awareness of our human condition in a more expansive way, in deep relationality with the earth? How can these rituals help us mend our destruction, restore what we have devastated, and help us repair our death-dealing desires?

Lastly, how can your church pray with those who are suffering, and with the earth itself?

How can we work toward understanding what the earth might be, and how can we honor it and act in right relation with it? If we want to start our work as resurrection people, we need to think and decide what we will do. As we finish this infected Holy Week, let us pause and pray-think about the inventory Bruno Latour gave us below. Since the new ways of the world are deeply related to the ways of our prayers, let us consider these questions in terms of our prayers during this time and how Holy Week can call us to an entire holy world and a entire holy year.

Latour asks us to think and pray about these questions, first individually, then collectively.

1. What currently suspended activities would you like *not* to return to normal?

2. Describe why each of these activities seems harmful, superfluous, senseless, or dangerous, and in what way its disappearance, suspension, or substitution would make other activities easier or more pertinent to our right relation with the earth and with each other.

3. Given the suspension of activities, what measures would you suggest to facilitate the transition to new activities that would have to be made by workers, employees, business owners? How can we as churches support those movements, helping the members of our churches to re-enter the society with measures of fairness and care especially for those hurting the most?

4. Which activities that are currently suspended would you like to see start over, grow, or even be totally recreated from zero? Examples: What about thinking life without police in your community? What about producing locally and supporting small farmers? On a larger

scale, what about agrarian reform? And no predatory fishing, lower consumption of meat, and limits to energy usage? What would all that mean locally and nationally?

5. Describe why this activity you chose seems positive to you and how it would make other activities that you prefer easier or more pertinent, and why it helps combat those you consider unfavorable.

What measures would you suggest to help workers, employees, business owners acquire the skills, means, and tools to restart, develop, or create this activity? How can these measures be related to churches, their members, their missions, and the communities around them? How can we think of new democracy without racism and with the earth and the waters, soil, animals and all species as fully part of our life together?

10

Praying with the Night

> En route to the floor of the ocean the diver first passes through the "belt of the fishes." This is a wide band of light reflected from the surface of the sea. From this area, he moves to a depth of water that cannot be penetrated by light above the surface. It is dark, foreboding and eerie. The diver's immediate reaction is apt to be one of fear and sometimes a sudden spasm of panic that soon passes. As he drops deeper and deeper into the abyss, slowly his eyes begin to pick up the luminous darkness; what was fear is relaxed and he moves into the lower region with confidence and peculiar vision.
>
> —HOWARD THURMAN[1]

HOWARD THURMAN SPEAKS OF "luminous darkness." This term is what guides me in this chapter, evoking the movement between and within light and darkness, as a dance that reveals and hides and asks us for new eyes and new visions. In order to see our luminous darkness, we must be like a diver who goes through layers of realities and perceptions that prepare us to venture into the next place, until we find our own abyss. It is only there, within our own abyss, that we are finally able to see our own luminous darkness. It is a journey that demands a conscious choice, an ever growing awareness of ourselves. Thurman follows the passage above with the words of the psalmist:

> If I say, Surely the darkness shall cover me
> Even the night shall be light about me . . .
> The darkness and the light are both alike to Thee.[2]

1. Thurman, *Luminous Darkness*, xvii–xviii.
2. Psalm 139:11–12.

Before the Introduction

It is hard to pray for the night to come. Perhaps many of us still fear the night, its mysterious, uncontrollable nature, and the parts of us living there that we do not know, cannot see, or cannot handle. In the night we can be lost, or we can find ourselves. In the night we can feel alone or learn that we live in a different kind of inhabited world, with other presences we just don't know yet. Once we approach the night without fear, we learn skills to live during the night, but also during the day. If we are not afraid of the night, we will be much less afraid of the day. As Psalm 91:5–6 says,

> You will not fear the terror of the night,
>> or the arrow that flies by day,
>> or the pestilence that stalks in darkness,
>> or the destruction that wastes at noonday.

We will not fear, because we learned the lesson as in verses 1 and 2 of the same psalm:

> You who live in the shelter of the Most High,
> Will say to the Lord, "My refuge and my fortress,
>> my God, in whom I trust."

The Most High is everywhere, abiding deep down in the earth and in the shadows beneath the earth. Night and day can be shelters or places of desolation, but wherever we might be, we have to find our trust within, in the light and darkness of the One who created the day and the night.

In our common imagery, the night has mostly been a time and a place that holds feelings of fear, vulnerability, anxiety, adversity, lack of control, and the approach of the end. I grew up fearing the night. At home, when my father went to bed and I could no longer see the light under the door, I was terribly scared. Or when I, a city boy, would go to the countryside and look at the trees in the dark, I felt at the doorstep of the unknown and of all of the monsters that lived there. Then I started to be afraid of becoming blind. Every time I felt this I came close to fainting. This essay is a way of understanding these persistent fears and talking to my soul and in so doing, to offer something to yours.

I am realizing that darkness is part of who I am and that it lives within my luminosity, just as my luminosity is dependent on my darkness. It is within this space of oneness and ambiguity that I am called to pray: to pray the night, to pray with the night.

I cannot remember when or where I read the sentence, "Everything I know about my light I learned from my darkness," but I know that it helped me to realize that the night was not my enemy. It offered me the perception of the night as a loving teacher, one living within me and with whom I could walk without wanting to run away. But how to understand that vast and deep darkness that is the night of the world? I began to understand when I heard Pedro Casaldáliga, my favorite theologian, say, "Only by living the dark night of the poor is it possible to live God's day. The stars can only be seen at night."[3]

If the wrestling of the poor and the cry of the earth do not visit me day and night, I cannot hear the sounds of the night or understand the light of the day. Through the conflicts of my soul and the struggles of the poor, I have a sense of a circularity that abandons the *telos* of Christologies and of the Christian faith. I do not approach an end; I live in the full circularity of the now. If the now is lived in fullness, the future of that now is already here and the past of that now is fully re-lived. Past, present, and future are ubications of the same life happening fully at this very place and time, right here and now, with the whole earth breathing here with me.

Introduction

The notion of darkness is a very rich one and I hope it can help us think about our lives and ministries.[4] I am using "darkness" in a very broad sense and with both its negative and its positive aspects. Darkness is both a real and an imaginary place. Darkness lives outside and inside me without duality. Darkness is part of the extreme violence in the world today, violence perpetrated by humans towards ourselves, towards other humans, towards animals and other living creatures, towards the earth. Darkness is the end of life on Earth. But darkness is also our luminosity, a light that penetrates the deepest places to create joy and freedom. Darkness is the beginning of life on Earth. Darkness is all the thick places we inhabit.

Listen with me to words about darkness. Achille Mbembe describes darkness as frighteningly beautiful:

> The darkness of the night—an opaque mask, yet so penetrable—imbued me, every time, with an indescribable fear with its legion of fireflies which were repeatedly said to germinate in each one a ghost, with its dismal chants of rusty flavor, salty from the corruptions of witchcraft, that kind of stoning, of perverse and

---

3. Casaldáliga, "Na minha idade."
4. This chapter was originally created to be spoken to a group of pastors.

immeasurable exhaustion that resisted the wreckage of the day and the ages of the world, with the skull of the caves.[5]

The poet Luis Rosales puts it confidently:

> We will go by night, when the shadow
>
> of the whole earth comes together,
>
> by night, when the road
>
> smells of rosemary and sedge,
>
> we will go by night, by night,
>
> we will go without moon, without moon,
>
> for in order to find the fountain
>
> only our thirst can light the way.[6]

Chet Raymo, in his work *The Soul of the Night*, relates the night to the wilderness:

> There is a tendency for us to flee from the wild silence and the wild dark, to pack up our gods and hunker down behind city walls, to turn the gods into idols, to kowtow before them and approach their precincts only in the official robes of office. And when we are in the temples, then who will hear the voice crying in the wilderness? Who will hear the reed shaken by the wind?[7]

Hear the way the biblical prophet sees no distinction in God, who is light and darkness:

> I will give you the treasures of darkness and riches hidden in secret places, so that you may know that it is I, the LORD, the God of Israel, who call you by your name. (Isa 45:3 NRSV)

And how Mary inhabits the night as a hidden treasure from God:

> And Mary answered and said, "I will teach you about what is hidden from you."[8]

There is no light that can save us from the night. We try so hard: we have lights on everywhere, trying to hide the darkness of the world and ourselves. But the winter solstice always comes back to remind us of who

---

5. Mbembe, *Sair da Grande Noite*, 33.
6. Rosales, *Antología*, 283.
7. Raymo, cited in Taylor, *Learning to Walk in the Dark*, loc. 1, Kindle.
8. Gospel of Mary 5:7, in King, *Gospel of Mary of Magdala*, 15.

we are. Darkness we are. The glorious darkness. Clark Strand, a Buddhist author and teacher, writes:

> In the modern world, petroleum may drive our engines but our consciousness is driven by light. And what it drives us to is excess, in every imaginable form.
>
> Beginning in the late 19th century, the availability of cheap, effective lighting extended the range of waking human consciousness, effectively adding more hours onto the day—for work, for entertainment, for discovery, for consumption; for every activity except sleep, that nightly act of renunciation. Darkness was the only power that has ever put the human agenda on hold.
>
> Advances in science, industry, medicine and nearly every other area of human enterprise resulted from the influx of light. . . .
>
> The only casualty was darkness, a thing of seemingly little value. But that was only because we had forgotten what darkness was for. In times past people took to their beds at nightfall, but not merely to sleep. They touched one another, told stories and, with so much night to work with, woke in the middle of it to a darkness so luxurious it teased visions from the mind and divine visitations that helped to guide their course through life. Now that deeper darkness has turned against us. The hour of the wolf we call it—that predatory insomnia that makes billions for big pharma. It was once the hour of God.[9]

That fear of the night has birthed many metaphors, so real and vivid that they visit our days and our nights. The transatlantic Western colonial formulations of race and the blackening of people as different, lower, and fearsome still control our minds, our daily lives, and politics today. It is what makes us create redlining, control the electoral process, build jails, cross the street when we see a Black person in front of us, ban people from Muslim countries, build walls against brown people from the South, and put pipelines in the sacred territories of Indigenous people. This kind of darkness shows us who we are in the world. What should be called light, we name darkness:

> The darkness of a world without jails where all Black people are free.
>
> The darkness of a world without borders.
>
> The darkness of a world in motion with people who do not look like us.

9. Strand, "Bring On the Dark."

> The darkness of a world without Christianity as its epicenter.
>
> The darkness of a God without full and endless light.
>
> The darkness of a life without the safety of the only light (and shadow) of what we know.

How then do we engage darkness as a precious gift of life and the darkness that comes to us as fear and terror, so that we embrace darkness and understand it?

My thought here is that by embracing a wealth of possibilities within the notion of darkness, we can also find language to deal with the darkness of ourselves, the darkness of God, and the darkness of the world. The life abundant that Jesus promises to us has both light and darkness in it. The light of God can only be manifested where there is darkness; without darkness there is no light. We are creatures of the night and of the day and we must learn to have a positive sense of darkness. Then we will be able to speak, preach, care, listen, and offer solidarity to others based on the luminous darkness of ourselves within the darkness and light of the world.

The Darkness of Others

La Noche

For many in the Latinx community, *la noche* involves a particular set of values and understandings. When someone says *buenas noches*, they are saying both hello and good-bye. The ability to say *buenas noches* as both arrival and departure can propitiate movements and strategies of survival.

The night, for the Latinx community, is a place to hide and shift identities. A place to resist, to move away, beyond borders, away from the scrutiny of power and surveillance. Night is a tricky place where everything is malleable and can move according to the needs of the present. *La noche* is both a dangerous place where we can be destroyed and an ally where we escape control and devise ways to survive and strategies for life to continue. As María DeGuzmán says,

> I would point out that transhistorical, transcultural elements such as night, shadows, masks, and veils carry a particular historical and cultural charge at a particular time in the history of any given culture, where culture is understood not as a closed circuit but as permeated by other cultures.[10]

---

10. DeGuzmán, *Buenas Noches, American Culture*, loc. 22, Kindle.

La noche is a decolonial space: a place to be what we are, openly or disguised, a place for tricksters to appear, the *coyote*[11] to disguise himself and others, and the waters to carry those who are crossing to the other side. Still, the colonial powers always threaten the decolonial forms of disguise and knowledge. The *coyotes* can be coopted by a system of violence and brutality. When we do not know the night and the waters we are crossing, we can be killed. The night is risky. *La noche* carries the possibilities of political movements and aesthetic practices, ones that challenge the oppressive conditions of existence and the limits of art and survival.

Illustration of this aesthetico-political practice is the mention of night in Cuban-American author Cristina García's novel *A Handbook to Luck*:

> Under cover of night, the character Marta Claros flees the civil war in El Salvador and her abusive husband, who works on the firing squad killing rebels for the U.S.-backed military government: Marta had never seen a sky this dark. There was no moon, and the stars seemed to hide in the Black folds of midnight. The silence was so complete that Marta feared life itself had withdrawn from these parts. At any moment she might cross the border from one world to the next, imperceptibly, like death. The coyote said that a night like this was good cover, that the yanquis' fiercest lights couldn't penetrate it.[12]

The night for the Latinx community is the inhabitation of the other *Americanos*, the ones below the borders. Since the fullness of America is only given to "certain" Americans, the living of the American identity is parsed by the government, pondered, negotiated, strategized, and only given to those who can get citizenship, or be worthy of such a form of humanity.

The permanent fabricated crisis at the borders between the US and Mexico has several purposes. The borders fuel the militarization as a state policy, it creates investment for private profit, and through its power dynamics it defines what this country is, defining its own identity over against the shady people on the other side.

The present "crisis" at the southern borders enhances the inhabitation of the night: darkness is a path to *el Norte* where *coyotes* are luminaries of the night. Under the cover of night, Central and Latin Americans are no more than the shadow of the real Americans who carry the might of modernity stamped on the flag of the United States. US American identity casts a thick shadow on foreign status, on immigrants, on "others." Along with Blacks,

---

11. A *coyote* is a person who smuggles migrants, usually over the Mexican border.

12. García, *Handbook to Luck*, quoted in DeGuzmán, *Buenas Noches, American Culture*, 1.

Indigenous, and Muslims, people from Central and South American countries are thus dangerous since they threaten the very existence of our light.

In the militarization of the borders, the lights of civility are cast over the shadows of uncivility of those beyond the wall, as if a humanity full of light must carry its own shadows in order to keep its light intact. No wonder the border patrols put immigrants in cages. Immigrants are indeed viewed as animals who crawl in the night. Border patrols with all-terrain vehicles, surveillance cameras, drones, helicopters, are all weapons of light to capture those who sneak in from the night. The money spent on border surveillance is a way of keeping the notion of US identity afloat. The enemy is the very condition of possibility for US identity.

Even now our ancestors who lived in this land for ages are cast into the shadow of the light of the Empire. Because of the "enlightened" project of the Empire, Latinx people have had to learn the secrets and tricks of the night in order to survive. They have had to learn to represent themselves in many ways, and resist the darkness of jail. The night is filled with beasts, spirits, and creatures that we do not know and cannot control. The night is a threat, and its creatures can possess since we are not ready to negotiate with or expel them properly. There is no constancy, no patterns, no full knowledge during the night. No invocation of justice, of honor, of humanity is enough to change the status of immigrants as not fully human. Instead, every appeal for security measures, every announcement of walls being built, ends up creating new forms of oppression, bias, violence, and death. At night, as well as during the day, immigrants have to live in unruly territories.

Again, what we do not realize is that the shadow we cast becomes our own light and we end up living under that shadow we project, which in turn dims the very light we were hoping to shine. We only see deepening of the darkness we were hoping to cast away. Worse, we become creatures not of the night with its fullness but creatures of shadows that are deeper than the shadows of the light we have cast. We become the frightening darkness we have been trying to avoid.

We cannot control the night, just as those who inhabit the night cannot control the spirits of the night. This spirit-filled environment of the night has been a rich source for the magical realism of Latin American literature, *lo real maravilloso*, a term coined by Alejo Carpentier.[13] Magical realism is the imagination of the night run free during the day. The unconscious and the conscious live together as a way of finding life in its fullness.

---

13. Carpentier, *De lo real maravilloso americano*.

They Will Be Coming for Us That Night

For African Americans, the night has long been a place of resistance and danger. It was during the night that people who were enslaved planned their escape. They forged paths and constructed maps (often sung) through waters with the help of signs in the skies, with hidden signs, strategies, and forms of survival and re-existence.

Paths and forests and waters of the Underground Railroad, bushes, homes, churches, became places of escape, windows into dreams and transformations. The night was the place where a future of freedom was planned with persistence, strength, sweat, and blood, in which a new world was created. But the struggle of African Americans for fullness of life is far from ended. Prisons have taken the place of slavery. They are a place imagined by night, hidden from the public's awareness, and placed into the budget of governments that create a school-to-prison pipeline to lock up the poor, especially African Americans. Prison is the en-light-ened panopticon to keep watch on those who belong to the night.[14] It is clear that the necropolitics of the US government want to keep African Americans in the shadows of society or the darkness of night in the prison system, without any chance of coming back to society. Prisons are the perpetuation of the night for people who are not allowed to live in the light of the day.

On November 19, 1970, after the philosopher and activist Angela Davis's arrest, early in her eighteen-month incarceration, the writer James Baldwin wrote to her in "An Open Letter to My Sister, Miss Angela Davis":

> Dear Sister:
> One might have hoped that, by this hour, the very sight of chains on Black flesh, or the very sight of chains, would be so intolerable a sight for the American people, and so unbearable a memory, that they would themselves spontaneously rise up and strike off the manacles. But, no, they appear to glory in their chains; now, more than ever, they appear to measure their safety in chains and corpses.
>
> The enormous revolution in Black consciousness which has occurred in your generation, my dear sister, means the beginning or the end of America. Some of us, white and Black, know how great a price has already been paid to bring into existence a new consciousness, a new people, an unprecedented nation. If we know, and do nothing, we are worse than the murderers hired in our name.

---

14. See Alexander, *The New Jim Crow*.

If we know, then we must fight for your life as though it were our own—which it is—and render impassable with our bodies the corridor to the gas chamber. For, if they take you in the morning, they will be coming for us that night. Therefore: peace,

Brother James[15]

Dreaming and Living in the Night: Our Luminous Darkness

The Algerian-French writer Albert Camus wrote a short story, "The Adulterous Woman,"[16] in which Janine, a married woman who is full of life and passion, is frustrated by the existence she leads with a husband who does not notice her passion and vitality. One night, while they are traveling, she leaves Marcel in a hotel room and while he sleeps, she goes out into the night. It is at night that Janine feels her full self, filled with excitement and desires and a sense of freedom she had never felt before. As she goes deeper into the night, she goes deeper into this experience with her body, heart, and soul and is enthralled by the immensity of this time. At the end, she lies down on her back and sees that the stars are all looking at her. The night becomes a place of freedom, of becoming who Janine felt she could fully be, a time in which she found the space of liberation that the daytime never allowed her to have. Janine's experience is the experience of so many whose lives are frustrated, incomplete, unnoticed, and not fully lived.

It is also at night that people with "unruly" sexualities can find a certain kind of fullness, away from the gaze of hatred and prejudice of those who cannot deal with the freedom of persons who dare to challenge the social norms and to be who they fully are. At night, alone, pastors can be their full selves, with all their imperfections and limitations. At night, serious people can become clowns and play. At night, we enter into an expansive fluidity, a queerness of the Spirit, and ponder the fullness of life. At night, we can also find the time we all need for rest and renewal.

At night, we have visions and witness apparitions. There is strangeness. The walls that separate reality and fiction erode, and we enter into places and realities we cannot control, with fictions that are more real than the real. Specters of other forms of rationality decompose our knowledges and notions of self. We find a part of ourselves that we are drawn to, fearful of: Madness! We see what we do not like or want. We are taken without permission to places we must visit.

15. Baldwin, "Open Letter to My Sister."
16. Camus, *Exile and the Kingdom*, 3–26.

The night is filled with dreams and nightmares. In our dreams we are told of the past and the future and of a present presented to us in codes, images, sequences that we cannot create when we are conscious. At night, our unconscious shows us what we are made of and to what we are really paying attention without realizing or knowing it.

Davi Kopenawa, an Indigenous Yanomami shaman in the Amazon, says that we white people—and by "white people" he means all of us who are not Indigenous—are so full of ourselves that we cannot think of nature as being a part of us, or of ourselves as belonging to the earth. He says that our lungs are filled with smoke because we cannot see much beyond ourselves. He adds, "Whites do not dream far like we do. They sleep a lot, but they only dream about themselves."[17]

The earth is so far removed from our conscious and unconscious realities, so far from what truly matters to us, that trees and seeds, fish and waters, mountains and meadows are never a part of our humanity. Only now, haunted by a terrifying virus, might we be visited by dreams of ghostly creatures devouring our world. We cannot deal with the darkness of our world because we cannot deal with the darkness of our own lives. We, creatures of the light and darkness, are turning everything into darkness, destabilizing the balance and movement between light and darkness.

Religions have always dwelled on light and darkness. Many religions have night prayers. Hinduism has the Hour of God, where meditation or yoga has to be done before sunrise. The Buddha's enlightenment is said to have occurred between 2:00 and 4:00 a.m. In Islam, the Hour of God is called *Tahajjud*, the "Night Prayer." Some forms of Judaism have the *Tikkun Chatzot*, the "Midnight Repair."[18] Christianity has Jesus praying to God in the middle of the night in the Garden of Gethsemane and the night prayer of monastic communities.

The night hours are the prime time for many forms of awakening and for an enhanced ability to see. To pray with the night is to find the courage to venture into darkness unknown so that we can find the luminosity of our darkness, the darkness of the world and the darkness of ourselves. The world has created too many lights to distract us from the night, the night of ourselves and the nights of others who are suffering.

Marc Ellis speaks of the ways the prophet wrestles with light in a way that gives us a sense of the complexity of the relation between light and darkness:

---

17. Kopenawa, *Ends of the World*, locs. 2112–16, Kindle.
18. Strand, *Waking Up to the Dark*, loc. 15, Kindle.

> The deeper grasp, that entry into history, the ability to see suffering and hope, to gather light in the darkness. To hold it all together. This is the prophet's task . . . Gathering light . . . In the darkness. Not from it. Not to announce light, which is too easy. Just seeing glimpses. Witnessing to the possibility of light. Horizon light.[19]

It is this deep wrestling with the light and darkness that makes the individual and collective prophet's light shine. If we are faithful to our abyss in fullness and like the prophet who "refuses to be an abyss voyeur," we might be able to find this luminous darkness.[20]

We Christians

I wonder how many Christians have learned to enter into the night or have walked deeply in the night. Our spirituality as Christians has not helped us to deal with either darkness or the night. Of the world. Of ourselves. We hide, we run, we cover, we become oblivious. Some of us might refer to John of the Cross and the dark night of the soul,[21] but very few of us can linger intentionally in the darkness.

Liturgically we have Lent: we delve into darkness with the somber ritual reminding us that we come from ashes and that to ashes we shall return. I always wonder how these forty days of shadows and darkness are lived by some Christian churches. The most I hear from people is about refraining from eating chocolate or drinking Diet Coke. I wonder about the practices of fasting, walks into the night, drawing near the darkness.

We seem to go from Ash Wednesday to Easter Sunday too quickly, not plunging more deeply into the Triduum itself. We do not go deeply into the night of Holy Saturday; we do not take much time to stop and be still. We move too quickly to the lights of Easter.

We do not pay much attention to the winter solstice, the longest night of the year. Instead, we cannot wait to light the next candle of Advent, anticipating the light of Christ who makes all darkness disappear. As for Christmas, we have cleansed the story from all of its darkness and messiness. We do not talk much about the dark night of Mary and Joseph. They were on their own, refugees away from home and without solace. They held fears of childbirth without any help or support. We do not talk about the lack of a place for them to stay or the smelly manger in which they finally stopped for

---

19. Ellis, *Finding Our Voice*, 17.
20. Ellis, *Finding Our Voice*, 23.
21. John of the Cross, *Dark Night of the Soul*.

shelter. We do not comment much on the story that when Jesus was born, he was surrounded by animals, the first to greet him, the first to love him. We do not dwell on the fearsome, lonely nights Mary and Joseph and Jesus lived. We make it all romantic, filled with lights. We rob the precious darkness from the story because we cannot bear to live without light.

Some Christian monks and nuns pray the Night Office, a regular prayer in the deep hours of the night. A monk writes of this prayer:

> There is a freshness of spirit, an emptiness of mind, a depth of heart, which we don't have during the day. The structure of the Night Office: singing the Psalms, listening to the readings, praying in silence, allows one to remain a long time recollected without any notable effort and to continue the "prayer of the heart." The Night Office always began after midnight and lasts for about two hours. This was incomparably the best time for being with God.[22]

Perhaps we need a God of darkness as much as a God of light. Unless we are able to venture into the darkness of the world, of ourselves and in the darkness of forests, we will never be able to see to the luminous darkness of our soul, of the earth, and of God. Without this thick darkness in the heart of life we are disconnected from nature and ourselves.

Until we move from thinking that darkness must be something to get rid of and move away from and not something to which and in which we belong, our sermons will have too much superficial lights and very little truth. A Buddhist friend said to me: "I am tired of Christians, especially Protestants, who want to be a lamp on the hill all the time. They are so entrenched in their own light that they can't listen to their own darkness and the darkness of the world."

We come from darkness and to darkness we shall return. We need to rediscover that while we are alive. Part of the work in our spiritual journey must be to disassociate darkness from sin, from ignorance, from hell, from fear, from pain and suffering. It must also be to disconnect darkness from Black people, brown people, LGBTQIA folks, Indigenous people, and foreigners. Christians need to gain a renewed understanding of darkness as part of their spirituality. Our connection to God is there to be discovered.

Unless we give ourselves to the darkness, we will never be able to deal with a world without borders. Without the darkness of the unknown, we cannot reach the safety of what we imagine we know. Without the darkness within, we will never see the light. Without the darkness of God, we cannot see the light of Jesus.

---

22. Strand, *Waking Up to the Dark*, 15.

My Own Darkness

The Christian faith has a great darkness running beneath it. In both the Jewish and the Christian faiths, we view the earth starting in darkness and light coming out of darkness only afterwards. The story of the birth of Jesus is filled with darkness. Jesus's time in the desert is filled with darkness. His ministry is filled with darkness. He goes into deep darkness at the end of his life. Without darkness we cannot understand this faith. That is why I had such a hard time understanding faith in years past. I was caught into a binary where God's light was the necessary denial of darkness.

I grew up afraid of anything that took life out of order. The absurd, that which we cannot explain, took possession of me and I started to live under the fear of all forms of the absurd: going blind, becoming quadriplegic, getting a chronic illness, losing a loved one, traveling, doing something wrong, saying something out of order, making a mistake, doing something unforgivable, getting locked in an airplane or an elevator. I lived through a soundtrack of fears until I realized that I could not hide my sunshine from my own darkness. It was and has been a long journey to learn about my fears and why they are there and to begin speaking to them until they disappear, until the one who fears inside of me does not fear anymore.

When I turned fifty, this long work on myself started to bear fruit. After years of therapy and prayer and meditation, looking deep inside, I started to learn more about myself. Becoming a father made me realize that unless I know myself, I cannot know my children. As I write this, my son has begun to ask me what would happen if he became deaf or blind. This reminded me of my eight-year-old self asking this same question but with nobody to answer it. I finally could respond to my own self as a little boy by responding to my son. I asked him how he would feel about it and he said he would be really sad. I agreed with him and said that yes, it could be very frightening. I added that we have to find a way to keep going, right? Later I showed him videos about Hellen Keller and how she was able to live her life fully as a person who was blind and deaf. My son said, "She had such bad luck!" and I replied, "This is life too." The fullness of life (John 10:10) is not only the good things but about everything we call life. Everything is a part of it, the good, the bad and everything between these too. There are ways to find gratitude in everything. Our darkness can be our light!

Our light has to be able to see the lights of other religious traditions, of other people and allow oneself to be enlightened by other lights and other forms of light. The Christian light we carry is not the only light in the world.[23] The light of Jesus shines upon spaces for us to see other forms

---

23. See chapter 7 in this book, "Praying with the People of Axé: An Interreligious Dialogue."

of light, life, resistance, and awareness. And the best way to learn how to deal with our darkness and our light is to learn from people who have lived under the shadow of death into the longest night.

Cornel West says that in the face of adversity, Black folks respond with style, smile, freedom, compassion, courage, and laughter.[24] To respond to catastrophic histories and events and to the darkness of the world, we have to delve into our luminous darkness, where we have the style, freedom, and potency that keep us all going through the night.

---

24. West, interview on *The Laura Flanders Show*, June 9, 2015, https://www.youtube.com/watch?v=nHsHhj329T4.

11

Praying with a Lost Heart

A Decolonial Prayer

Dear God, G*, Goddess

Querida/o/x Deus/Deusa,

Estimadx Dios,

    I call on you not knowing how to call you. I don't know in the grips of what principality I am when I say your name. When I pronounce your name, am I under the wings of your love or the paws of something evil? Who am I speaking with when I address you as my God? And hear, O God, I mean not you but those who are actually with me when I utter your name. Whose project am I a part of when I offer myself to you? How can I escape the spirit of the world, especially a nationalistic world, when I speak to you? How can I make the *you* I say not become my property or part of my compulsions and consumptions? How do I say your name by losing myself in the fullness of my own dis-appropriation?[1]

    I would rather start my prayer by speaking somebody else's words, appropriating the voice of a precious Vietnamese sister and the words with which she (does not) pray(s):

> Somewhere in the process the flowers wither and the whole world smells of open wounds. The peculiar odor of fire powder, dust and dirt, concrete and steel; the very odor of blood, carbolic acid, decaying insides and burnt carnality has been trapped for some time in the air, but only the child in me—a child of the war—notices it. The wounded adult-me weeps at the sight of wreckage, loudly deplores the tragedies, vocally condemns the abuses, then visually gets inoculated with the constant replay on screen of serialized

---

1. "A veces le llamo S/N (sin nombre), a veces dios-cómplice, a veces nada. Como a menudo lo he explicado, pienso que cada cual tiene derecho a inventar su propio dios y a diseñar su propia gnosis." Pániker, *Adiós a casi todo*, locs. 32–34, Kindle.

destruction. And, when the shock has faded, finds it quasi natural to move about band-aided with an invisible muffler. The dis-ease goes on unacknowledged. The toxic spill effect, felt but largely unseen, is slowly laying waste in the overexposed cities—these immense man-made wildernesses where its inhabitants caught in between walls of metal, zinc or concrete have little access to the light innerscape of blood flowers.

Again, the heart meanders for no one knows why. Sudan, Tiber, Iraq, Afghanistan, Palestine, Rwanda, Congo, Burma, and . . . and . . . and, with the recurring specters of Bosnia, Kosovo, South Africa, Cambodia, Vietnam. What is it that makes both talks and silences stained with shame? Everyone readily comes up with an answer and everyone is eager to fill in the blanks. But once raised, the question never fails to fold back, returning to just where one thinks one last knows. Rising like the murmurs of an underground river, it persists in infinite whisperings, striking randomly when it is least expected. Could it be the sound? The places in sight? The lie, the fear, the excess, or, *that shadow of a frail body in flight*? Sometimes the mind freezes and the heart goes on fasting: name, nation, identity, citizenship disappear. *Once I was a human.*[2]

My sister helps me name my inability to speak after seeing so many human cruelties and unnamable disasters. For when I present myself to you in prayer, I am ashamed of what we have become, a form of human species that has been able to build wonderful things but in this process of creation has destroyed everything. I am now speaking to you from the end of what we call life, at the edge of our common living, at the dusk of our civilizations. I come to you not knowing how to answer you in the places where my brothers and sisters are. Do you see that miserable child drinking dirty water from the city grounds? That is where my sisters and brothers are, O God. My problem in praying to you is that I don't know how to tell you why they are there, with their frail bodies, at the end of their ability to hold on.

So I call your name from an "offshore call center," a center outside of the real centers of life, under those who own these centers and crush us. I call you from a non-place, a stance of vulnerability, where my voice is blurred with the voices of millions of people whose death is necessary so others can live. I call from a non-place where human beings are called "human resources." I am sorry: in these places people speak with accents. I pray that you understand my prayer even if I don't understand myself.

---

2. Minh-ha, *Lovecidal*, 1, italics original.

I am calling on you from one of the non-places that function as subsidiaries of the modern thinking of Europe, the worldview of the United States, and the growing control by China. From a temporary non-place where my voice sounds nasal, underdeveloped, unfinished, using very slow speed internet. It's not drugs, God. And yet, it is hard not to live under any kind of drugs, prescribed or not, to keep up with our times. O God, how you have changed through the years! How did you make it here?

I remember when, in my naiveté, I thought the objectivity of my thinking was my salvation. I could reach the skies of proper academic work and be counted among the intellectuals! That eventually got me a very nice job, which I still have. But now, I realize, these forms of objectivity were another trap of the profit motive orienting all forms of education these days. May I still believe that I have some agency in this? Do my own people have agency here? My delusional and triumphalist academic work is what preserves me. Have I become trapped in the rationalization of the European enlightenment that tells me, "Either Greek-Western thinking or barbarism!"?

I am holding myself back from telling you about all of the deaths and oppression that are stored in my visual memory, but I don't want to bother you with the obvious. I confess that I can only pray like Walter Benjamin, who saw the angel of history, looking back and seeing all the debris of tragedies piling up in human history, death and graves and demolitions. All that the angel of history tells us is that more afflictions are coming—the past clearly shows it. Instead of finding something new, something that will help us re-create the world accordingly, we are going to encounter again the historical demons we did not face in the past.

God of all disasters, how do we learn to move towards the future without assurances of transformation, and with the certainty that unfathomable disasters are coming our way? Can your presence enable us to travel within dangerous memories of the past so that our future can be more than the self-enclosed destinies of our doomed rhetoric of progress and naïve hope? From this call center, serving the big centers of theology, I pray that I see and feel the *angelus novus* alive in me, *doing me* every morning and folding its wings every night if possible, illuminating both our past and future, as to reorder our present in new worlds of possibilities for this earth, for all of us. From this call center I cry to you, O God. I pray that I can see beyond the pillage of bodies everywhere; I pray that I can listen to sounds beyond the sounds of bullets and of deathly silence; I pray that I can smell the scent of flowers and the forests beyond the strong acid, dry smell of the earth burning for our consumption; I pray that I can drink and swim in the waters of rivers and the sea while we still have water to drink and ocean life is still there; I pray that I can hear somebody else pray to you, other than you, not

You; I pray that I can touch the bodies of my grandchildren with the lightness of an open, viable future; I pray that I can taste the salty waters of my tears turning into honeydew in the mouth of all those who will come after me.

But God, I confess it is so hard. Again, I call your name from the assholes of the Americas, the shitty places to which nobody pays attention, the call centers of broken-bodied, broken-hearted, and broken-spirited people. Those who are the damned, doubly disfigured people, those who try to self-renovate and self-disguise through resistance and assimilation so as to keep going with their lives hanging by a thread.[3] Disfiguring and being disfigured, time and again, Indigenous, Blacks, women, children, queer people, Palestinians, poor people. They are mine and I am theirs, even when the very *us* embedded in *theirs* is so difficult to describe, even when we are pitted against each other for the sake of sacred wars, capitalist consumerism, and political conquest. May I never forget the only thing I may know: we share the same humus/humanness, the same stardust that composes us, the same glory, the same earth, the same wind, the same wonder.

I call you from the centers of power about the offshore center calls, to talk to you about *decolonialidad*. That word is bullshit as is everything else, but perhaps it is a necessary one, which contains the hopes of disentangling our vocabulary, our prayer grammar, our imperial forms of knowledge and other forms of knowing, so that we can birth old and new ways of living and being and praying.

From these call centers I call on you, O God! They are places of faith that render your name so frail. When we speak your name from these places we are thrown into ambiguities. And for both yes and no and maybe, I pray to you, O God, O my soul, you who are the source of creativity, renewal, feistiness, and fetishism. As I pray, I name you, my God, but a God only conceived in terms of a collectivity, as long as collectivity means deliverance and liberation. A God so much mine that you can only belong to others. Like your/my/our people, I can only pray to you in the plural, the plural of myself in them, and their polydoxy in me. For I can only count myself in the many, possessed that I am by the many winds of your Spirit, by the many living and nonliving creatures that I am woven with, and braided through the ancestries of the world and all the forms of lives of the earth. It is under this consciousness of this maddening "garment of mutuality" that I keep myself sane—my madness being one that can only be tamed by the plurality of people and the many spirits in me. So I pray,

---

3. Chow, *Not like a Native Speaker*, 8.

O God, that no one ever casts away all the people who live in me. Without them I am silenced, I am extinguished.

These call centers are from the *cú do mundo*, which is filled with discardable people, those whose skin cannot bear worth, whose souls have no value, those who have been vanished from the centers of power, those displaced and kept at a distance from the actual places where the services take place, those who now live in the shadows of our illuminated misery. These call centers are also sites where the earth calls your name groaning in pain. Can you hear them?

Can you see the recent new turnings of the world, O God of the disenfranchised? A new blood-shed turn that unites nationalism, militarism, right-wing religion, fascism, extractivism, and patriarchy is threatening to endanger us even more. They are pressing into the ongoing fragility of our systems of self-sustenance: depression, isolation, fears, violence, alienation, addiction, panic, all countless forms of instability.

One of the formal expressions of this conservatism, fascist white supremacy, capitalism, and right-wing religion is the work of political theorist Yoram Hazony, who has proclaimed the new forms of "national community" and identities in which he refreshes the old moral loyalty to nation, family, and property into more expanded ways of gluing the constitution of a nation to the structures of the self.[4]

O God, I hear the same things from your professed servant, the neofascist president of Brazil, Jair Messias Bolsonaro, who wants the patriarchal ruling elites to continue to sustain the upper hand over minorities who need to assimilate or be excluded. The ruling "nations" are the ones who set aside and control the offshore centers of power and exploitation. They are scavengers of natural and human resources, depleting their means until exhaustion and then throwing them away. They are but patriarchal fascist movements after the use of law for their own fulfillment and the destruction of the women and children.

O God, have you created us wired to capitalism so we can only understand and live in consumeristic ways? Is our brain malleable so we can adapt to our own destruction? Or is it the global capitalism that shapes our brain in ways that we cannot escape? Is the plasticity of our brain a form of

---

4. Hazony is a proponent of a form of free state where "a majority nation whose cultural dominance is plain and unquestioned, and against which resistance appears to be futile. Such a majority nation is strong enough not to fear challenges from national minorities, and so is able to grant them rights and liberties without damaging the internal integrity of the state. For the most part, they therefore assimilate themselves into the system of expectations established by the constitutional and religious culture of the majority nation, learning its language and resorting to violence only on rare occasions." Hazony, *Virtue of Nationalism*, 165.

adaptation to the systems or is it flexibility that makes us submit to forms of power?[5] I pray that our prayer practices can help us live in the Spirit of plasticity so we can engage situations by saying NO to forms of capitalism that destroy or prevent life in all forms.

But God of all and no disciplines, my vocation is also my malady. My professional advancement depends on parochialism and self-regard. The weakness being the impossibility to have a conversation outside of the field of liturgy where other forms of knowledge must always turn back to the God-given liturgical knowledges, assurances, and assessments. Prayers in books and altars away from the people. Our universal prayers praise you, but do nothing for the real situations of real people. I wonder about our speaking out of both sides of our mouths when we say our prayers: on one side we say our litany of confessions about the things we do and should not do, but on the other side of our lips we silence the litanies of injustices churches keep speaking because of neoliberal capitalism.

Forgive me, God, for my wariness, but it is becoming increasingly more difficult to defend you. Or to defend you as I defend myself? Or to indict you as I also indict my own field? I don't know so I come to you. God of all the answers, help me here with some questions I have. Are you on the side of the good guys or the bad guys? My conundrum is this: I teach liturgy, and I am supposed to teach the history, acts, gestures, thoughts, and modes of being a Christian by way of the doings of the liturgy, something fundamental in every religion. I wonder whether what I am teaching is nothing more than a nuanced source of reinforced coloniality, just another tool in the master's toolbox.[6] Am I fair to you when I say that a lot of the history of the church is filled with the smell of putrefied bodies killed and destroyed by your church in your name? Am I too harsh if I say that the church in Latin America was mostly a racist, capitalist, white supremacist catalyst for greed, arrogance, and defilement, or that the white Christian churches in the US are really nothing but a tale of the slavocrat, patriarchal, capitalistic elite? I confess, for you already know it, my questions are forms of answers which are so difficult to move away from without moving away from You, the you I thought was always so near.

If I am not making you mad or bothering you too much, I also want to press a little more and ask about worship books. Can we still use them? People say that our prayer books have the wisdom of the past and that they can give us a trajectory of your movements in history. They say it is wonderful to continue to pray the same prayers your people have prayed

---

5. Malabou, *What Should We Do with Our Brain?*
6. Lorde, *The Master's Tools Will Never Dismantle the Master's House.*

for ages. They say these books come close to what the early church did. But let me confess this to you, O God from whom nothing is hidden. I have my suspicions. That those books only carry the wisdom of some people especially from the *Norte*, and we are supposed to repeat them like parrots as the universal Christian religion. And worse: that we can only be authentic, valid Christians, if we can recite the books and do exactly what the books tell us to do. Thus, the formula of my teaching, in order to have my students pass the exams of their churches, is "Be the best parrots you can be; if you can believe in it, even better!" When I teach, I must acquire enough knowledge so I can continue speaking in your hallowed name. With all of that, I wonder, am I confessing the unholy expectation of the church, the necessary duplicity of my students' religious tasks or my own complicity and lack of courage? For all of that I beg for forgiveness.

Can the denominational books of prayers offer anything good? Or are they pretty much psychological ways of organizing and comforting the souls of bodies drenched in capitalism? Are they prayers that do not do much beyond smoothing the path of class struggle? On the other hand, there are these new "cool" churches that avoid the liturgical books and are bound to the efficacy of their faith, making prayers an instrumentalization of the capitalistic society as they rush to become a sub-product of the neoliberal economic environment of our time. They pray mighty prayers, extemporaneously, and promise promises to enhance the empire of the individual, while destroying the ecosystems and basic commonalities. They are very different in their collective and individual approach to you and to life, but they are exactly the same in their leanings towards capitalism.

I wonder: Where is the best place to pray to you? In churches where people bow down to patriarchal priests with pointy hats, in liberal Protestant churches that keep the same patriarchal structures, or in new churches with horrendous "cool" liturgies and racist pastors? How do we Christians unlearn the prayer of greed and undo the desire for social ascension? How do we foster a society that leads us not into the temptation of full monetary indebtedness and emptiness?

I wonder: When did the Christian faith become a high commodity, one shaped by colonialism, and fully lived in the gospel proclaimed by suburban churches and lower-class theologies of prosperity? When was it that we got so detached from the earth and incarnated a new trinity described by Eduardo Viveiros de Castro as "State the Father, Market the Son, and Reason/Science the Holy Spirit"?[7] This trinitarian structure holds together the totality of the self that owns everything. As my friend Ken

---

7. Viveiros de Castro, "A revolução faz o bom tempo."

Sawyer, with whom I pray all the time, rightly said, "Self the Father, Self the Son, and Self the Holy Spirit."[8]

The offshore prayer call places I am imagining calling to you from are filled with people whose lives are meaningless to many Self-trinitarian Christians whose only concern is to properly own their own lives.

I once heard that the devil is not your opposite, O God, but your twisted self, the one who sneaks in and does the evil work in us without our perceiving its presence. I wonder why we were never clever enough to see the work of the devil turning Christianity into a major driving force of colonialism and capitalism, with Protestantism in a major alliance with the Market. Why, since the time of Jesus, have very few Christians been angry with the money-changers of our day, the merchants and the business people? I assume that you might still be angry at these people, but what do you do when they own the church? Are you still part of this business-entrepreneurial organization called church? Or have you been pushed out by your business partners, downsized or outsourced, no longer essential to the business model? Aren't you frustrated that your announced kin(g)dom of God has become this institution we call church? But surely there are some parts of this church that look like you: it was because of the church that I got where I am now, so I have seen real love happening.

Professor James Cone once told me over lunch that the church is a very small thing everywhere. From his experience with the institutional church in the US, he told me, "It is very hard to find the church, but it exists!"

You know too well, God, that since Constantine we have sold our soul to the powers that be. We have swum in the fullness of patriarchy and we still do. We became an empire and we continue to be. Your name has been spoken mostly in vain since that time with exceptions when your name truly matters for "the least of these." And then, O God, since the Reformation, Christianity has been fundamental to the very structure of expansion through colonization. Christianity became a modern Western enterprise, an apparatus for the conquering machine of the West. During colonization, patriarchy kissed whiteness, fucked non-European people, and gave birth to colonialism and all its racist murderous siblings. God have mercy on us, for the (we the) devil won this battle!

Since the Reformation we have learned to read the Bible differently. And we learned from our Reformed leaders that a little bit of usury was not that bad, that crushing peasants was necessary in order to obey the Princes and continue to be the church. Under your banner, the church was

---

8. Ken Sawyer, Professor of Church History, in reading and praying this text with me.

sanctified with power and money and used the people as resources for its wealth. By allying the Bible with the middle classes, it served the elite. The Reformation churches lost sight of the poor and forgot about your plans of justice and preference for the poor. We Christians mirrored the Hebrew covenant between you and Abraham with a covenantal love with conquering Emperors! The Protestant churches became like the Catholics they had rebuked. With the holy Crusades, we destroyed every enemy on the way, especially the Jews, who—we believed—had clearly betrayed us! The new covenant expanded, and Protestant churches jumped on the wave of capitalism, helping the system to be organized, appeased, controlled and appreciated. Churches boomed everywhere, missions went overseas, colonization took over the world, and Christian white supremacy flourished! It made sense to say, "God is good all the time!"

Please receive my litany of laments, O God.

I lament that Calvin was in favor of a little usury.

I lament that Luther supported the crushing of the peasants and bashed the Jews.

I lament that Christians provided capitalism with great theological thinking and normalized capitalism's actions.

I lament that early capitalism borrowed the doctrine of Providence and the invisible hand of God to organize the understanding of the Market[9] that controlled everything.

I lament that Adam Smith's *Wealth of Nations*[10] used the notion of your invisible hand as the invisible hand that organizes and controls the market.

I lament that the capitalist system learned to work on a profoundly faulty aspect of the human soul.

I lament that what was supposed to be the means of grace and love turned into the crushing of sinners, including the Jews and peasants in Europe.

I lament that the doctrine of the total corruption or depravity helped to establish rules of monetary transactions.

I lament the perverse thinking of Christians who saw us in such horrendous ways, even though we are both *homo demens* (delusional beings) and *homo ludens* (playful beings).

I lament the ways in which the economic imagination used the delusional part of ourselves and the use of sin, moral limitation, and human

---

9. Throughout this chapter and the book, I use the notion of the financialized market in two ways: Market (capitalized) as almost a divine institution, and market (lowercase) as a human creation that can be dismantled.

10. Smith, *Wealth of Nations*.

brokenness as the conditions for capitalism to build its whole ground where the renting system lends money to people knowing that many of them will never be able to repay it.

I lament that the economic covenant is now made in the hope of profit and destruction.

I lament that human "sin" became the place where economic greed meets human limitations, the crux of our own self-destruction, where human perversion becomes the axis that organizes the ways we live.

I lament that many of us have lost our sense of awareness and enlightenment and are turning our species against its own self.

I lament that the Reformation inaugurated a covenant between the Christian faith and the new emerging market and its political powers. This covenant lasted for a long time. I lament that the construction of the liberal market coincided with the growth of Protestant churches. These churches never condemned the economic market, but instead, replicated the model of the market into their own structures.

I lament that the unquenchable desire of God became the ceaseless desire of desiring desire for things.

I lament that even to this day, Protestant churches mirror the market: a vast majority of small and medium churches are disappearing and a few big, rich churches are thriving; a few pastors are paid like CEOs, while the majority of pastors are struggling to make ends meet; the size of endowments is more important than the size of student debt; rich donors are honored more than people working in places being dismantled by state abandonment and violence. As I lament, we don't deny, O God, that there has always been a faithful relationship between the Christian faith and the middle and upper classes in the United States, but we can no longer deny that the poor have been completely silenced and excluded from public conversation.

But God, everything comes to an end, and this very satisfactory covenant didn't last. With the structure of the market going from liberal to neoliberal, capitalism broke its covenant with the Protestant and Catholic churches and affiliated itself with neo-Pentecostal churches. We never thought that capitalism would break this sacred covenant, but it did. Now many Christian churches, seminaries, and other institutions are at a loss because they don't know how to survive. We have learned to trust wholeheartedly in the Market and not in you, and now our faith keeps fluctuating with the market. Any Christian institution in the First World today depends fundamentally on budget, not necessarily on faith. There is no Christianity without budgets.

As we have had plenty of opportunities to see in history, O God, capitalism as an autophagic system orients and adapts itself according to the most pressing opportunities. Once capitalism saw it didn't need the official church anymore, that they didn't have the importance in the culture that Christianity and Christians used to have, it started calling individual pastors to do the dirty job of teaching people to bow down to God by way of aligning themselves with corrupt systems with the promise that, if they teach their people that everything is only a matter of inner faith and that whatever they desire can be satisfied, they would be rewarded. In liberal capitalism, pastors are running out of jobs and churches closing, while denominations are still carrying loads of old money. Surely, they are still a part of the system and it doesn't seem they will break with it. Liberal capitalism fosters an alliance between liberal theologies and Protestant churches.

The new theological need of the neoliberal market is to organize itself around other forms of theology and the Prosperity Gospel, where You are the richest king ever. It seems to be a great deal. Besides the eternal rehashing of old toothless liberal theologies, the neoliberal economic system matches new Prosperity Gospel churches in powerful ways. Among the chief differences, Prosperity Gospel churches will bring in the money and make their own budget with the enrichment of pastors while Protestant church pastors will have a specific salary, cash flow, and budget to keep and possibly an endowment to secure. While Protestant churches do not need to talk about desires because its members have the basics for life: house, car, school for their children, and health care, Prosperity Gospel churches must speak of desires and consumerism openly, aiming at going up in the social chain and, depending on people's social location, acquiring a first or second or third car. While Protestant churches have members and have to keep up old buildings, Prosperity Gospel churches don't have members and are always building newer and bigger buildings, which are signs of their faith to God.

The victims of the historical forms of capitalism and the current neoliberal system who are now in offshore praying places have to cope with the precarization of their own lives, the necro-politics of nation-states, the increasing vulnerability of their lives, and a faith that engulfs them even back into this system of domination.

O God, we could go on, but you know what happened to us! The cross of Jesus Christ was turned from a symbol of violence and humiliation into candies—strawberry lollipops sold in Christian stores, attesting to the lucrative financial marketing potential for US Christians. In a nutshell, we Christians were able to entangle faith, money, whiteness, patriarchy, heterosexism, and classism, and intertwine it all in many forms of perpetual racism. Nonetheless, the financial gain was quite good. We were able to build religious empires made of money where Jesus Christ is used as its major patron. Just in the US, religion is worth $1.2 trillion a year.[11] A triumph for sure! I am just not sure if the triumph is yours, O God, or whether it is ours and/or the Devil's. This is the face of the Christian gospel and I wonder how you feel about it.

That is why, God of the poor, my mind and my heart wonder about those Christians who remain faithful, those of whom James Cone said are the real church of Jesus Christ, those who persist and hold on to the prophetic voice of Jesus and continue to resist oppression and death here and there, the ones who carry a faith that is fully lived in precarious places around the globe, in poverty-stricken situations, in offshore call centers where people keep on calling your name.

Now, O God, my voice trembles and drifts away, my self is divided and broken, not knowing how to organize myself in the face of so many conflicts and contradictions. But if you, O God, stay with me and have mercy on me and the changes of the tonalities of my voice, I will say this to you as if, and only as if, I am telling it to the world.

There is coloniality everywhere in my faith. How do I give an account of the "coloniality of power"[12] through the intricacies of many grammars of faith and forms of living faithfully, O God? How does Christian religious formation through songs, prayers, sermons, worship spaces, stories, and theologies hold onto cosmologies and forms of living that can both liberate and oppress people? I wonder about how every one of my senses, filled with coloniality, prevents me from fully saying your name. Whose name am I saying when I say your name? Am I saying the name of the one who destroyed my people and stole their land? Are you, O God, really good all the time?

In addition to inhabiting my vocabulary and my grammar, coloniality holds sway even over my sense of home. Where do I belong? How can I be less divided while living in such radically different worlds within the Americas? Surely I need to learn to be less Brazilian in the US and less of the US in Brazil. "Why do you do that?" is a constant question I have to answer, and I always freeze when this angry question is thrown at me, in both interpersonal and institutional cases, often with threats to me of proper consequences for my behavior. My immigrant experiences are filled with contradictions. When I think "correctly," I make my way around here, even as I am reminded that I am from somewhere else. When I go to Brazil, my own people remind me that I haven't been there for a while and

---

11. "U.S. Religion Is Worth $1.2T/Year."
12. Quijano, "Coloniality of Power."

I now belong elsewhere. Then I remember a reflection by our brother Luis N. Rivera-Pagán and add it to my prayer:

> Diaspora entails dislocation, displacement, but also a painful and complex process of forging new strategies to articulate cultural differences and identifications. In the Western cosmopolis, with its heterogeneous and frequently conflicting ethnocultural minorities that belie the mythical e pluribus unum, the émigré exists in ambivalent tension.[13]

God, my prayer doesn't have a ground. My dislocation is lodged in my soul and manifests itself in the awkward movements of my body and the overshowing of my emotions. Dislodged from a mythical place of fullness, my dislocation cannot be compared to the displacement of those who are truly scattered around the world today: those displaced by war, running away from threats, living in refugee camps, trying to hang in there with those who pray in the misplaced, forgotten offshore call centers of our world. Where are you for these people, my God of love?

These offshore call centers are purposefully created in order to be hidden and forgotten. The call centers offer artificial care to the affluent within the sterile world of finances and extort every single penny from middle-class people who want to survive or, better, to get the deals that will help them climb the social ladder.[14] These offshore call centers are also accompanied by porous borders and are places of heavy militarization, turning immigrants into "illegal," "sick," and "dangerous" "terrorists." God, did you see the caravans of migrants from Central America? Where do they belong? Their countries are filled with violence and when they come to the US, mothers, *tíos*, and *niños* are threatened with military weapons. O God, where do immigrants belong? Do they belong to you? If "belong" means "to be with," as a character in Coetzee's *Slow Man* observes, immigrants do not belong anywhere because the "I" of the immigrant is always detached from the "we": "I am not the we of anyone."[15]

---

13. Rivera-Pagán, "Towards a Decolonial Theology," 47.

14. See Martin Scorsese's movie *The Wolf of Wall Street*.

15. "I had three doses of the immigrant experience, not just one, so it imprinted itself quite deeply. First when I was uprooted as a child and brought to Australia; then when I declared my independence and returned to France; then when I gave up on France and came back to Australia. 'Is this where I belong?' I asked with each move. 'Is this my true home?' 'You went back to France—I forgot about that. One day you must tell me more about that period of your life. But what is the answer to your question? Is this your true home?' She waves a hand in a gesture that encompasses not just the room in which they are sitting but also the city and, beyond that, the hills and mountains and deserts of the continent. He shrugs. 'I have always found it a very English concept,

As we move around, sometimes we find the *we* of our *I*. It happened to me when I was saved by a friend who said that we belong to the *shalom* of God. Whatever that means, it provided me with an *oikos*, a home, a household, a place. It also happened when I found the nest of my wife and children. And it happens in my daily walk, with what I learned from the Buddhist monk Thich Nhat Hanh, who invites to pray with each step:

> I have arrived. I am home.
>
> In the here. In the now.
>
> I am solid. I am free.
>
> In the ultimate I dwell.[16]

All of these welcoming occasions happened to me because I was given an official document. I am legal, God of all documents. Because I am a man, because I pass as a white guy, and mostly for not speaking in some places, I was accepted as a citizen. And now I wonder: How do I learn to belong to God's *shalom* in the midst of my undocumented people? How do I get rid of the fear that my adoptive children will be ashamed of my broken English and thick accent, or that I might eventually embarrass them just for being brown in the US? How can I learn to always arrive at each step without confusion and separation? Or without speaking your name in vain?

O God, I need your help, for I still feel that coloniality is at the heart of my prayer. Just as it owns my vocabulary, coloniality defines how I pray and behave, controlling my knees and my neck, its dirty hands on my jugular in case I move too much. Where do I go to find you, my God? Prayer books are both a source of peace and—mostly—utter foreignness. The hymn that I learned in my first years at my family's Presbyterian church and that I still sing gives me peace through its foreign ways. The author was a British man named Sabine Baring-Gould and the title of the hymn is "Now the Day is Over."[17]

---

home. Hearth and home, say the English. To them, home is the place where the fire burns in the hearth, where you come to warm yourself. The one place where you will not be left out in the cold. No, I am not warm here.' He waves a hand in a gesture that imitates hers, parodies it. 'I seem to be cold wherever I go. Is that not what you said of me: You cold man?' The woman is silent. 'Among the French, as you know, there is no home. Among the French to be at home is to be among ourselves, among our kind. I am not at home in France. Transparently not. I am not the we of anyone." Coetzee, *Slow Man*, locs. 179–80, Kindle.

16. Nhat Hanh, *Breathe, You Are Alive*, 114.

17. Sabine Baring-Gould, "Now the Day Is Over" (1865):

> Now the day is over, night is drawing nigh,

The hymn says so much to me, is so much a part of me, is so much a radical otherness in me, through such an unspoken acculturation/assimilation/liberation. If, as Augustine has taught us, singing is praying twice, does that mean that when I am singing my colonizer's song I am being doubly colonized? Doubly defaced? Doubly deceived? Does that mean that the healing power of this song in my heart and the sense of protection I always felt when I sang it were doubly wrong? Was it improper for me to sing it when Christianity was the language of those who taught me more than songs and prayers but morals and ways of living, even as they stole everything from my people?

How can I even say that, when the church gave me everything I have and took me away from poverty? Should I get rid of these hymns and find a new song? What is in fact my own song? If this hymn is not mine, what song is? What makes something mine and what makes something a[n] [mis]appropriation? How much is "colonial Latino Christendom"[18] the holder of power elsewhere? How do we fight this? How do I learn what is mere parroting of somebody else's power and create and generate narratives of liberation and transformation for my own people, even if the narrative comes from outside and it is mixed with the narratives of my own people? What are we to do with worship books and Indigenous practices? Can I call Bob Marley's "Redemption Song" my theme song when I am not Jamaican or Rastafarian? Help us, O God, to understand that there is no pure culture or essentialized race: help us to understand that isolation of groups from each other and notions of race without expansive mutualities and diverse bodies are exactly what kills us. May Bob Marley become my elder and my guide so I can sing his song.

As I move towards finishing this prayer, I must say that in spite of speaking too much here, I have been tempted to go into aphasia. Especially when I hear about the endless destruction of Black people, Indigenous people, the poor, and the earth. Especially when I think that the gospel of

---

Shadows of the evening steal across the sky.
Jesus, give the weary calm and sweet repose;
With Thy tend'rest blessing may our eyelids close.
Grant to little children visions bright of Thee;
Guard the sailors tossing on the deep blue sea.
Comfort ev'ry suff'rer watching late in pain;
Those who plan some evil from their sin restrain.
When the morning wakens, then may I arise
Pure, and fresh, and sinless in Thy holy eyes.

18. Dussel, "Epistemological Decolonization," 33.

Jesus is about love, no harm, caring, and honor. But love is nowhere to be found. Then "love" becomes the code for domination, for nationalism, for oppression. I love you so much that I must turn you into something like me, or else kill you for the sake of the world. Love decoded is read "coloniality." So much love in our world is in service to false gods!

Unless love is embodied in material gestures of transformation and acts of liberation, we are only using it for dominance. Unless love is the awareness of the killing of people and the destruction of the earth, love is nothing more than a tool in the master's tool box. As our brother Ignacio Ellacuría so vividly said, "Those who make themselves deaf and blind, because they think that [the open wound of injustice and suffering] is not a religious problem, these are the lukewarm that God, disgusted, has already vomited out of his mouth."[19]

Everything is stolen and appropriated by this colonial love. Even our dreams are colonized, O God. Our unconscious has been taken over by centuries of oppression, and the loss of our dreams is tantamount to our current natural and social disaster. The extent of our disaster is the size of the destruction of the earth. We cannot think or feel anything else than our own desires and entitlement. We cannot hear the earth groaning. We cannot adjust our lives to the limits and pace of the earth. We cannot let the earth orient our rhythms. Development and progress are never to be challenged. Even our sense of humanity is now deeply attached to our ability to develop and progress. If we do not always produce something that results in progress or efficiency, we are not living up to our full potential. The result is that we become more detached from the earth, eating poisonous food and becoming sick, anxious, and depressed.

God, in these times of increasing instability and insecurity, we cannot root our spirituality in you if your name entails a separation between heaven and Earth, a dualism between transcendence and immanence. We must start listening to the voices of Earth by listening to those who listen to the earth. Sylvia Marcos tells us of a movement of Mesoamerican women presenting a mutuality of relations, complementarities, and intersectionalities as fundamental to Indigenous forms of spiritualities. She writes,

> As Comandanta Esther insisted in her address to the Mexican Congress, complementarity embraces everything in nature. She explained that earth is life, is nature, and we are all part of it. This simple phrase expresses the interconnectedness of all beings in the Mesoamerican cosmos. Beings are not separable from one another. This principle engenders a very particular

---

19. Ellacuría, *Escritos teológicos*, 135. My translation.

form of human collectivity with little tendency to individuation. This sense of connectedness has been found consistently within contemporary indigenous medical systems and also in the first historical primary sources. The "I" cannot be abstracted from its surroundings. There is a permanent transit between the inside and the outside. . . . The international indigenous movements . . . acknowledge the damage that diverse colonialisms have done to their worldviews and have begun to echo one another concerning the value of recovering their own spiritualities and cosmologies.[20]

How can we make the *I* become a *we*, O God? Our *we* is much too entranced by our own selves and our own noises. We do not listen to the birds, we cannot hear the water, we do not pause to hear the sounds of the earth. The coloniality of white academic scholarship has deemed thinking and breathing with the earth a weaker form of scholarship.

God of our lives, help us, the *we*, perform other than our known forms of prayers. Prayers and performances that haunt the site of the oppressor. May these offshore call centers be a double sign of vengeance: vengeance by the poor, who will sooner or later invade the boundaries of gentrified white supremacist zip codes; vengeance by the earth, which will get rid of us at the right time. Surely these call centers will be changed so as to pray and to pronounce your name. The faithful ones from everywhere among the poor will remind us of the possibility of the gospel of Jesus Christ!

I feel the Spirit nudging me for a good word here before I end my prayer. I am reminded of Howard Thurman's wisdom: "Don't ask yourself what the world needs. Ask yourself what makes you come alive and then go do that. Because what the world needs is people who have come alive."[21] I am also reminded of the wisdom that admonishes us to plant trees we will never see but under whose shade our grandchildren will rest.

May this prayer, O God, help us engage with the Memory of Fire as remembered by our brother Eduardo Galeano, who prayed: "I believe in memory not as a place of arrival, but as point of departure—a catapult throwing you into present times, allowing you to imagine the future instead of accepting it."[22]

I am sorry I spoke so much. Forgive me, O God, for being so diffuse, for not addressing just one thing wholeheartedly, for letting my mind follow the wanderings of my heart, for the heaviness of my inconsistencies. If I

---

20. Marcos, "Mesoamerican Women's Indigenous Spirituality," 85.
21. Thurman, cited in Bailie, *Violence Unveiled*, xv.
22. Galeano, *Memory of Fire Trilogy*, locs. 1379–80, Kindle.

pray, it is because I hope this prayer can be received by you and encompassed within the multitude of your mercy. Merciful One, I beg for mercy! I pray trusting the words of Scripture:

> Likewise the Spirit helps us in our weakness; for we do not know how to pray as we ought, but that very Spirit intercedes with sighs too deep for words. And God, who searches the heart, knows what is the mind of the Spirit, because the Spirit intercedes for the saints according to the will of God. (Rom 8:26–27 NRSV)

In the name of the *we*-refugee-undocumented-immigrant-lynched Jesus Christ, whose life was killed by state-sanctified violence for all of the call centers of this world, I pray.

12

Praying with the End of the World

> It may be that when we no longer know what to do we have come to our real work and that when we no longer know which way to go we have begun our real journey. The mind that is not baffled is not employed. The impeded stream is the one that sings.
>
> —Wendell Berry[1]

In order to pray with people from the ends of the world, we must learn how to pray *with the end of the world*, which means witnessing closely with those whose worlds have ended so many times. Praying with the end of the world means learning to be prepared for the worst while building as best we can for another world that will come after this one has ended. Thus, to pray means *to put soul into consciousness*, as we saw earlier,[2] and to be aware of the worlds that are ending, offering compassion and presence to those who are dying, while we form, illuminate, and point to forms of resurrection within these dying worlds—in order that, perhaps, a new world can emerge.

For this to happen we must listen and learn with Indigenous peoples, whose worlds have ended so many times through colonial settlers' campaigns of genocide and theft of their lands. We must listen and learn with Black people, whose worlds have ended so many times through slavery, apartheid, and prisons. When Breonna Taylor, George Floyd, Ahmaud Arbery, and João Pedro Matos Pinto were killed, Black and Indigenous worlds collapsed one more time. We must learn with Brown people, whose worlds have ended so many times thanks to NAFTA, the continuous vicious colonization of Central and Latin America, the building of walls, and the deportation and abuse of undocumented immigrants. With our own children

---

1. Berry, *Standing by Words*, loc. 104, Kindle.
2. See the introduction and the reference to Guimarães Rosa.

in cages, our world has ended once again. We must learn with Palestinians, who suffer ceaseless ethnic cleansing and bloodshed at the hands of the state of Israel. Every time Palestinians are required to show proof of identity to enter their own land, their world ends. We must learn with the Dalits of India, whose inhumane treatment is beyond the pale. Every time a Dalit has to use bare hands to clean a latrine, their world ends.

To pray with the end of the world is to learn about these worlds, the forms of colonial power that crushed them, and why those worlds succumbed to those powers. But to pray with the end of the world is also to know how these particular worlds have survived, why they are still here, and what gives them the strength and stubbornness to continue living. It is to understand how these worlds' structures of life, their beliefs, their spiritual and religious forms of resistance and re-existence have continued, and why their people continue to sing and gesture into being new forms of life.

Our historical moment is a time of death and possible resurrection. Due to ecological devastation, it seems everyone is arriving at the end of the world. Scientists have been telling us we don't have much time to change, and that we must transform our ways of living. Yet, we do not seem to hear those warnings. Our entire world is being consumed by our desires, and we are literally killing ourselves. Our demands for food and consumer goods burn forests, deplete oceans, and extinguish many forms of life. We have severed every single form of relationship with the earth: emotional, cosmological, spiritual, social, cultural. Our bodies live as if disconnected from the earth, untouched, unhinged. It is the same with our homes, our churches, and our spiritualities. Our confusion is such that we have allowed fears of all kinds to seize our hearts. Our religions do not allow for much connection with the earth, and even God's presence throughout the earth seems rarified or regulated under a minimal potency of glory. We are out of touch with ourselves, with what we know, and with what we don't know. We are unable to know or say what we desire, but our demands blind us to what we ought to know. Our world cannot sustain these forms of human madness. Brazilian philosopher Déborah Danowski says that there is no longer enough Earth for the whole world.[3]

We are living under multiple forms of climate disaster negationism, a form of denial that has historical consequences. Danowski traces the development of the term *négationnisme*: "Since 1987, [it] has been used in this way by French historian Henry Rousso, to denounce Holocaust revisionists, who said that there had been no extermination camps, that there had been

---

3. Danowski, "Não tem mais mundo." My translation.

no genocide of Jews, etc."[4] Danowski also reminds us that the French term *négationnisme* is translated into English as

> denial, negation. One meaning is to deny, to negate; another is to be in denial, to be in negation, not wanting to believe, which can be understood, briefly, as the psychic mechanism necessary to prevent the subject from further suffering—and psychoanalysis has taught us that there are many pathological forms of this refusal of reality, of the twisting of reality.[5]

Negationism or denial of the climate calamity happens in at least three ways. One form of negationism is the honestly held belief that all this talk about climate change is a hoax, fake news, a leftist excuse to control politics, a communist invention—so we'll just keep living as usual.

Another form of negationism is the phenomenon of powerful politicians and corporations manufacturing and paying for studies and publicity presenting climate change as a hoax, when they know very well the sorts of disasters that loom on the horizon. In *Dónde aterrizar* (Where to Land), Bruno Latour describes how global elites have engendered processes of denial and geopolitical and economic changes through their patterns of ownership, theft, and abuse of the earth.[6] This small global elite is aware of the disasters it is imposing on us all, and of how it is fostering the end of the world. Its members have abandoned the people and no longer even pretend they want to construct a healthy society for all. To put it simply, they lie, and they don't care. Instead, they build underground bunkers for survival[7] and plan on relocating to Mars and creating other forms of life there.[8] However, for every action there is a reaction; a single movement creates a ripple effect. Our violent lifestyles lead in turn to the earth's reacting with increasing violence. As Latour writes, "The reaction of some implies the reaction of others; both react to a reaction, much more radical, which is that of Earth, which has stopped fending off the blows and returns them with more and more

---

4. Danowski, "Não tem mais mundo."

5. Danowski, "Não tem mais mundo."

6. In chapter 5 of *Donde aterrizar*, Latour writes, "If until the 1990s modernization could be associated with progress, emancipation, wealth, comfort, luxury and, above all, rationality, the ferocity of deregulation, the explosion of inequalities and the abandonment of solidarity, on the other hand, have made modernization an arbitrary decision made in favor of a few. The best of worlds became the worst." Latour, *Dónde aterrizar*, loc. 286, Kindle.

7. See Osnos, "Doomsday Prep for the Super-Rich," and O'Connell, "Why Silicon Valley Billionaires Are Prepping."

8. Wall, "Billionaires Wanted to Fund Private Mars Colony."

violence."[9] Our current situation does not bode well for a future open to our children, much less our grandchildren.

Finally, we see a third form of negationism in the ways in which people like us—families, churches, intellectuals, and the academy—all seem to agree in different ways that climate disasters are indeed coming, but cannot muster a reaction, change their lifestyles, increase their awareness, and engage in forceful action that would demand politicians and government enact meaningful change.

There are three reasons for this final type of negationism: first, the belief that God will intervene and fix everything; second, the conviction that somebody will eventually find a way out, and we will be fine in the end; and third, that since we don't know what to do, we can't deal with this horrid news, and we stop listening to it. In one of my courses on climate disasters, a student sent me an email after the first class, saying "Professor, I can't deal with this . . . it is way too overwhelming and I get anxious and depressed, I am sorry, I cannot take this class." We experience this emotion because we feel disconnected and alone. If we learn to live and pray in solidarity, we will know that our strength is never our individual strength alone, but the potency of many gatherings assembled together from many places and wisdoms. We cannot live in this world of billions of humans feeling alone and disconnected. We must engage in the work of prayer and solidarity. As Paulo Freire says, "Solidarity requires that one enter into the situation of those with whom one is solidary; it is a radical posture. . . . True solidarity with the oppressed means fighting at their side to transform the objective reality which has made them these 'beings for another.'"[10]

Prayer is a way of answering this denial, avoiding hiding, and being honest: honest about our own destructiveness, honest about our fears, and honest about God and what God means to us. Once we are honest about our condition, prayers can be gestures that keep forms of solidarities alive, preventing us from losing our own humanity, our connection, our ability to wonder, to sing, to pursue justice, and to help us build threads of life that are common to us all. Thus, if we do not pray in the manner of being for one another, we will not be able to go on.

We have been marked by pedagogies of cruelty,[11] which teach us to normalize forms of death and violence in our societies. These pedagogies try to displace solidarity and compassion and impose upon us a sense of powerlessness and indifference. These forms of violence are making us all

---

9. Latour, *Dónde aterrizar*, 293.
10. Freire, *Pedagogy of the Oppressed* (Penguin, 1996), 31.
11. Carvalhaes, "Pedagogies of Cruelty."

sick: human societies, animal societies, the waters, and the earth. When the earth gets sick, we get sick, too. We are living at a time in which we are losing our worlds. COVID-19 took away our world, white supremacy steals worlds from people of color, and now our collective future has been taken away thanks to ecological destruction. Under these circumstances, prayer can be an antidote to denial and negation, anxiety and depression—and it can also lead to the creation of a new world, in line with what we have read on street walls around the world during the pandemic: A different end of the world is possible. Perhaps our prayers can begin with the poet Aimé Césaire's question:

> What can I do?
> I must begin.
> Begin what?
> The only thing in the world worth beginning:
> The End of the World, no less.[12]

How can we begin with the end of the world at hand? By not running away. Not by giving up, but by giving in to the end of the world. Perhaps the prayer "Come, Holy Spirit" can provide a model of this time. When we are afraid, we tend to recoil into our own cocoon, hoping something will happen to change the situation. We lower our expectations and wait for happiness to show up at some point. To go after a new world is too much work, we think. However, it is incumbent upon us to help initiate this new world with a sense of shared responsibility, where everyone is deeply implicated in the present situation. Prayer can help us gain the strength to join the struggle, to join a growing awareness that can be expanded even more when religious solidarities, social coalitions, and alliances of many kinds of places and organizations engage in bringing forth and creating forces to demand the end of this world. This process entails going deep into our colonized history and facing up to our individual despairs and anxieties. Vincent Lloyd, a professor of theology and religious studies and director of Africana studies at Villanova University, writes,

> Demanding the end of the world implies that interlocking systems of domination (anti-Blackness, patriarchy, capitalism, settler colonialism) have captured the world. It also makes a claim of faith: The world is never fully captured by domination. There is always a remainder. Because domination has infected our language and our perception, we cannot point to that remainder

---

12. Césaire, *Return to My Native Land*, 60.

and name it. But in song, poetry, dance, protest, and prayer we can conjure it now, and we can project it into the future, visioning a world without domination, after the world's end. New life awaits after the end of the world.[13]

Demanding, reminding, perceiving, and visioning are ways of awakening to a new world, a world that undoes the one we know and builds a new one that is coming. Today forms of power and oppression are being shaken, and they will be undone. A new time is opening up to us. New *charismata* are populating the earth. We are in the midst of a crisis, living into a time of in-betweenness where the old has not left us, yet the new has not yet fully arrived. Political philosopher Antonio Gramsci explains powerfully why, for example, the rise of fascism is a symptom of these old forms of power approaching their end: "This crisis consists precisely in the fact that the old is dying and the new cannot be born; in this interregnum a great variety of morbid symptoms appear.[14]

In this in-betweenness, we must pray with an awareness of this change and gain a little clarity about how to pray that the old leave us and the new arrive. We must learn how to cast out the monsters of this time while we still have time. So we begin in between the end of this world and the aftermath of this world's end by avoiding hope. We do not need to sugarcoat our situation with promises of a better life, as if everything will be all right in the end. Indulging in such palliatives will only delay our process of renewal. However, we have to know that before it starts to get better, it will get worse. We don't need a gospel that offers a pill to numb us against the pain of the world and anesthetize our feelings, transforming them into illusions that will only lead to our own demise. Hope is a response to fear. It often builds on dependence, and it can easily be used by those in power. Thus, instead of hope, we require courage and desire! Courage to face this time of monsters, and desire to create and foster new worlds after the end of our current world.

Brazilian psychoanalyst Christian Ingo Lenz Dunker tells us more about hope and our desire:

> Hope is the effect of desire, not its cause. Retire the conversation around optimism or pessimism and leave it to moralists and coaches. Instead, let us reconstruct happiness by reconciling ourselves with the fact that desire cannot be conditioned to anything, for at this very moment, the fog of guilt and the shadows of fear will clear and we will discover, in this darkest hour, that it is only here that we recognize who, after all, we can count

---

13. Lloyd, "The End of the World."
14. Gramsci, *Prison Notebooks*, 276.

on. No one would need to give reasons for us to get involved in our desire.... For this reason, desire also operates better in a state of productive and uncompromising solitude than in a turbulent mass. When we realize that we have given up our most precious dreams in exchange for empty words, or the illusion of easy and inconsequential happiness, there is at least one benefit. We understand that happiness is costly, and that losing it is like losing freedom.[15]

This way of understanding desire can establish a home through the work of prayer. Saint Augustine said that in prayer we desire the happiness that God can give us. "When the Apostle tells us: Pray without ceasing (1 Thess 5:16), he means this: Desire unceasingly that life of happiness which is nothing if not eternal, and ask it of him alone who is able to give it."[16] Our task here is to turn from the idea of eternal life as a thing of the future, and work from the knowledge that eternal life is right now, that we are fully loved in the present. Not for the fulfilment of oneself or self-infatuation, but rather, fully present *with* the whole earth as we listen to each other in care and gratitude. We then place the future of eternal life in God's hands, but the eternal life of here and now is ours to build by the grace of God, fully build here in our present: fully alive, fully eternal with God in desiring life in fullness for the earth and all its inhabitants.

Prayer and meditation will then desire into being the forces that will enable relationship between humans and non-humans, between the earth and the universes. Desiring this deep connection with the earth, we will become who we already are: the air we breathe, the soil we stand on, the wind who guides us, and the fire that both extinguishes what needs to vanish and gives us warmth to keep us alive. Prayers then will be about desires opening up practices that restore our collective life, both within ourselves and with the earth, wherever we live. Prayers and meditations will be exercises of mutual desire to sustain and support life everywhere, to dwell with those living at the end of the world, to fight each other's fights, sustain our collective wisdom, empower ourselves within our own struggles, and change our forms of knowledge and faith. Prayers and meditations will act as interventions, forms of bridging the knowledges of local populations to stand firm against the universality of any religion.

Prayers and meditations will open themselves to mutual power and to leadership by women, Indigenous peoples, and rural workers. Prayers and meditations will be suffused by multiple feminisms that break down any

---

15. Dunker, "Como encontrar a felicidade."
16. Augustine of Hippo, *Letter* 130, chapter 9.

form of hierarchical male power and pray the prayers of all women, especially women of color. Prayers and meditations will be the means of cracking open the present, when so many things are ending and we are grieving and struggling to breathe: prayers as means of cracking open the present to postpone the end of the world, but also as ways of modeling new forms of being after the world's end.

Prayer will become a dedication of our whole life to learn, to feel, to share, to gain awareness of how racism lives in our bodies, and to know that only a small part of white supremacy exists "in our cognitive brains. For the most part, white supremacy lives in our bodies. In fact, white supremacy would be better termed white-body supremacy."[17] And prayer will allow us to become conscious of the fact that sexual, class, and racialized forms of relationships present in various forms of "practices of dominance are simultaneously knitted into the interstices of multiple institutions as well as into everyday life."[18] These forms of awareness can build local networks of resistance against any form of oppression, moving against governments, and predatory corporations, breaking down existing forms of power, and making use of jurisprudence to distribute land to all. Prayer will become desire that imbues consciousness with soul through practices of poetry, wonderings, walks along rivers and in forests, the restoration of biomes, the healing of animals, and the renewal of the earth.

In the essay "There Is No Fire Without Air," Argentine professor and feminist activist Verónica Gago tells us how the work of transnational feminists struggling across the globe continues to create resistance that takes the form of resonant acts that build and sustain political memory, even in the midst of the COVID-19 pandemic. As an example of desires embodied in gesture, Gago asks how a collective can organize and use the street. For her, "Whether it is a mobilization, a strike, or an occupation, actions (or their suspension) have a rhythm and composition (a tangle of memory and future) through which air circulates, making sparks ignite."[19]

If we can engage in prayer as action, with rhythm and composition, we can circulate air that will spark a fire. Prayers are then compositions of new responses, new gestures of transformation, fire-starters, and builders of memories both past and future.

In this way, prayers do not cede either the space of dreams or political and ecological demands. The desire for our common happiness starts by bringing us closer to the earth, becoming kin of other species, and caring

---

17. Menakem, *My Grandmother's Hands*, loc. ix, Kindle.
18. Alexander, *Pedagogies of Crossing*, loc. 4, Kindle.
19. Gago, "There Is No Fire without Air."

for all there is. To attach prayer to the earth, we must again get close to the ground and claim our belonging where we are, in the earth, where our sense of identity and belonging begin, calling on those who came before us, honoring the Indigenous people whose lands were stolen, and creating forms of life woven in reciprocity and restoration. Our prayers, desires, bodies, cultures, and the earth, all join together in mutual respect, collective flourishing, and common sustainable life. Each prayer breathing life, each desire fostering collective living, each dream being visited by a tree or a river; working for the restoration of dead areas, working for racist laws to be abolished. In this way, we will postpone the end of the earth by creating new sustainable worlds on Earth. Airton Krenak, a leader of the Krenak Indigenous nation in Brazil, says in *Ideas to Postpone the End of the World*, "My provocation about postponing the end of the world is exactly that I can always tell one more story. If we can do that, we will be postponing the end."[20]

Surely prayers cannot do it all, but they can provide a small space in which stories can be retold, and where we can respond to the world's catastrophic destructions by desiring a new life—until we are able to attend to our dreams and until dreams are transformed into a life lived beyond ourselves. Dreams made of trees, plants, animals, stars, rivers, mountains, and every human being. If we understand—fueled by dreams made of trees, plants, animals, stars, rivers, mountains, and every human being—that our life is deeply involved, affected by, and utterly entangled with every human and non-human form of life, we will discover that our mode of living has limits. We will then make use only of what our local portion of the earth can provide. We will take care of our gardens, our animals, our rivers, our trees, and our oceans. If we pray and desire and dream with a more expansive form of life, we will care for the collective and the common good and will not become trapped by the demands of the individual.

Prayer, desire, dream, action, and wondering together can enable us to find a freedom we have not yet fully lived, because only a few have been able to experience it thus far. We cannot take freedom for granted. As Dunker writes about freedom and the work of happiness,

> Before, it seemed (that freedom was) free and without cost, but now, its absence appears to suffocate us. This is the great lesson that the worst moments (of history) leave for us: self-criticism and shame are better companions for writing history than guilt or hope. This morale of resistance is important so that we may dream of a happiness that is not divine merit or grace received from magical godparents, but that can, however, be taken from us

---

20. Krenak, *Ideias para adiar o fim do mundo*, locs. 19–20, Apple Books.

by tyrants of occasion. Happiness is a precious and rare encounter, not a state of bliss. It is an achievement and a task for each one, just like the lesser happiness and morale of the survivor: happy to be alive. This too shall pass, says the Jewish saying.[21]

Through prayer a paradoxical movement takes place in our desires: we must give up our desires at the end of the world and live into the desire for the present, for the arrival of a new world. We must desire at the end of the world with our bodies attuned to the small voice that speaks from places we are not used to perceiving. We can be grateful for what we have wherever we are as a way of pushing our way forward without being destroyed by systems of fear, debt, poverty, destruction, insecurity, and death. From out of mourning and grief, we will move with gratitude into more expansive forms of life and renewal. And we will be prepared:

> So when you wake up to life, next time, step carefully, because the weight of your happiness is part of the dream for all of us.[22]

Prayer is dreaming. May we awaken to a world that is altered by our prayers, and prayers altered by our dreams.

---

21. Dunker, "Como encontrar a felicidade."
22. Dunker, "Como encontrar a felicidade."

Conclusion

Orienting Our Hearts to Live Better

At my age, everything fits in a prayer.

—Pedro Casaldáliga[1]

In a class on prayer at the Hispanic Summer Program, Ana María Rodríguez Alfonso wrote a searing story about her prayer life. Ana María called it a forgotten prayer.[2] It goes something like this:

> A few years ago I went through various changes in my life of faith. I have belonged to a church where I learned everything about my Christian life and the importance of prayer. Every night I spent a long time praying before going to sleep. Prayer became my refuge. My family was completely against my new faith and I had to read the Bible under the street light and forced myself to pray in complete silence.
>
> Praying in silence was not easy for me. Over the years I understood that I suffered from post-traumatic stress disorder (PTSD). For several years I suffered the consequences of poverty, verbal and psychological abuse, physical and sexual violence, and a profound abandonment that accompanied me until the moment I felt an indescribable closeness to the Divine. Every moment of prayer was the moment when the pain and anguish

---

1. Casaldáliga, "Na minha idade, tudo cabe em uma oração."
2. Story used with permission of Ana María Rodríguez Alfonso, who also asked that her real name be kept. I want to say a word of gratitude to Ana María but also to all of my incredible students who were in the class "Praying in Times of COVID-19 and Other Disasters" in the 2020 Hispanic Summer Program. They were the first to read the first draft of this book: Maria Isabel Salazar, Mark Anthony Hernández, Adriana Rivera, Martin Tapia, Jess Navarette, Sally Marie Foster, Diana Rosa Ramos Garcia, Yadira Martinez, Omar Isaac Ortiz, and Jonathan Paredes. My gratitude to you all!

of so many years could come to the fore. Prayer was my safe place, a place where no one could harm me. When I was praying, the Divine was there, embracing all the broken pieces of my humanity like a mother embraces her child. I felt protected by a Divine shield. As the psalmist said, I was protected inside a mighty tower. I felt so comfortable that I could cry and express everything I felt inside and at the end, I could get up with my spirit full again and my afflictions seemed to be gone.

This amazing experience lasted a couple of years until my family forbade me to go back to church. It was only many years later that I return to a new church. But in this new church, I learned that everything I had experienced with God before was wrong. The teachings I received went so deep inside of me that I could not pray anymore. I became afraid, since I thought I had done everything wrong. My safe place was gone. My life fell apart so quickly that I didn't have a floor to fall on. My cry now was alone, without the Divine shield, without anyone. I left that church, but I forgot to pray. For years I did not want to pray.

Lately, I started to reconcile myself with prayer. Slowly, I started praying again, here and there. I have discovered that prayer for me was as fundamental as breathing. I have been rebuilding my safe place again, where I join God in new warm and loving embraces.

This story moved me deeply and made me think that prayer is like a nest we build little by little, with whatever materials we can find to give ourselves protection. Once we are safe enough, we need to take flight and venture into other skies. For no nest will last for one's entire life. Ana María built a nest and lost it. She had to build it again. To build a prayer nest one needs time, patience, and a lot of work. And then there are rest, alertness, care, pause, and other forms of life being built. Over time, though, our life changes and the nest doesn't function anymore. For a nest only serves for a season. Then off we go. We learn with Ultima, the grandmother of Antonio, a little boy learning with her about life and the power of the earth in the novel of Rudolfo A. Anaya, *Bless Me, Ultima*, that change is part of our strength: "You are growing, and growth is change. Accept the change, make it a part of your strength."[3]

We start orienting our hearts by knowing that change and transformation are a constant part of life. And this constant work of change is the work of building the nest, resting, and flying again. Knowing ourselves and the ways of our mutual life, moving around paradoxes, being cared for and

---

3. Anaya, *Bless Me, Ultima*, 245.

taking care, learning to live in abandonment and to live a life of embraces, going from and through the end of times and into the beginning of a new world after the end of the world.

The work of prayer is a work of our archives, the depth of ourselves, the depth of histories, the depth of wisdom, and the depth of the earth. Alexis Pauline Gumbs tells us in *After the End of the World* about her own archives: "the archive of dirt: what we did; the archive of sky: what we become; the archive of fire: rate of change and the archive of ocean: origin."[4] In naming these archives, Gumbs is decolonizing herself; she is moving deeply into territories hidden, taken away, destroyed by forces of death. By digging into our personal and collective archives, we find our collective history, destiny, and freedom. That is the orientation of our hearts.

Prayer is an inner practice that leads us to conversion and interior transformation. Prayer is also an outer practice that can change the world. Inside and outside are constantly being reshaped together for life to be healed, transformed, challenged, expanded—until we finally become free with the world.

If you have come this far in the book, I hope you have wrestled with some of the issues raised here and found some materials to build your own nest, knowing that your nest—with your life and the life of your community—is at stake, and thus the lives of all the living creatures, the rocks, and the whole world.

If the prayer materials offered here are too much for you at this time, set them aside. Use only what you think you can use for your nest, for what is coming to you now. Perhaps this book will speak to you more at a later time. Orient yourself according to your own needs. Pray, desire, dream, excavate, touch the ground; for these movements of the heart, body, and soul are networks of solidarity and life together. Pray as an exercise of your entire being with the earth. Pray not necessarily knowing everything. Prayer grants us a knowledge of God that is only found in the unknown. A life of prayer is not one that keeps building brick upon brick on the edifice of belief but rather, an itinerary that pays attention to where we have been, where we live, where we are heading, and to all the forms of life and death surrounding us.

Prayer, as we have seen, is *ora et labora*, prayer (which also includes rest) and work amidst the piling up of the debris of our world, carrying the grief of so many human deaths, animal extinctions, and unbearable Earth destruction. In these moments, Jesus will pray for us until we are able to pray again. Then, when we are ready again, we pick up the prayer and start

---

4. Gumbs, *After the End of the World*. These words are some of the chapter titles in her magnificent book.

all over again. Like the endless work of Saint Francis physically repairing the structure of the San Damiano church in Italy. Like the endless work of Sisyphus pushing the boulder up the mountain; in a new perspective on the myth, it is also a work of love. One day, the church will be ready, and we will rejoice! One day, the boulder will stay put, the curse will be undone, the boulder will dissipate—or the mountainous terrain will level out. I leave you with a prayer by the poet Paul Celan, the last line of his poem "Vast, Glowing Vault":

The world is gone, I must carry you.[5]

Shall we pray?

---

5. Celan, "Die Welt ist fort, ich muß dich tragen," in Derrida, *Sovereignties in Question*, 158.

Afterword

—Marc H. Ellis

PRAYING WITH EVERY (LOST) heart, for (a darker) faith, with (and at) the end of the (natural) world. Can the pages we just read be our way to a future—after? Since, from varied traditions and cultures, we all come after.

Yet at the end of things is our beginning. Since, I believe and, I think, Cláudio Carvalhaes believes, that after, there is always enough left to begin again. Though the situation is so dire, so urgent, at times in these pages, we wonder. Is our world already gone?

Cláudio has taken us on his journey which, now, is ours, too. And what a journey it is. Through liberation theologies. Through nature and its demise. Through prayer experiments and liturgical seasons. To religions and spiritualities other than his own. If we can identify his own religion. Is Cláudio Carvalhaes (still) a Christian?

Some might ask this, as I have, for as a Jew, traveling around the world, I have encountered many different forms of Christian life. What is Christianity, I ask, in its varied traditional forms and as these forms evolve? Is Christianity a power to oppress or a pathway toward liberation? Can Christianity be both and at the same time? Cláudio thinks so. What a tangle!

As a Jew, I come after the Holocaust. But as a Jew of Conscience, I also come after Israel—after what Israel has done and is doing to the Palestinian people. Cláudio, as a Christian, comes after imperial and colonial Christianity—and what both have done and are doing to his people, country, and continent. These afters are within us; history and the present are deep within our interior life. And as Cláudio points out, they exist within our prayer life, too.

How do we move forward after the traditions that command us are emptied of their ethics? The cycle of violence and atrocity, through our histories now at the heart of our covenants, is often deflected and repressed. But Cláudio places that cycle at the center of our prayer life, as an almost insurmountable challenge. Once we are aware, our questions deepen. Where is God in this cycle of violence and atrocity, if anywhere? Can we call on God in prayer—after? Cláudio is uncertain.

Cláudio searches in the public places of liturgy and church life, but he is at his most gut-wrenching and enlightening—courageous!—when he opens his heart to the world and to us. How often our spiritual leaders and thinkers hide themselves in religion and thought! As if something outside themselves is at stake but everything inside is safe and secure. Closeted, criticism becomes a safe haven. Closeted, pronouncements become a lashing out. Closeted, both become a wager for career advancement.

In these pages, Cláudio Carvalhaes becomes a question. To himself. For us. He writes books, teaches at a prestigious seminary, is invited to give endowed lectures and liturgies. His newfound privilege includes travels to places where others live like he once did—poor, dispossessed, under the boot. He and his cohorts are welcomed by those who have little or nothing. His question mark is ours: Can he, with his compatriots, save those he visits, prays with, and speaks for?

Cláudio isn't convinced by the attention he receives. Instead, it makes the confusion he feels more intense. Has he, a victim of empire, become an accomplice?

Reading his book and revisiting his broken places, I feel Cláudio is on a dangerous path. If and where he will land is uncertain. Shall we follow?

Even when you come from the margins, and are accepted, exile looms for those who cannot abide another form of speaking-for-others hypocrisy. Exile most often comes from above but sometimes, unexpectedly, by those who have previously accompanied you. Rhetoric aside, self-interest is often more powerful than our commitment to others.

Reading as Cláudio's story unfolds, I wonder: Can Cláudio survive yet another dispossession? Is he, subconsciously, for the sake of his soul, courting one?

As I finished his book, I thought of Cláudio as part of what I call the Late Style Prophetic. Initially, I applied this category in a specifically Jewish sense, the Jewish tradition being the root of the prophetic. But now I see branches everywhere. The Late Style Prophetic is Jewish—but not only.

By Late Style Prophetic, I mean the prophetic tradition come alive in its deconstruction and in its committed waywardness, visible wailing, and solitude—as a form of dystopic solidarity.

As I envision it, the Late Style Prophetic comes at the end of our various traditions, including the prophetic tradition itself.

Will the prophets continue to appear if they are unable to tap into the prophetic tradition itself? Can the prophetic community survive if it is itself doubly exiled?

So, for example, the prophet, once called by God, can no longer call on God. If there is a God who moves in history. Claiming God no longer makes sense, since the very ground of return and promise is too violated. The prophetic community, which gathers around the doomed prophet, is itself on the rails, thrown about, on the run, and quite aware of its own failings.

The prophet and the prophetic are on their own. Which is to say, out on a limb, with little support, untethered, open to the winds, rising only to fall.

In Cláudio's words and rhythms, I do not hear "Reclaim Jesus!" or "Be a true Christian and we will be saved!" It is too late for these clarion calls, the calls themselves being so tainted with violence and atrocity.

No, Cláudio Carvalhaes is now within a broader tradition of faith and struggle; he carries the remnants of his Christian past into what I call the New Diaspora. The New Diaspora is the place where exiles from every religious tradition, culture, and geographic region find themselves once they realize their inheritance has no future as a whole or, even in part, by itself. In this community of exiles, what remains are the shattered fragments of what was. In the New Diaspora there is no ability to construct a new whole or even the intention to do so. Yet when reclaimed for ourselves and shared with others at certain moments on the journey, our shattered fragments can be life-giving.

En route, Cláudio Carvalhaes has shared the shattered fragments which, at this moment, are left within him. It is now our turn to continue the journey with him.

Bibliography

Ai, Weiwei, dir. *Human Flow*. 24 Media Films, 2017.
Alexander, M. Jacqui. *Pedagogies of Crossing: Meditations on Feminism, Sexual Politics, Memory, and the Sacred*. Perverse Modernities. Durham: Duke University Press, 2006.
Alexander, Michelle. *The New Jim Crow: Mass Incarceration in the Age of Colorblindness*. New York: New Press, 2012.
Allen, Theodore W. *The Invention of the White Race*. 2 vols. 2nd ed. London: Verso, 2012.
Alves, Rubem. *Perguntaram-me se eu acredito em Deus*. Translated by Emily Everett. São Paulo: Editora Planeta do Brasil, 2007.
———. "Sobre Política e Jardinagem." In *Melhores Crônicas de Rubem Alves*, 26–30. Campinas, SP, Brazil: Editora Papirus, 2012.
Anaya, Rudolfo A. *Bless Me, Ultima*. New York: Grand Central, 2013.
"Artist Creates 'Letter from a Birmingham Jail' Memes to Stop People from Whitewashing MLK." *Mic*, January 16, 2017. https://mic.com/articles/165598/artist-creates-letters-from-birmingham-jail-memes-to-stop-people-from-whitewashing-mlk#.bzIDoXy1V.
Augustine of Hippo. "*Letter* 130 (AD 412)." Translated by J. G. Cunningham. https://www.newadvent.org/fathers/1102130.htm.
Bailie, Gil. *Violence Unveiled: Humanity at the Crossroads*. New York: Crossroad, 1996.
Baldwin, James. "An Open Letter to My Sister, Miss Angela Davis." *The New York Review of Books*, January 7, 1971. https://www.nybooks.com/articles/1971/01/07/an-open-letter-to-my-sister-miss-angela-davis/.
Baring-Gould, Sabine. "Now the Day Is Over." In *The Lutheran Hymnal*, 654. St. Louis: Concordia, 1941.
Baschet, Jérôme. "COVID-19: O século XXI Começa Agora." Translated by Ana Luiza Braga. https://n-1edicoes.org/017.
Benjamin, Walter. "On the Concept of History." https://www.sfu.ca/~andrewf/CONCEPT2.html.
Berger, Teresa. *Women's Ways of Worship: Gender Analysis and Liturgical History*. New York: Pueblo, 1999.
Berry, Wendell. *Standing by Words: Essays*. Berkeley: Counterpoint, 1983.
Betcher, Sharon V. "Take My Yoga upon You: A Spiritual *Pli* for the Global City." In *Polydoxy: Theology of Multiplicity and Relation*, edited by Catherine Keller and Laurel C. Schneider, 57–80. New York: Routledge, 2011.

Boff, Leonardo. "Post-COVID-19: How Should Cosmology and Ethics Respond? (I)." https://leonardoboff.org/2020/06/07/post-covid-19-how-should-cosmology-and-ethics-respond-i/.

———. "Post-COVID-19: What Cosmology and Ethics to Incorporate (II)." https://leonardoboff.org/2020/06/14/post-covid-19-what-cosmology-and-ethics-to-incorporate-ii/.

———. "Prefiro o silêncio de Buda à tagarelice dos teólogos." Interview on the *Viver com Fé* Brazilian television program. http://gnt.globo.com/programas/viver-com-fe/videos/2306495.htm.

Breton, André. *Mad Love = L'amour fou*. Lincoln: University of Nebraska Press, 1987.

Brum, Eliane. *Brasil, Construtor de Ruínas*. Porto Alegre: Arquipélago Editorial, 2019. Kindle.

———. *The Collector of Leftover Souls: Dispatches from Brazil*. London: Granta, 2019.

———. "O futuro pós-coronavírus já está em disputa." *El País*, world edition, April 8, 2020. https://brasil.elpais.com/opiniao/2020-04-08/o-futuro-pos-coronavirus-ja-esta-em-disputa.html.

Buarque, Chico, and Edú Lobo. "Salmo." Álbum de Teatro. São Paulo: Sony-BM, 1996.

Butler, Judith. "Thinking in Alliance: An Interview with Judith Butler." *Verso Books* (blog). https://www.versobooks.com/blogs/3718-thinking-in-alliance-an-interview-with-judith-butler.

Camus, Albert. *Exile and the Kingdom*. Translated by Justin O'Brien. New York: Vintage, 1958.

Caputo, John D. *The Prayers and Tears of Jacques Derrida: Religion Without Religion*. Bloomington: Indiana University Press, 1997.

Carpentier, Alejo. *De lo real maravilloso americano*. Mexico: Universidad Nacional Autonoma de Mexico, 2004.

Carvalhaes, Cláudio. *Eucharist and Globalization: Redrawing the Borders of Eucharistic Hospitality*. Eugene, OR: Pickwick, 2013.

———. "*Lex Naturae*: A New Way into a Liturgical Political Theology." In *T&T Clark Handbook to Political Theology*, edited by Rubén Rosário Rodriguez, 449–66. New York: T. & T. Clark, 2019.

———, ed. *Liturgies from Below: Praying with People at the Ends of the World*. Nashville: Abingdon, 2020.

———. "Pedagogies of Cruelty." *The Wabash Center* (blog), May 20, 2020. https://www.wabashcenter.wabash.edu/2020/05/pedagogies-of-cruelty/.

———. "A Prayer Song for Alan Kurdi, a Three-Year-Old Boy from Syria Who Drowned in the Mediterranean Sea." https://www.youtube.com/watch?v=ghWWDN08-GQ.

———. "Praying Each Other's Prayers: An Inter-religious Approach." In *Post-Colonial Practice of Ministry*, edited by Kwok Pui-lan and Stephen Burns, 137–50. Lanham, MD: Lexington, 2016.

———. "White Reasoning and What Is Common in Our Common Worship?" *Call to Worship: Liturgy, Music, Preaching, and the Arts* 49 (2017) 19–27.

Casaldáliga, Pedro. "Na minha idade, tudo cabe em uma oração." February 17, 2018. http://www.ihu.unisinos.br/78-noticias/576146-pedro-casaldaliga-na-minha-idade-tudo-cabe-em-uma-oracao.

Casaldaliga, Pedro, and Pedro Tierra. "Missa dos Quilombos." Music by Milton Nascimento. Compact Disc Digital Audio: PolyGram do Brasil Ltda, 1982. http://www.servicioskoinonia.org/Casaldaliga/poesia/quilombos.htm.
Césaire, Aimé. *Return to My Native Land*. Translated by John Berger and Anna Bostock. Baltimore: Penguin, 1969.
Chow, Rey. *Not like a Native Speaker: On Languaging as a Postcolonial Experience*. New York: Columbia University Press, 2014.
Chryssavgis, John. *In the Heart of the Desert: The Spirituality of the Desert Fathers and Mothers*. Bloomington, IN: World Wisdom, 2008.
Churton, Edward. *The Early English Church*. London: J. Burns, 1840.
Coetzee, J. M. *Slow Man*. New York: Penguin, 2005.
Cone, James H. *The Cross and the Lynching Tree*. Maryknoll, NY: Orbis, 2011.
Copeland, M. Shawn. "Eucharist, Racism, and Black Bodies." In *Enfleshing Freedom: Body, Race, and Being*, 107–28. Minneapolis: Fortress, 2009.
Danowski, Déborah. "Não tem mais mundo pra todo mundo." https://n-1edicoes.org/081.
Danowski, Déborah, and Eduardo Viveiros de Castro. *The Ends of the World*. Translated by Rodrigo Nunes. Malden, MA: Polity, 2017.
Děd, Lal. *I, Lalla: The Poems of Lal Děd*. Translated by Ranjit Hoskote. New York: Penguin Global, 2013.
DeGuzmán, María. *Buenas Noches, American Culture: Latina/o Aesthetics of Night*. Bloomington: Indiana University Press, 2012.
Derrida, Jacques. *Aporias*. Translated by Thomas Dutoit. Stanford: Stanford University Press, 1993.
———. *Parages*. Edited by John P. Leavey. Translated by Tom Conley et al. Stanford: Stanford University Press, 2010.
———. *Psyche: Inventions of the Other*. Translated by Catherine Porter. Stanford: Stanford University Press, 2008.
———. *Sovereignties in Question: The Poetics of Paul Celan*. New York: Fordham University Press, 2005.
Douglas, Kelly Brown. *Stand Your Ground: Black Bodies and the Justice of God*. Maryknoll, NY: Orbis, 2015.
Du Bois, W. E. B. *Prayers for Dark People*. Edited by Herbert Aptheker. Amherst: University of Massachusetts Press, 1980.
Dunker, Christian Ingo Lenz. "Como encontrar a felicidade em tempos sombrios: Três passos para olhar o futuro." *The Intercept*, October 25, 2019. https://theintercept.com/2019/10/25/felicidade-tempos-sombrios/.
Dussel, Enrique. "Epistemological Decolonization of Theology." In *Decolonial Christianities: Latinx and Latin American Perspectives*, edited by Raimundo Barreto and Roberto Sirvent, 25–42. London: Palgrave, 2019.
Ellacuría, Ignacio. *Escritos teológicos*. Vol. 2. San Salvador: UCA Editores, 2000.
Ellis, Marc H. *Finding Our Voice: Embodying the Prophetic and Other Misadventures*. Eugene, OR: Cascade, 2018.
Espín, Orlando O. *Idol and Grace: On Traditioning and Subversive Hope*. Maryknoll, NY: Orbis, 2014.
Evagrios the Solitary (of Pontus). *On Prayer: One Hundred and Fifty-Three Texts*. In *The Philokalia: The Complete Text*. Translated and edited by G. E. H. Palmer et al. https://archive.org/stream/Philokalia-TheCompleteText/Philokalia-Complete-Text_djvu.txt.

Evangelical Lutheran Church in America. *Evangelical Lutheran Worship: Pew Edition*. Minneapolis: Fortress, 2006.

Fanon, Frantz. *Black Skins, White Masks*. New York: Grove, 1967.

Flatow, Nicole. "DOJ Finds Unconstitutional Solitary Confinement of Mentally Ill for Months, Years in Pennsylvania." http://thinkprogress.org/justice/2013/06/06/2114821/doj-finds-unconstitutional-solitary-confinement-of-mentally-ill-for-months-years-in-pennsylvania/?mobile=nc.

Foucault, Michel. *The Archaeology of Knowledge and the Discourse on Language*. New York: Vintage, 1982.

Freire, Paulo. *Cartas à Guiné-Bissau: Registros de uma experiencia em processo*. Rio de Janeiro: Editora Paz e Terra, 1978.

———. *Pedagogy of the Oppressed*. Translated by Myra Bergman Ramos. New York: Continuum, 1968.

———. *Pedagogy of the Oppressed*. Translated by Myra Bergman Ramos. New rev. ed. London: Penguin, 1996.

Gago, Verónica. "There Is No Fire Without Air." Translated by Amanda Sommer Lotspike. *ConTactos* (HemiPress). https://contactos.tome.press/no-fire-without-air/.

Galbreath, Paul. *Leading into the World*. Vital Worship, Healthy Congregations. New York: Rowman & Littlefield, 2014.

Galeano, Eduardo. *The Memory of Fire Trilogy: Genesis, Faces and Masks, and Century of the Wind*. New York: Open Road, 2014.

———. *Open Veins of Latin America: Five Centuries of the Pillage of a Continent*. New York: Monthly Review Press, 1997.

García, Cristina. *A Handbook to Luck*. New York: Knopf, 2007.

Gebara, Ivone. "Liturgia e teologia, uma nota dissonante." In *Teologia do Culto: Entre o Altar e o Mundo; Aportes Multidisciplinares da Liturgia*, edited by Cláudio Carvalhaes. São Paulo: Fonte Editorial, 2012.

Gil, Gilberto. "Bolsonaro me inspira a oração." https://www.metropoles.com/brasil/gilberto-gil-bolsonaro-me-inspira-a-oracao.

Glick, Daniel. "The Big Thaw: As the Climate Warms, How Much, and How Quickly, Will Earth's Glaciers Melt?" https://www.nationalgeographic.com/environment/global-warming/big-thaw/.

Gomes, Roberto. *A crítica da razão tupiniquim*. São Paulo: FTD, 1994.

Gómez-Barris, Macarena. *The Extractive Zone: Social Ecologies and Decolonial Perspectives*. Durham: Duke University Press, 2017.

Gramsci, Antonio. *Selections from the Prison Notebooks of Antonio Gramsci*. Edited and translated by Quintin Hoare and Geoffrey Nowell Smith. New York: International, 1971.

Gumbs, Alexis Pauline. *M Archive: After the End of the World*. Durham: Duke University Press, 2018.

Haldeman, Scott. *Towards Liturgies That Reconcile: Race and Ritual among African-American and European-American Protestants*. New York: Routledge: 2016.

Haraway, Donna. "Making Kin: Anthropocene, Capitalocene, Plantationocene, Chthulucene." In *Staying with the Trouble: Making Kin in the Chthulucene*. Durham: Duke University Press, 2016.

Harney, Stefano, and Fred Moten. *The Undercommons: Fugitive Planning & Black Study*. New York: Minor Compositions, 2013.

Hazony, Yoram. *The Virtue of Nationalism*. New York: Basic Books, 2018.
Heng, Geraldine. "The Invention of Race in the Middle Ages I: Race Studies, Modernity, and the Middle Ages." *Literature Compass* 8 (2011) 315–31.
Heschel, Abraham Joshua. *I Asked for Wonder: A Spiritual Anthology*. New York: Crossroad, 1983.
———. "On Prayer." In *Moral Grandeur and Spiritual Audacity: Essays by Abraham Joshua Heschel*, edited by Susannah Heschel, 257–67. New York: Farrar, Straus & Giroux, 1997.
Holmer, Paul L. *The Grammar of Faith*. San Francisco: Harper & Row, 1978.
Hosseini, Khaled. *Sea Prayer*. New York: Riverhead, 2018.
Irarrázaval, Diego. "Salvação Indígena y Afro-Americana." In *Teologia pluralista libertadora intercontinental*, edited by José M. Vigil et al. São Paulo: Paulinas, 2008.
Isasi-Díaz, Ada María. *Mujerista Theology: A Theology for the Twenty-First Century*. Maryknoll, NY: Orbis, 2013.
Jennings, Willie James. *The Christian Imagination: Theology and the Origins of Race*. New Haven: Yale University Press, 2010.
Jenson, Matt. *The Gravity of Sin: Augustine, Luther and Barth on "homo incurvatus in se"*. London: T. & T. Clark, 2007.
Joh, Wonhee Anne. *Heart of the Cross: A Postcolonial Christology*. Louisville: Westminster John Knox, 2006.
John of the Cross. *Dark Night of the Soul*. Mineola, NY: Dover, 2003.
Johnson, Jay Emerson. *Divine Communion: A Eucharistic Theology of Sexual Intimacy*. New York: Seabury, 2013.
Joon-ho, Bon, dir. *Parasite*. Seoul, South Korea: Barunson E&A, 2018.
Julian of Norwich. *Revelations of Divine Love*. https://www.gutenberg.org/files/52958/52958-h/52958-h.htm.
Junker, Tércio Bretanha. *Prophetic Liturgy: Toward a Transforming Christian Praxis*. Eugene, OR: Pickwick, 2014.
Kaufman, Amanda. "Here Is the Story Behind the Horrific Photo of the Man and Toddler Drowning at the Border." *Boston Globe*, June 26, 2019. https://www.bostonglobe.com/news/nation/2019/06/26/here-story-behind-horrific-photo-man-and-toddler-drowning-border/GdG1TRH99pURcdRdJujJhL/story.html.
Kim, Nami, and Wonhee Anne Joh, eds. *Feminist Praxis against U.S. Militarism*. Postcolonial and Decolonial Studies in Religion and Theology. Lanham, MD: Lexington, 2019.
Kimmerer, Robin Wall. *Braiding Sweetgrass: Indigenous Wisdom, Scientific Knowledge, and the Teachings of Plants*. Helena, MT: Milkweed, 2013.
———. *Gathering Moss: A Natural and Cultural History of Mosses*. Corvallis: Oregon State University Press, 2003.
King, Karen L. *The Gospel of Mary of Magdala: Jesus and the First Woman Apostle*. Santa Rosa, CA: Polebridge, 2003.
King Jr., Martin Luther. "A Knock at Midnight." In *A Testament of Hope: The Essential Writings and Speeches of Martin Luther King, Jr.*, edited by James Melvin Washington. San Francisco: HarperSanFrancisco, 1991.
———. "Letter from Birmingham City Jail." In *A Testament of Hope: The Essential Writings and Speeches of Martin Luther King, Jr.*, edited by James Melvin Washington, 289–302. New York: HarperCollins, 1991.

———. "Letter from Birmingham Jail." In *The Radical King*, edited and introduced by Cornel West, 127–45. Boston: Beacon, 2015.

———. "The Other America." Speech given April 14, 1967, at Memorial Auditorium, Stanford University. https://kinginstitute.stanford.edu/news/50-years-ago-martin-luther-king-jr-speaks-stanford-university.

Kopenawa, Davi, and Bruce Albert. *The Falling Sky: Words of a Yanomami Shaman*. Cambridge: Belknap Press of Harvard University Press, 2013.

Kotrosits, Maia. *The Lives of Objects: Material Culture, Experience, and the Real in the History of Early Christianity*. Class 200: New Studies in Religion. Chicago: University of Chicago Press, 2020.

———. *Rethinking Early Christian Identity: Affect, Violence, and Belonging*. Minneapolis: Fortress, 2015.

Krenak, Ailton. *Ideias para adiar o fim do mundo*. São Paulo: Companhia das Lestras, 2019.

Lathrop, Gordon W. *Holy Ground: A Liturgical Cosmology*. Minneapolis: Fortress, 2009.

———. *Holy People: A Liturgical Ecclesiology*. Minneapolis: Fortress, 1999.

———. *Holy Things: A Liturgical Theology*. Minneapolis: Fortress, 1993.

Latour, Bruno. *Dónde aterrizar: Cómo orientarse en política*. Madrid: Penguin Random House Grupo Editorial España, 2019.

———. "Imaginar gestos que barrem o retorno da produção pré-crise." Translated by Déborah Danowski. *AOC-Media*, March 29, 2020. http://www.bruno-latour.fr/sites/default/files/downloads/P-202-AOC-03-20-PORTUGAIS_2.pdf.

———. "Is This a Dress Rehearsal?" *In the Moment* (blog of *Critical Inquiry*), March 26, 2020. https://critinq.wordpress.com/2020/03/26/is-this-a-dress-rehearsal/.

Leiman, Melvin. *The Political Economy of Racism*. Chicago: Haymarket, 2010.

Lispector, Clarice. "A experiência maior." In *Para não esquecer*. Rio de Janeiro: Rocco, 1999.

———. "Brasilia." In *Complete Stories*, 961–62. New York: New Directions, 2018.

———. *Todos os contos*. Edited and with a preface by Benjamin Moser. Rio de Janeiro: Editora Rocco, 2016.

Lloyd, Vincent. "The End of the World: Reflections from Black Activism." *Berkley Forum*, June 9, 2020. https://berkleycenter.georgetown.edu/responses/the-end-of-the-world-reflections-from-black-activism?fbclid=IwAR2Sq9HLyVylA8cFho3a9c5COrLX1T_dBAhozeNNK6_M2GtlN6um3szjbf4.

Lorde, Audre. *The Master's Tools Will Never Dismantle the Master's House*. New York: Penguin, 2018.

Lowery, Wesley. *They Can't Kill Us All: Ferguson, Baltimore, and a New Era in America's Racial Justice Movement*. Boston: Little, Brown, 2016.

Malabou, Catherine. *What Should We Do with Our Brain?* Translated by Sebastian Rand. New York: Fordham University Press, 2008.

Maraschin, Jaci. *A beleza da santidade: Ensaios de liturgia*. São Paulo: ASTE, 1996.

———. "The Transient Body: Sensibility and Spirituality." Paper presented at the event "Liturgy and Body," Union Theological Seminary, New York, October 20, 2003.

Marcos, Sylvia. "Mesoamerican Women's Indigenous Spirituality: Decolonizing Religious Beliefs." In *Decolonial Christianities: Latinx and Latin American Perspectives*, edited by Raimundo Barreto and Roberto Sirvent, 63–88. New Approaches to Religion and Power. London: Palgrave, 2019.

Marvell, Andrew. "To His Coy Mistress." In *The Complete Poems*, edited by Elizabeth Story Donno, 50–51. London: Penguin, 2005.

Mbembe, Achille. *Critique of Black Reason*. Durham: Duke University Press, 2017.
———. *Sair da Grande Noite: Ensaio Sobre a África Descolonizada*. Luanda, Angola: Edições Mulemba, 2014.
Mbiti, John S. *The Prayers of African Religion*. Maryknoll, NY: Orbis, 1976.
Menakem, Resmaa. *My Grandmother's Hands*. Las Vegas: Central Recovery, 2017.
Meyers, Ruth A. *Missional Worship, Worshipful Mission*. Grand Rapids: Eerdmans, 2014.
Mignolo, Walter, and Rolando Vazquez. "Decolonial AestheSis: Colonial Wounds/ Decolonial Healings." *Social Text*, July 15, 2013. https://socialtextjournal.org/periscope_article/decolonial-aesthesis-colonial-woundsdecolonial-healings/.
Minh-ha, Trinh T. *Lovecidal: Walking with the Disappeared*. New York: Fordham University Press, 2016.
Mitchell, Nathan D. *Meeting Mystery: Liturgy, Worship, Sacraments*. Maryknoll, NY: Orbis, 1984.
Netke, Shefali. "1550 Chairs Stacked Between Buildings." https://mymodernmet.com/doris-salcedo-1550-chairs-stacked/.
Nhat Hanh, Thich. *Breathe, You Are Alive: The Sutra on the Full Awareness of Breathing*. Berkeley: Parallax, 2008.
Nietzsche, Friedrich. *Thus Spake Zarathustra*. Mineola, NY: Dover, 1999.
Nodari, Alexandre. "'A vida oblíqua': o hetairismo ontológico segundo G. H." *O Eixo e a Roda: Revista d.e Literatura Brasileira* 24 (2015) 139–54.
O'Connell, Mark. "Why Silicon Valley Billionaires Are Prepping for the Apocalypse in New Zealand." *The Guardian*, February 15, 2018. https://www.theguardian.com/news/2018/feb/15/why-silicon-valley-billionaires-are-prepping-for-the-apocalypse-in-new-zealand.
Orwell, George. "Politics and the English Language." *Horizon*, April 1946. https://www.orwellfoundation.com/the-orwell-foundation/orwell/essays-and-other-works/politics-and-the-english-language/.
Osnos, Evan. "Doomsday Prep for the Super-Rich." *The New Yorker*, January 30, 2017. https://www.newyorker.com/magazine/2017/01/30/doomsday-prep-for-the-super-rich.
Oxfam. "World's Billionaires Have More Wealth than 4.6 Billion People." https://www.oxfam.org/en/press-releases/worlds-billionaires-have-more-wealth-46-billion-people.
Paintner, Christine Valters. *Earth, Our Original Monastery*. Notre Dame, IN: Sorin, 2020.
Pániker, Salvador. *Adiós a casi todo*. Diarios de Pániker 5. Barcelona: Penguin Random House Grupo Editorial España, 2017.
"Pentecostals: Christianity Reborn." *The Economist*, special report, December 19, 2006. https://www.economist.com/special-report/2006/12/19/christianity-reborn.
Pineda-Madrid, Nancy. *Suffering and Salvation in Ciudad Juarez*. Minneapolis: Fortress, 2011.
Ponciano, Jonathan. "The World's 25 Richest Billionaires Have Gained Nearly $255 Billion in Just Two Months." *Forbes*, May 23, 2020. https://www.forbes.com/sites/jonathanponciano/2020/05/22/billionaires-zuckerberg-bezos/#67da545e7ed6.
Prandi, Reginaldo. *Mitologia dos Orixás*. São Paulo: Companhia das Letras, 2007.
———. *Os Candomblés de São Paulo*. São Paulo: Hucitec-EDUSP, 1991.

Presbyterian Church (USA). *Book of Common Worship*. Louisville: Westminster John Knox, 2018.

Procter-Smith, Marjorie. *Praying with Our Eyes Open: Engendering Feminist Liturgical Prayer*. Nashville: Abingdon, 1995.

———. "Review Article: Liturgical Responses to Sexual and Domestic Violence." *Journal of Religion & Abuse* 8 (2006) 39–44.

Procter-Smith, Marjorie, and Janet R. Walton, eds. *Women at Worship: Interpretations of North American Diversity*. Louisville: Westminster John Knox, 1993.

Quijano, Anibal. "Coloniality of Power, Eurocentrism, and Latin America." *Nepantla: Views from South* 1 (2000) 533–80.

Redmont, Jane. *When in Doubt, Sing: Prayer in Daily Life*. New York: HarperCollins, 1999.

Reticker, Gini, dir. *Pray the Devil Back to Hell*. New York: Fork Films, 2008.

Rivera Cusicanqui, Silvia. *Ch'ixinakax utxiwa: On Decolonising Practices and Discourses*. Cambridge: Polity, 2020.

———. *Sociología de la imagen*. Buenos Aires: Tinta Limón, 2015.

Rivera-Pagán, Luis N. "Towards a Decolonial Theology: Perspectives from the Caribbean." In *Decolonial Christianities: Latinx and Latin American Perspectives*, edited by Raimundo Barreto and Roberto Sirvent, 43–62. London: Palgrave, 2019.

Rosa, João Guimarães. *Grande Sertão: Veredas*. São Paulo: Companhia das Letras, 2019.

Rosales, Jose Luis. In *Antología De Poesía Mística Española*, edited by Miguel de Santiago, 283. Barcelona: Verón Editores, 1998.

Rumi, Jalal al-Din. "Who Says Words with My Mouth?" In *The Essential Rumi*, edited by Coleman Barks, 2. Translated by Coleman Barks et al. New expanded ed. New York: HarperOne, 2004.

Safatle, Vladimir. *Quando as ruas queimam: Manifesto pela emergência*. São Paulo: N-1 Edições, 2017.

Said, Edward W. *Orientalism*. New York: Vintage, 1979.

Santiago, Miguel de, ed. *Antología de poesía mística española*. Barcelona: Verón Editores, 1998.

Santos, Boaventura de Sousa. *Epistemologies of the South: Justice Against Epistemicide*. New York: Routledge, 2014.

Scorsese, Martin, dir. *The Wolf of Wall Street*. Hollywood, CA: Paramount Pictures, 2013.

Seuss, Dr. [Theodore Geisel]. *The Lorax*. New York: Random House, 1971.

Sifton, Elisabeth. *The Serenity Prayer: Faith and Politics in Times of Peace and War*. New York: Norton, 2003.

Smith, Adam. *The Wealth of Nations*. New York: Modern Library, 1994.

Sosa, Mercedes. "Como la Cigarra." https://www.youtube.com/watch?v=FnxfPBIbcek.

Stewart, Benjamin M. *A Watered Garden: Christian Worship and Earth's Ecology*. Minneapolis: Fortress, 2009.

Strand, Clark. "Bring On the Dark." *New York Times*, December 20, 2014. https://www.nytimes.com/2014/12/20/opinion/why-we-need-the-winter-solstice.html.

———. *Waking Up to the Dark*. New York: Random House, 2018.

Sung, Jung Mo. *Desire, Market, Religion*. Reclaiming Liberation Theology. London: SCM, 2012.

Swaine, Jon, et al. "Young Black Men Killed by US Police at Highest Rate in Year of 1,134 Deaths." *The Guardian*, December 31, 2015. https://www.theguardian.com/us-news/2015/dec/31/the-counted-police-killings-2015-young-black-men.

Tamez, Elsa. *The Scandalous Message of James: Faith without Works Is Dead*. New York: Herder & Herder, 2002.

Taylor, Barbara Brown. *Learning to Walk in the Dark*. San Francisco: HarperOne, 2014.

Thompson, Susan. "A Flor de Piel: The Fragile Force of Doris Salcedo's Artwork." Blog of the Guggenheim Museum. https://www.guggenheim.org/blogs/checklist/a-flor-de-piel-the-fragile-force-of-doris-salcedos-artwork.

Thunberg, Greta, et al. *Our House Is on Fire: Scenes of a Family and a Planet in Crisis*. London: Penguin, 2020.

Thurman, Howard. *The Luminous Darkness: A Personal Interpretation of the Anatomy of Segregation and the Ground of Hope*. Richmond, IN: Friends United, 2014.

Toole, Mary M. *Handbook for Chaplains: Comfort My People*. New York: Paulist, 2006.

Townes, Emilie M. *Womanist Ethics and the Cultural Production of Evil*. New York: Palgrave Macmillan, 2006.

Tutu, Desmond. *An African Prayer Book*. New York: Doubleday, 2006.

———. *No Future without Forgiveness*. New York: Penguin Random House, 2009.

Untener, Kenneth. "The Mystery of the Romero Prayer." http://www.journeywithjesus.net/PoemsAndPrayers/Ken_Untener_A_Future_Not_Our_Own.shtml.

"U.S. Religion Is Worth $1.2T/Year, More than America's 10 Biggest Tech Companies, Combined." http://the-atlantic.blogspot.ch/2018/04/us-religion-is-worth-12tyear-more-than.html?m=1.

Valéry, Paul. *The Outlook for Intelligence*. Translated by Denise Folliot and Jackson Matthews. Princeton: University Press, 1989.

Van Fleteren, Frederick. "Interpretation, Assimilation, Appropriation: Recent Commentators on Augustine and His Tradition." In *Tradition and the Rule of Faith in the Early Church: Essays in Honor of Joseph T. Lienhard, S.J.*, edited by Ronnie J. Rombs and Alexander Y. Hwang, 270–85. Washington, DC: Catholic University of America Press, 2010.

Vellem, Vuyani. "Cracking the Skull of Racism in South Africa Post-1994." In *Who Is an African? Race, Identity, and Destiny in Post-apartheid South Africa*, edited by Roderick R. Hewitt and Chammah J. Kaunda. Minneapolis: Fortress, 2018.

Viveiros de Castro, Eduardo. "A revolução faz o bom tempo." Lecture given April 18, 2015, São Paulo, Brazil. https://www.youtube.com/watch?v=CjbU1jO6rmE.

Voon, Claire. "Doris Salcedo Fills a Public Square in Bogotá with the Names of Civil War Victims." *Hyperallergic*, October 12, 2016. https://hyperallergic.com/329579/doris-salcedo-fills-public-square-bogota-names-civil-war-victims/.

Wall, Mike. "Billionaires Wanted to Fund Private Mars Colony." *Space.com*, August 25, 2015. https://www.space.com/30357-mars-one-colony-billionaires-wanted.html.

Walsh, Bryan. "Alan Kurdi's Story: Behind the Most Heartbreaking Photo of 2015." *TIME*, December 29, 2015. https://time.com/4162306/alan-kurdi-syria-drowned-boy-refugee-crisis/.

Walton, Janet R. *Feminist Liturgy: A Matter of Justice*. Collegeville, MN: Liturgical, 2000.

West, Cornel. "Cornel West on Bernie Sanders, Michael Eric Dyson, Trans Rights, and B.B. King." *The Laura Flanders Show*. June 9, 2015. https://www.youtube.com/watch?v=nHsHhj329T4.

West, Traci C. "Liturgy: Church Worship and White Superiority." In *Disruptive Christian Ethics: When Racism and Women's Lives Matter*, 112–40. Louisville: Westminster John Knox, 2006.

Wilmore, Gayraud S. "Historical Perspective." In *The Cambridge Companion to Black Theology*, edited by Dwight N. Hopkins and Edward P. Antonio, 21. Cambridge: Cambridge University Press, 2012.

Wittgenstein, Ludwig. *Tractatus Logico-Philosophicus*. Translated by C. K. Ogden. Mineola, NY: Dover, 1998.

Wright, Timothy. *No Peace without Prayer: Encouraging Muslims and Christians to Pray Together; a Benedictine Approach*. Monastic Interreligious Dialogue. Collegeville, MN: Liturgical, 2013.

www.ingramcontent.com/pod-product-compliance
Lightning Source LLC
Chambersburg PA
CBHW071240230426
43668CB00011B/1516